TELLY ON TOAST

THE CRAZY LIFE OF A BREAKFAST TV PRODUCER

MICHELLE PORTER

QUERCIA MEDIA PUBLISHING

To my lovely husband Ian

I have lost many things in my life, but I am glad I found you.

BEFORE YOU START

If you want to find out more about Michelle's life behind the scenes on Breakfast TV, go to the website www.tellyon toast.com.

Also listen out for the podcast **Telly on Toast** where you can hear more stories from some well-known Breakfast TV faces and those working behind the scenes, plus tips on how to make a career in television.

While this book is based on fact, some of the stories happened a number of years ago, so please forgive the author if some of the stories are slightly different to other recollections. Some names of the people in this book have been changed for protection of some the people involved.

WHAT A TEASE!

"Can you cut a tease for the six o'clock menu?" my senior producer Kate asked me, looking up from her keyboard while still tapping away. Her long red nails clicked over the keys as she wrote and rewrote scripts that would later be read out on air.

"Of course," I said, trying to sound keen. I picked up my notebook, scribbled down what she had asked me, stood up from my desk and walked with what I hoped was a sense of purpose across the newsroom. To be honest though, I had no idea what she was talking about.

I had just started working on the UK's biggest breakfast show, *GMTV*, as an output producer.

Nine years after I had written my dissertation at university all about Breakfast TV, here I was actually working on it. After starting my career at LBC radio working with radio legends like Steve Allen and Pete Murray, I had just spent four happy years working on the London cable station Channel One, learning some of the tricks of the video trade. But, working on the main commercial breakfast show, on Britain's largest commercial network ITV was taking it to another level.

GMTV was the biggest breakfast show at the time, and everyone knew what a big deal it was. Pop bands lined up to appear on the show. In fact, just a few years before, The Spice Girls had made their TV debut there. Government and opposition politicians jostled to get a slot and get their point of view across to an audience of over five million viewers.

Just a week into the job and I was on my first night shift, working from nine at night until nine in the morning. I was supposed to be shadowing another output producer, but they had disappeared an hour before. No doubt for a quick nap before all the madness began.

It was five o'clock in the morning and the newsroom was alive with people chattering on phones or tapping away on their keyboards, talking to our correspondents around the country, briefing them on the day's story they would be covering in just an hour's time live on TV.

The televisions across the newsroom sprung into life, switching from ITV's night screen—a teletext service offering a preview of the day's TV schedule—to reruns of *Coronation Street* or *BBC Business Breakfast* if the televisions were tuned to our rival channel BBC.

Newsreader and presenter Penny Smith had already arrived and left the newsroom, her hair an unruly wet swirl from just coming out of the shower at home. She'd jumped straight into the car, arriving at 4am to her morning briefing from the overnight editor. She was now in the make-up room sipping a cup of Rooibos tea, being transformed by the make-up artists and hairdressers into a beautifully manicured newsreader, dressed in a brightly coloured jacket. In just over an hour, she would be telling our viewers the latest news as they woke up. Her co-presenter John Stapleton had just arrived too. In need of less hair and make-up, he sat in the corner of the newsroom reading the morning papers, trying to glean crucial bits of information and editorial on the stories he would be covering that morning.

I was on the fourth floor of the London studios on the Southbank. The London studios were home not only to *GMTV*, but also housed the production offices of some of Britain's biggest television shows like *An Audience with* ...pop stars like Rod Stewart and the Bee Gees, *This Morning* with Richard and Judy and *SMTV* and *CDUK* then hosted by two young fresh-faced presenters called Ant and Dec. During the day it buzzed with people working in telly but, at that time in the morning, the 22-storey building was eerily empty.

The sun was just rising in the east along the river Thames, casting a low orange glow across the building and sprinkling light onto the grimy side windows of the office, highlighting the fact that they needed a good clean.

Everyone was buzzing around the newsroom, like human bluebottle flies, stopping only briefly to grab a script or take a phone call from a guest or presenter. Everyone had a job to do, and pursued it with a confident purpose. Meanwhile, I had a job to do and I didn't have a clue how to do it.

I looked at the hastily scribbled note in my new black A4 hardback book bought specially from WH Smith for my new job. "Cut a tease for the six o'clock menu," read the words in front of me.

With no sign of the producer I was meant to shadow, I was flying solo, and I was just going to have to figure it out for myself.

I started with the menu bit. Surely, it must have something to do with breakfast, I thought. Was there a breakfast menu somewhere I had to look at and maybe cut something out of? The only place where you could find any food at that time in the morning was our kitchen, which just had a tea and coffee machine and a microwave containing remnants of the ready meals that had been heated up and then spattered in it overnight. The only other place was our green room where the bacon butties, buns and pastries had just arrived to feed the crew and later the guests who would be on the show.

I had never been to the Green Room, but I knew where it was. Green Rooms were the TV version of waiting rooms, where guests sat about before they went on the show. Unlike doctors' waiting rooms, they didn't have any out-of-date women's and gardening magazines to thumb through. Instead, there was usually a set of the morning's newspapers, a TV in one corner, a kettle and coffee machine, a fridge and a series of firm chairs for our guests to sit on. In the centre sat the coffee table with three plates, one with cheese rolls, one with bacon rolls and the other one with sticky buns on it.

Like most Green Rooms I had seen in the past, it wasn't green. TV types have told me that, in days gone by, the rooms were often populated with green pot plants to make them more relaxing for guests. Green was also said to be a soothing colour, to calm the guests before they went on air. In reality our Green Room was pretty small with hardly space for the guests, let alone any pot plants, and it was painted a pale shade of yellow like a tub of margarine.

I popped down to the third floor where our studio and Green Room were situated to see if I could find any sign of the elusive menu.

Darren–one of our camera operators–was just making himself a cup of tea.

"Is there a menu for breakfast at six o'clock?" I asked, looking at the walls, on the table and in the cupboards to see if I could find something vaguely resembling a menu.

He looked at me blankly. "I wish there was," he said, "I'm getting pretty sick of bacon or cheese rolls. Why have you heard something? If so, can I put in a request for some porridge?" he asked hopefully.

I hunted around outside the room as well. The TV gallery next to the Green Room had sprung into life. All the screens flickered with pictures of videos, weather graphics or live broadcasts getting ready to go on air, but there was no sign of a menu.

The make-up room was full of humming hairdryers and two presenters with heads buried in their programme briefs, trying to get their heads around the questions they would ask the people they were about to interview.

I shouted at Helen, one of the make-up artists trying to make myself heard over the whirring din. "Has anyone seen a breakfast menu?"

"Luvvies, the downstairs café opens at six," she said helpfully.

"They've got quite a good menu. You can even get nice smoothies there now."

At which point our weather presenter Andrea McLean looked up from her notes, her hair in rollers, and nodded in agreement.

As helpful as this information was, I didn't think it was the menu I was looking for.

I concluded I was taking the wrong track on this one. Cutting a tease for the six o'clock menu obviously didn't have anything to do with breakfast, but the idea of what on earth I was meant to do was still a mystery, and I was too embarrassed to admit it to anyone.

I decided to return to the newsroom and try another tack. To say I did not know anything about cutting a tease for the six o'clock menu was not completely true. I had a strong idea about one element. I thought I knew about the cutting bit. What I can tell you, is it had nothing to do with scissors or a knife, although in the past there had been a few razor blades involved.

In television, we used the term when we were editing together video or pictures–a term taken from the days of film–when they physically had to cut and splice tapes together to make an edit.

I had actually done a bit of cutting and splicing myself in my first job at LBC radio. There, we recorded the interviews on giant reels of tape the size of a large pizza. When you wanted to edit them, you had to physically splice the tape with a razor blade, find the bit you wanted to join it to and stick it back together again with tiny bits of thin white sticky tape.

Looking back, health and safety would have had a field day. In our workplace, there were newspapers, note pads, pens, tape machines and an array of razor blades strewn across the desks. Thankfully, I had no suicidal tendencies, but for an outsider it must have looked slightly odd.

Moving into television was a sharp learning curve. I was very good at finding stories and guests to interview; the problem was always the pictures. In radio you could just pick up a microphone and a recorder, record your interview and then you could just cut or edit the bits you wanted from it, maybe add a bit of your own voiceover, and voila! You had something ready to broadcast. However, for every story you put on television you had to think about the visuals—what people would see on the TV.

While it was perfectly okay to just show a clip or live interview of someone talking, you always had to think about what pictures you could cut to accompany them. If you were talking about the Prime Minister, you might have a video of him walking out of 10 Downing Street or standing at the dispatch box in the Houses of Parliament.

If it was a story about snow in the north, you needed to try to get hold of some video of the snow in Northumberland or at least some photographs you could show of the snowy scene. You either had to ask the video librarians if we had any library or stock footage, or we had to get the pictures sent from their original source, whether that was from Newcastle or New York and fed down the line either by satellite or cable.

Also, unlike these days when anyone can film and upload pictures onto their phones, using YouTube channels or social media, getting your pictures on Terrestrial TV in the late 1990s involved a lot more people.

There was the camera and sound operator who had originally shot the pictures, often with a producer director like me in tow to ask the questions, sometimes even a lighting director if it was a big interview. There were the production managers who helped you sort out the technical aspects of the shoot, the broadcast engineer who was responsible for feeding the pictures from one location to another. There was the video editor who helped you edit or cut the pictures and, finally, all the people in the gallery that helped to make sure the pictures went out on air.

First there was the director, who controlled and shouted out all the camera shots, the vision mixer who actually selected those shots on screen and the programme editor who created the running order and shouted in the presenter's ear. Then there was the production assistant, who did all the timings on the live show, the technical director who checked the quality of the pictures and sound, the autocue operator who controlled all the words that flashed in front of the presenters for them to read out. Inside the studio there were the lighting, camera and sound crews plus a floor manager or two who made sure everyone sat in the right spot at the right time and, of course, the presenters themselves who read out the link into the video or talked over the images you were showing.

Oh, and then there were the make-up artists, who had the most important and difficult job of all to make the presenters look bright and perky at 6am. This was no mean feat when you saw the state of some of them when they first arrived in the building. Waking up at three in the morning and lack of sleep is not good for anyone's complexion. Not only did their job include putting on eye makeup and lipstick it also involved covering up random pimples, spots and in the case of male presenters shaving rashes and bald patches.

Then there was the wardrobe team who had to buy, pick out and wash, press and iron their clothes. You are talking about a hell of a lot of people just to make one TV show.

In radio, I worked with presenters who turned up unwashed, dishevelled and, in some cases, topless when it got too hot in the studios. Listeners were none the wiser. The only leeway TV presenters had was that most people only saw them from the waist up, particularly the newsreaders behind the desk. When Penny Smith was just reading the news, she would often wear a smart jacket and blouse on top and jeans and training shoes underneath.

Having got the hang of editing or cutting pictures with the help of a video editor, who sat in a darkened suite surrounded by screens and knobs, I also had to learn all the technical terms. My time on UK Living and the London cable station Channel One had taught me a few of them. 'VT' stood for video tape, which often had a voiceover and told a particular story. Sometimes, though, they called it a package, although it had nothing to do with waxed brown paper sent first class by Royal Mail. It referred to the fact it was a finished piece of video that was ready to go out on air. Like a complete package.

A 'ulay' pronounced 'you lay' was short for underlay. It did not in any way involve a trip to a carpet shop. Instead, it was a term where you edited together some pictures that played out on air, while the presenter spoke UNDER the pictures to illustrate a story. Although this was even more confusing because at the BBC, our rival channel, they called it an olay, which was short for overlay, because the pictures went OVER the top of the person talking. When I first heard this term, I thought it had something to do with a certain face cream my nan used to use or I kept thinking of a tall dark Spanish flamenco dancer standing in the wings with his castanets ready to shout 'Olé', every time he was directed to do so.

Even more confusing was when you saw OOV in a script. I originally thought it meant to build up the excitement for a story ...like OOOOH, what's coming next? But I quickly learned it meant *out of vision*, yet another way to describe the fact that a presenter would be talking over or under some pictures just like a ulay or an olay.

A SOT was short for *sound on tape*, but in reality, it was a short interview clip of someone saying something in vision with no other pictures over the top of them. This was also called a *soundbite*. Originally, I imagined pictures of someone eating something, perhaps munching a large juicy Cox apple, with large sound effects to illustrate the point, but it actually turned out to be the same thing as the SOT; a short clip of someone talking.

Having got to grips with many television terms, there were still many that were a mystery to me. As I sat in that *GMTV* newsroom at five o'clock in the morning, a six o'clock 'menu tease' was one of them.

The menu part had drawn a blank, so I tried the other part. What about this tease? Who was I teasing? I have to say I could tease anyone if I knew them well, but I had only been in the job for just over a week and I didn't think my colleagues would have taken too kindly to me ribbing them about their dress sense or their bad choice of hairstyle.

The clock was ticking. It was now quarter past five and I knew I had to deliver this menu tease thing by six o'clock whatever it was. I took a punt that the cutting bit had something to do with editing.

Between five and six in the morning there was always a huge queue of producers trying to get into the three editing suites we had. We had to edit lots of videos before we went on air. Two and a half hours is a lot of time to fill and while much of it was live, there were also lots of SOTs and ulays to be cut.

At that time in the morning, producers tended to put down roots in the edit suites.

It was the TV equivalent of German tourists bagging a sunbed with their towels in the Costa del Sol. You made your claim early and then wouldn't budge.

There were two reasons for this. Firstly, they often had to update their news stories to cover any new storylines, so there was no point moving. Secondly and probably more importantly, they were too tired to move.

Like me, they had all been working since nine o'clock at night before, and by five the following morning their energy levels were close to zero.

Also, if you left, you often lost your slot and had to hover outside as some other producer had pounced. There was often an unofficial queueing system like a dance card. Editors would often receive requests to "go in next" from producers desperate to get their footage edited by the witching hour of 6am when we went on air. Producers frequently ended up bribing editors with biscuits, sweets and offers of extra tea so they could jump the queue.

With no idea what to do, and unaware of the queueing system, I walked into Edit One to find a producer slumped over the desk trying to nap. Nick the editor was sitting beside her.

"I need to cut a tease for the six o'clock menu," I said, trying to sound like I knew what I was talking about.

The producer uncurled herself from the desk and looked up at me sleepily. "A six o'clock menu tease on what?"

Trying not to give away the fact that I was completely ignorant. I turned on my heels and left the edit suite.

"I'll find out," I said and walked off before she could question me further. I ran back to the senior producer who was still furiously typing into her computer.

"Sorry Kate, what do you want a six o'clock menu tease on?" I said, trying not to sound stupid.

Kate paused and looked up from her keyboard. "The story you are producing," she said, looking at me oddly. "I need a six o'clock menu tease on dangerous dogs."

Now this was making more sense. The previous evening at the start of the shift we had all been assigned stories to look after overnight. My stories that night were dangerous dogs and our Hollywood gossip slot with our LA correspondent in America.

I went back to Edit One where Nick was now on his own. The other producer had sloped off to make some breakfast.

"I need to do a six o'clock menu tease on dangerous dogs, but I don't have a clue how to do it," I confessed.

"Don't worry," said Nick. "I'll help you." He then explained that a menu tease was a ten second script you wrote for the presenter to say over moving pictures in the form of a ulay. The menu tease would tell people, or entice them, about what was coming up on the show.

On the top of every hour, or just before, there was a menu teasing two or three stories. The day before another young child had been mauled by a Staffordshire bull terrier and we were debating whether people should be able to still keep this breed as a pet in the UK or whether they should be banned?

With just fifteen minutes to go, Nick had helped me to cut my first menu tease and I proudly watched as Penny and John read out my script under the pictures of a snarling dog that I had found from our video library.

I had managed to get away with it. I had navigated a six o'clock menu tease without anyone finding out how little I knew.

Now I just had to learn the rest of it.

2

CROSSED WIRES

'Who said TV was glamorous?' I thought to myself as I wriggled along on my stomach. The tufts from the school carpet left a thin layer of beige fluff on my brand-new black work jacket and trousers.

We had just gone live on *GMTV* and while I was inching along on my stomach, trying not to make a noise, the then Home Secretary Jack Straw was just centimetres away from me, busy telling our presenters Eamonn Holmes and Fiona Phillips about a new government initiative.

He was oblivious to the scene going on behind him. In front of him, the ITN TV camera operator, a head teacher, ten young school children and five government officials, could see exactly what was going on. The viewers at home may have just been seeing a government minister talking, but those present could also see behind him a TV producer doing a very good impression of a large black-suited worm, wriggling along the ground.

To make matters worse, two of the young school children decided it was much more fun to join me than to stand and listen to a member of the British government talking. They too dropped to the floor and started crawling towards me. "You can be the snake and I'll be the wiggly worm," whispered the little girl to us both. "No, I'm the snake," said the little boy, pushing her to one side. "And I am going to eat you both all up!" He made a loud gobbling noise.

To be fair, at this point I really hoped that he would eat me all up or at least the ground would. Rather than standing calmly beside the camera operator, I was on the floor covered in beige fluff and involved in some imaginary worm game with two six-year-olds. This really was not how I had imagined my first *live* broadcast to be on Breakfast TV.

When I told people, I worked in television everyone always had the same response. "Oooh, how exciting." Quickly followed by "How glamorous, what celebrities have you met?" The reality was very different. Over my years in Breakfast TV, yes, I did get to meet some very well-known people and, yes, I did get to have some amazing experiences, but behind the scenes as a TV producer involved long hours, hard work and thinking on your feet to overcome any number of obstacles. Whether it be trying to sort technical problems, managing the fragile egos of celebrities or dealing with unruly presenters or pets.

It also involved dealing with politicians.

In Breakfast Television news, you often covered the same stories at the same time as other networks. BBC Breakfast and Sky also had morning shows, and they too were looking to cover the news that people were waking up to, whether it was updating a developing story, or a new government announcement that day.

Many big organisations often embargoed their stories, in other words, stipulating a time that the story was released to the media, in many cases often to target the breakfast TV and radio market. The government in particular, liked launching new initiatives or policies early in the morning, hoping to set the news agenda of the day.

This particular morning, I had been sent along to make sure that the Home Secretary Jack Straw sat down for our interview at exactly the right time. It was my first time producing a live broadcast for *GMTV*. Not surprisingly I wanted it to go well. I had had lots of experience producing television from a TV gallery, but I had never done anything live on location and I was keen to try to create a good impression.

Having been told I was going to be with a government minister, I went out and bought a new black suit from Next. Television production offices are normally filled with scruffy individuals wearing jeans, but if you were a reporter or going along to produce something involving members of the government you tended to try to be more smartly dressed.

I had a new black jacket, white blouse and black pencil skirt, with black patent court shoes. I had never dealt with live TV interviews with government ministers before, but I assumed they would appreciate me dressing appropriately for the occasion.

We had a slot of 7.40am. The problem was he was also doing interviews with *BBC Breakfast* and *Sky News*. *Sky News* were just after us at 7.50, while *BBC Breakfast* had an interview organised with Jack Straw at eight o'clock. Their producers had no interest in making sure he got onto *GMTV* on time. In fact, they often hindered it, running late with their interviews or grabbing the government minister early for their own network.

My job was to make sure he sat down at exactly the right time and stayed there for our allotted four minutes.

Before the Home Secretary arrived, I was nervous about the interview, but I couldn't have been more prepared. I had my script, my brief and a list of questions that the presenters would be asking him.

I met the cameraman outside the school. At 6am they let me in to set up our camera position. Not only did we need to have a different one to the other broadcasters, but also, we wanted to get the best shot with the best background. Eager to make sure we got the prime position I had actually arrived at 5.30, but all I did was wait outside for half an hour.

Being so early in the morning, I had totally forgotten that not everyone was up at dawn and neither was the school caretaker. I sat in the cameraman's car waiting to see any sign of life at the school gates. At 6am the caretaker finally appeared and let us in.

Having entered the school, we looked for the best spot to film. We needed a location that had enough light either coming from the window or from overhead lights, but not so bright that it would cast shadows over the guests. We didn't want to shoot against a window, or the interviewee would be in silhouette. It was April so the sun had already risen, but we also had some lights just in case. We had to find a location quiet enough so we could clearly hear what the guest was saying. We knew there would be many people turning up, so we chose a classroom away from the main reception area and started to set up.

There was still no sign of the soundman, however. I called the number on our call sheet to find out where he was.

A croaky voice answered the phone. "Didn't you get the message? I had to call in sick today, I woke up feeling terrible," he said and hung up.

No, I had not got the news. I phoned up the production desk and explained my annoyance at not being told.

"Who's going to replace him?"

"We can't just magic sound people out of thin air at four in the morning," he said sarcastically.

"It's an easy down-the-line with Jack Straw so the cameraman should be able to manage it."

This was not the news I wanted to hear when I was producing my first ever live broadcast.

I tried to calm myself down. This wasn't the end of the world. It was just one interview with Jack Straw sitting on a chair. All it needed was someone to put one microphone and earpiece on him. What could possibly go wrong?

The cameraman set up his camera and then laid out two cables, one for the microphone we would clip onto the minister's lapel and one with an earpiece so that he could hear what was going on back in the studio in Central London and, more importantly, hear the presenters' questions. The picture and the sound were working perfectly. At 6.30, we were all set up and ready to go.

The problem was politicians; in particular, government ministers were notorious for cutting it fine. An hour passed and there was no sign of Jack Straw. By 7.25, the Home Secretary had only just turned up at the school. The head teacher, a hoard of press photographers and a gaggle of schoolchildren immediately rushed to meet him.

With just fifteen minutes until the interview, I really wanted him to come with me into our quiet classroom and sit straight down, but Jack Straw had other ideas. He was showing no sign of sitting anywhere, chatting away to the throng of people who surrounded him.

I had only been working in Breakfast TV for a few months, so I really didn't know the etiquette regarding this. Did I let him chat, and then hold up a big sign with *GMTV* on it like someone waiting at an airport arrivals lounge? Or did I need to go over and firmly escort him to where our camera was set up? He was, after all, a government minister, and I was a lowly TV producer.

With eight minutes to go, I decided to do the latter. I walked up and introduced myself to one of his press team, who was standing in a corner checking his phone for messages.

"Good morning, my name is Michelle Porter from *GMTV*." I said, trying to lower my voice to sound a little bit more authoritative.

"Would it be possible for Mr Straw to come with me and sit down for his interview please?"

The press officer looked at his watch and at the paper schedule he had in front of him.

"Just give him a few more minutes, he'll be over to you shortly." He said and went back to his notes.

I started to panic. It was all very well giving him a *few more minutes* but, by my calculations, that would only give me five minutes to escort him down the corridor to the classroom, then get him sat down and miked up for the interview.

My heart was thumping. This was my first broadcast, and I desperately wanted it to go well. I waited for another minute and then decided I could wait no more.

Spotting the Home Secretary with his back to me, I marched over and asked in my low, firm voice.

"Mr Straw, I'm here with *GMTV* and we have an interview with you now, can I kindly ask you to accompany me and sit down please?"

I trembled as I said it, worried that I was being too forceful with the minister, but I had a job to do. Either I wasn't talking loud enough or maybe words had not come out of my mouth at all. There was no reaction. He completely ignored me and carried on chatting. His back was still firmly turned away from me.

Either he was trying to prove that he was in charge or he was just being downright rude. I didn't have time to consider which, I just had a job to do. I tried again. This time though, my voice had risen several decibels so I sounded like a strangled cat.

"Mr Straw, you have an interview with *GMTV* in two minutes, please can you come with me and sit down." My words again received no acknowledgement from him.

By now, the senior producer in the gallery was on the phone to me asking why they still had an empty seat, rather than Jack Straw sitting in it. There was nothing left but to go for it. I tapped him on his left shoulder. He jumped and spun round, alarmed.

"Hello," he said. "How can I help you?"

"Mr Straw. Please will you listen to me. I work for *GMTV* and I really need you to come with me for our interview," My voice was up to straggled gerbil level, trying to control the panic in my vocal cords.

"Yes of course," he said, checking his watch and glancing over to his press officer who nodded his approval that it was indeed time to follow me.

"I'm sorry I didn't hear you before. I'm a little deaf in my left ear."

This explained a lot. I had been standing behind him just to the left, so he obviously hadn't heard my requests. He hadn't been rude after all. I was so embarrassed. Not only had I spent the last two minutes shouting at a government minister, but I had been shouting at a partially deaf one.

I would have given him a grovelling apology, but I didn't have time for that. I escorted him to our camera position in the little classroom and sat him down. The whole gaggle of officials, school children and teachers followed him. This wasn't ideal as there would be a chance they would make a noise, but I didn't have time to shoo them away.

There was less than a minute to go until we were *live*. The cameraman hastily put a lapel mike on Jack Straw's suit, and handed him an earpiece to put into his left ear, so he could hear what the studio was saying.

"I'm really sorry," said Jack Straw. "Can I put the earpiece in my right ear? I can hear better in that one."

The cameraman obliged, hastily adjusted the wiring behind his back and handed it to him to put in his right ear. Jack Straw popped the earpiece into his ear and we were all set.

By now, there were just thirty seconds to go until the broadcast, so we both ran back to behind the camera to make sure the minister was framed up and in focus and the studio could hear him as they were just wrapping up the previous item and coming to him imminently. I stood back, relieved that I had achieved my one job, getting him to sit down. I tried to catch my breath and felt pleased with myself. I phoned the gallery to tell them. "He's there and ready to go," I said, but I had spoken too soon.

The problem was that the cable had been set up for his left ear, so putting it in his right meant that it had to stretch that bit further and was very tight around the back of Jack Straw's neck. Every time he turned his head, the cable at the back connected to the camera popped out and disconnected from the earpiece.

"You'll have to go and fix it," whispered the cameraman. "I can't leave the camera." He waved me in the direction of the Home Secretary.

Running behind Jack Straw, I fumbled for the two separated wires and through sweaty palms managed to clip them back together.

"Yes, Fiona, I can hear you?" said Jack Straw just as I reconnected the wires, at which point I realised we were now live on the show. There was no escape. I was trapped behind the back of a government minister and I couldn't get out. There was no way I could pop out from behind him like a Jack-in-the-box or, in my case, a Jill-in-the-box and walk off.

I just imagined viewers watching around their breakfast tables at home as a random woman appeared. I was going to have to leave some other way. I was stuck crouched behind a member of the UK government and I had nowhere to go.

I thought about just staying there, but soon realised I couldn't spend the full four minutes like this. For a start, it would have been very disconcerting for the Home Secretary, having a producer breathing down his neck behind him. For another, I didn't think my pencil skirt would hold out that long. It was currently tightly wrapped around my knees. I also didn't think I could sit still for that long. I always was a terrible fidget. He was about the same size as me so any slight movement and you would have seen an odd arm or ear appearing behind him, which would have been very distracting for the viewers at home.

I had to think on my feet or, rather, my stomach. There was nothing else for it. I dropped to the ground, lay flat on the ground and started crawling, using my arms to propel me along the school carpet. I was so close to the floor I could smell the combined odour of children's feet and ground-in biscuits.

The two children came to join me. Rather than concentrating on what Mr Straw had to say, everyone in the room had their eyes trained on this crazy producer wriggling along the floor, playing at being a worm with two small children.

Having wriggled a safe distance out of the shot, I decided it was safe to get up. There was just one-minute left on the interview. I went and stood beside the cameraman for the remainder of the time trying to make out the previous excruciating three minutes had not just happened.

I had done my job, I had got Jack Straw to sit down, on time and before our Breakfast TV rivals could snatch him.

I had completed my first live broadcast for breakfast television. I had many career highlights in my time working on Breakfast TV, but this was definitely an early low one. To viewers watching at home, they would have seen none of my panic or last-minute drama, but I knew full well what had happened and had a fluff-covered suit to prove it.

3

HOLMES SWEET HOLMES

Working on *GMTV*, I became used to answering the same question. In fact, I lost count of the number of times people asked me about it. The person would start the conversation with "I love watching Eamonn and Fiona. They seem lovely on TV, but what are they *really* like?"

As an employee of the company, I was obliged to say that they were lovely to work with, but now I don't work there anymore, I can reveal the truth!

Fiona Phillips is a great presenter and fun to work with. Eamonn Holmes is an extremely talented television presenter, but he is also one of the most annoying. On the plus side he was one of the best male presenters I knew who could go from light to shade without skipping a beat. What I mean by that is that in one moment he could be having a laugh with Fiona Phillips on the sofa, the next he would be introducing an item about a family that had suffered a terrible tragedy, but he always got the tone exactly right.

Using just the right words mixed with a pinch of Irish charm he could put ordinary families at their ease and just as easily lull politicians into a false sense of security with a light-hearted quip, before delivering a killer question that went straight for the jugular.

I'll come to the annoying part in a moment.

When I joined *GMTV*, Eamonn and Fiona were the main presenters. Fiona had previously been the LA correspondent, but when Anthea Turner left the show, she was put forward as her temporary replacement. Eamonn and Fiona immediately gelled on screen and she became a permanent fixture. They had great chemistry. Both were strong journalists, but they also knew how to be down-to-earth, and have a bit of fun in the morning. The viewers loved them and the ratings for the show were huge, far outstripping our BBC rivals. My parents loved watching them, too.

When I joined the show, both my mum and dad were really proud and watched religiously each morning, particularly if they knew I was working on that day's show. What was frustrating, though, was that my mum remembered more about what Eamonn and Fiona had said than the item I had spent hours slogging over.

Our phone conversation would go something like this:

"Hi Mum, did you watch the show this morning?"

"Yes, of course. I loved Fiona's jacket today and wasn't it funny when she and Eamonn had that joke about the Welsh tart?"

"Yes, that was funny." I remembered Fiona had been talking about eating a tart and Eamonn had asked her if it was a Welsh one. They had then both had a giggle about Welsh tarts. Fiona had Welsh parents so her love of Wales and all things Welsh was a running theme through the show.

I tried again. "But did you see my item about the MMR vaccine?"

At the time, Scottish doctor Andrew Wakefield had released a paper in the Lancet suggesting that having the measles, mumps, and rubella vaccine could increase a child's risk of being autistic. I had spent hours trying to track down parents who were now thinking of not giving their child the vaccine after what he had written. I had found some worried parents, but it had taken several hours to persuade them to come on the show. The result was a very fiery live debate on both sides of the argument.

"Ah yes, that was very interesting," said Mum. Hurray! She'd seen it, I patted myself on the back for that one. "But Eamonn obviously wasn't happy that Manchester United lost this morning." She replied without skipping a beat.

Initially I was miffed that she had spent more time noticing what the presenters had been talking about, than the story I had spent a whole day trying to organise. But then I realised I shouldn't take it personally. You could produce the most fantastic piece of television, but people ultimately tuned in for the presenters. If they didn't like the presenting team, then they would switch to the other channel.

The fact that they pulled in such big audiences meant that the stories I produced were seen by a much bigger audience than the shows I had worked on previously. Millions rather than thousands of people were watching this show.

Having watched Eamonn and Fiona on TV before I joined, I was very nervous about meeting them. As an output producer, I didn't have to deal with them directly as that was the job of the overnight editor and the senior producer, but I would see them walk past me when I was outside the studio and they always smiled and said hello.

The closest I came to them in the six months was watching them read out the link or tease that I had written. If they didn't change it as they read it, I felt immensely proud, as I realised, I had learnt to adapt my scripts to their voice. In other words, saying things how they would naturally say them. Fifty per cent of the time I cracked it, the other fifty Eamonn or Fiona would either tweak it slightly or completely change it.

About nine months after I joined *GMTV*, I was on a day shift as an output producer. There were two producers and a researcher on each shift with a senior producer in charge of us. Gerry, who was the editor at the time, called me into the office, along with Malcolm the deputy editor.

"Michelle, we've been really pleased with your work here at *GMTV*." I was really surprised. Compliments did not come easily from these two. "We were wondering what your career plans were?"

I was a bit taken aback. I had only been at the job for less than a year, and still felt I was learning how to produce things for a breakfast television audience. I tried to think of an appropriate response. I obviously wanted to get promoted at some point, but I didn't want to come across as too cocky, less than a year into the job.

"How would you like to be a senior producer?" Gerry asked before I had a chance to respond.

"Well obviously I'd like to step up to the position sometime in the future," I replied, trying to sound keen, but not *too* keen.

"How about today?" he said.

I was very flattered by their confidence in me.

"Nicola has phoned in sick, so we would like you to cover her," Malcolm added.

Now this was making more sense. The senior producer was ill and they were in a hole and they needed someone to get them out of it.

"But I've never done it before," I said. I had noticed that normally people who did the job had a few shadow shifts first.

"Don't worry, I'm sure you'll pick it up and I'll be there to help you," Malcolm said, giving a nervous laugh.

I wasn't sure if the nervous laugh was about me doing the job or him actually helping me.

And so, I started as an acting senior producer on that day. To put it mildly I was terrified. In front of me was a huge grid of lines that made up the running order. Two and half hours of television had to be filled every day with proper TV items - scripts and videos and underlays that would later end up on the show. I had to decide which items I thought would work best in each slot, plus the length of each segment and what went in them.

Although I had producers to help me write the items, I was responsible for writing all the introductions and the teases - which I now knew how to do- and checking and rewriting the bits that the other producers had written. I also had to present all the items in the three o'clock programme planning meeting to get the blessing or not of the senior team. We only had so many slots in the show and the editor naturally wanted to make sure we put stories that would give us the best ratings.

Sometimes you would have worked all day setting up stories, only for the editor to throw them out at 3pm and you were left with two or three big gaps in the show. To be fair to Malcolm, though, if there was a hole in the show when he left for the evening, he would still be phoning in at 8pm with ideas on how to fill it.

When you worked overnight you had to update all the scripts ready for the executive editor who would come in at 2am.

The first time I spoke to Eamonn was on a night shift. He had phoned up to speak to that night's executive editor, a jolly man called Simon. Simon was nicknamed 'The Admiral' because watching him was just like watching the captain steering the ship in the television gallery.

Running a Breakfast TV show definitely wasn't plain sailing. All sorts of chaos could be going on around him, there could be breaking news, late arriving guests, technical glitches and all manner of script changes, but Simon would firmly shout instructions to both the presenters and the studio about what to do next. If an item was drifting on too long, Simon would flick the microphone on and speak to the presenters in their earpieces and quietly tell them to move on. Eight out of ten times they did what he said, on the other occasions, he would just tweak the timings on other items on the show to accommodate.

At two o'clock in the morning the newsroom could be a cold and gloomy place. Simon would pitch up and immediately inject his energy and humour into the proceedings. He was like a human Red Bull, giving an instant boost to everyone around him. I learnt a lot from him about how much time you needed to give to items to let them breathe or how you could shave a minute off one item and give it to another to make it all add up to the right time in the running order.

One morning I was sitting at my desk waiting for Simon to arrive. It was just before 2am when I picked up the phone. It was Eamonn. I was surprised to receive his call as he normally didn't show up until 6.30am. I thought at this time he would be fast asleep.

He appeared to be in a good mood. I soon discovered why. He was in a car on the way back from Manchester after watching his beloved football team Manchester United win 2-0 against Chelsea.

"Is the Admiral there?" He asked.

"He's not in yet, do you want me to pass on a message?" I said nervously.

To my surprise he had no message but wanted my help.

"Can you do something for me?"

This was the first time Eamonn had asked me directly to do anything, so I wanted to get it right.

"I was watching Ally McBeal last night and there's a funny dancing baby, I also saw it on the website. Can you look it up for me and get it ready for the show this morning? I'd love to talk about it on the programme later."

This might sound like an easy request, but this was the early days of the internet. We had just one computer linked up to the web which sat in the corner of the office blinking away like a tiny lighthouse. Most people were afraid to touch it.

I had done a course on the internet in a local internet cafe, but I still hadn't used it much. "Can you give me the web address?" I said nervously. I didn't want to mess up my first encounter with Eamonn.

"H T T P S colon forward slash forward slash Ally McBeal dot com," he said.

I asked him to repeat it one more time. The Ally McBeal bit was easy but the H's, the T's and the colons at the beginning were really confusing me.

I wrote it down, but still wasn't sure I had written it down correctly, but I didn't have the nerve to ask him to say it for a third time. This was before the days of Google or Yahoo, so I had to get the address exactly right or otherwise the internet wouldn't find it.

For the next two hours I kept running to the lone computer that had the internet on it and tried typing in every permutation I could think of. Every time 'page not found' kept blinking back at me.

I didn't want to admit to anyone that I couldn't find the site, but I was getting desperate. I checked I had put a colon, I checked the spelling of her name, I checked with forward slashes and backslashes. Finally, I admitted defeat and quietly asked someone in our IT department.

"Did you put it in upper or lower case?"

"Upper case or course," I said. "It needs to be lower case." came the reply.

Who puts something like that in lower case I wondered, but I was soon to discover everyone on the internet did. It worked and I finally found the website I was looking for, but that was just the start of it. I then had to work out how to get the dancing baby from the computer onto video and on the show. At that time, you couldn't record the screen or email it to someone, so I had to find a camera to film it with. After another hour of searching, I finally had the piece filmed and edited and ready in the rundown to be used as a video when Eamonn brought it up in the conversation.

I was really proud of myself for doing it, but sadly it never made it to air, my hours of work were wasted. Eamonn and Fiona were so busy talking about something else that Eamonn never talked about Ally McBeal, so we never broadcast it.

This was a producer's worst nightmare, watching your item go from white to blue on the rundown. This meant it was being put on hold. This was just a simple clip, but often you could have spent the whole day or night researching, scripting and editing a video, only for it never to see the light of day. It was very demoralising, particularly after a night shift when you were tired, but you had to just learn not to let it get to you.

But this wasn't the most annoying thing about Eamonn.

While other presenters like Fiona would turn up hours before the show started to read their briefs and get up to date on the morning's news. Eamonn would arrive at 6.30am, but sometimes just ten minutes before he went on air and just wing it.

The irritating part was he would still do it brilliantly. It was like the boy at school who did no revision for his exams, but would then pass them with flying colours getting a grade A. While I was the one who always spent hours revising and still only got a B.

The runner would fax him through all the briefs for the show the night before, but he often hadn't read them. I remember on many occasions either Simon or myself standing outside his dressing room briefing him in his briefs. We were shouting through the dressing room door, while he was in his underpants on the other side changing into his suit. I soon perfected the art of shouting the basics of the story in less than a minute.

While I was worried that he hadn't had time to straighten his tie, let alone work out who the hell he was interviewing. He would breeze into the studio with just minutes to spare, sit down and just do it.

Lots of times the opening titles to the show would be running and Eamonn still hadn't taken his seat. Only once do I remember him not making it in time, but he brushed it off with a witty one liner. Often during the ad breaks you would see him reading the brief for the next story he was talking about. I often wondered how on earth he could take it all in, but he did and always did a great job of interviewing people.

The rare mistake he did make, he got away with, using his Irish charm. He was rarely lost for words. Even during an interview with magician David Blaine, he managed to keep talking, even when David decided to say nothing.

Another annoying thing he did was call me Meesh. My name is Michelle and I didn't like it shortened, I would tolerate Meeshelle, or even Shelley, but definitely not Shelle or Meesh.

He was the only person who called me Meesh and still does and gets away with it. If anyone else did I would immediately snap back at them. The crazy thing with Eamonn is even if he was saying something you didn't like, with his soothing Irish lilt, it didn't sound half as bad, in fact you actually felt he was being nice.

Years later I was at a reception held at St James Palace in London for the Northern Ireland Tourist Board. It was a black-tie affair and I was wearing a strapless black ruffled dress.

The great and good from Northern Ireland were there including Barry McGuigan, Christine Lampard, Dennis Taylor and Van Morrison. I didn't know until I arrived but the evening was compered by Eamonn, one of their most famous exports.

Eamonn spotted me in the crowd. By now he had left *GMTV* ten years before and was working at Sky and This Morning.

"Ah Meesh," he said. "How are you?" I tried not to bristle. "What are you up to? Where are you working now?"

"I'm still working on ITV Breakfast," I said.

"Oh," he said, sounding surprised. "I thought you would have left years ago."

I didn't know how to respond to that. There was an awkward silence.

"Congratulations by the way."

I didn't know what he was congratulating me on. Was it for staying the course on Breakfast TV?

"When's it due?" He said, pointing at my stomach.

I was shocked. I may have put on a few pounds since I had last seen him, but I would hardly describe the ruffle in my dress as bump-like.

"Eamonn I'm not pregnant." I responded, pulling down my dress to try and prove it.

"Are you not?" said Eamonn in his charming Irish drawl. "That's strange, because you look like you are."

I was flabbergasted, but not surprised. I should have been shocked and offended, instead it just made me smile. Once again Eamonn had delivered a killer line coated in his smooth

Irish tones. Somehow, he could make you feel special, even when insulting you.

He disappeared into the crowd, before I could respond. Moving effortlessly between celebrities. Joking with one and having a serious conversation with another.

I learnt many things from Eamonn, but the best skill I perfected was to be able to brief presenters and guests in break next speed. Standing behind that dressing room door you quickly mastered the technique. If you couldn't tell someone in sixty seconds the key points, they needed to talk about in a four-minute interview, then you hadn't understood the story.

And Eamonn took just sixty seconds to get to the heart of the story. Like it or not. He was annoyingly good at it.

4
_____

IT WILL BE ALRIGHT IN THE MORNING

There is something weird about going to work in the dark when everyone else is heading in the other direction, and coming home in broad daylight as everyone is just starting their day. In my case, it also means you find yourself asleep in all manner of places.

It was 9.30 in the morning and I was in an empty rail carriage with the train driver of the 8.37 from Waterloo. He looked shocked to see me. Not for the first time I had fallen asleep on the journey home, after a night shift, but this was the first time I had ended up in the railway sidings.

"You're not supposed to be here. You're not insured," he said indignantly.

"I didn't do it on purpose." I replied sheepishly. "It's just that no one noticed me in the carriage and the next thing I knew, here I am,"

I am sure he thought I had been on an all-night bender. "I work on Breakfast TV," I explained. "I've just done a night shift. I'm exhausted and I just want to go home to bed."

His face softened. "Ah," he said. "That explains everything."

Working on Breakfast TV is like working in no other part of television. For a start, it's live television every weekday. There are no summer breaks, days off for bank holidays or Easter holidays, every weekday except Christmas Day, Boxing Day and New Year's Day, there was a show to produce. This included working on Sundays, to get ready for Monday's show.

The other main difference to this and any other normal job is the time of the day you had to work. Every weekday morning viewers tuned into the latest news or stories they were waking up to from 6am to 8.30am. The problem was in order to see those stories, poor souls like me had to work all night to produce them. If you weren't working nights, you often had to get up very early in the morning, often three or four o'clock to either come into the studio to produce your item, or direct a live out on location.

I lost count of the number of times that people didn't clock the fact that in order to appear on Breakfast TV, they actually had to get up early to do it.

"Can't we just do the interview later in the day?" one PR asked me. "My client doesn't like early mornings."

"No," I would reply. "The clue is in the title, Good Morning Television–it has to happen live in the morning! We are on air from 6am to 8.30am."

The PR looked horrified. "You mean my client has to get up at six o'clock to be in the studio for 6.30 and then they'll be on air at 7.20? Who on earth is up at that time of the day watching?" she exclaimed snootily.

"About five million people," I replied.

"I think it might be worth your client's effort to get up early one day, and bear a thought for all the studio crew and staff who have been there all night or from two in the morning."

She was suitably chastised.

When I first started at *GMTV*, I used to work on our output team. There was a day team and a night team and we used to alternate a week of days and then a week of nights. The day team who worked from ten in the morning to ten at night were responsible for writing scripts and videos for the news stories that we had already planned for the next day. Things like a new report you knew that was coming out, or a fixed event like Halloween or Fireworks night. The night team were responsible for finishing off those stories or updating them as the story developed during the night. Or you could be working on a breaking news story coming in from around the world.

There was a real mix of stories. It could be anything from a new initiative by the Government, to covering wildfires in California. A human-interest story about a family with a child with life limiting illness through to a story about the baking hot weather. Every time you walked into the newsroom you never knew what you would be working on. Every day was a fresh set of stories and videos to cut.

As anyone who has ever done them will know, working night shifts are not good for you. I know many people spend years of their lives working in the twilight hours. I have huge respect for those people – doctors, nurses, police, street cleaners, security to name just a few. I did just five years of night shifts and that was plenty. On the way into work, everyone else is heading back home to curl up in front of the telly with their evening meal, on the way back, when you leave work the following morning, you are fighting your way through commuters charging to get to work in the other direction.

Night shifts also did weird things to your body. For a start, you were eating cereal when most people were having their evening meal. You would then head into the office where you would have your lunch around midnight. As the night wore on, you started to get peckish again around 4am, just as the daily buns and pastries arrived. You then had your busiest period of the shift when you went on air from 6am to 8.30am. Having then outputted the show you then headed home, often after consuming yet another breakfast.

I always remember the feeling you get between two and three in the morning. Your body temperature drops and suddenly you feel incredibly vulnerable. Decisions that seem perfectly normal and easy to make during the day such as what you are going to have for dinner, or where you are going out that weekend, seem incredibly difficult to make at that time in the morning.

I would get so cold that my hands would become numb and I would start to shiver. I kept a large cardigan and a blanket in my drawer, and would wrap them tightly around my legs, while I carried on typing. You often saw producers sitting in their coats, huddled around little heaters to try to keep warm. It was also common to find them slumped on their desks, trying to grab a quick nap before the busy period of the shift started, when we went on air.

One producer we knew used to disappear for hours on end. We never did find out where she was hiding, but we assumed she had found an unlocked dressing room or a nice sofa somewhere in the building to sleep on.

One programme editor I worked with even used to fall asleep when we were live on air. I remember sitting next to him in the gallery – which is a noisy place at the best of times. One minute he was talking to the presenters. The next he had his eyes shut, snatching forty winks during an ad break. An ad could be blasting out extolling the virtues of Kellogg's corn flakes, while he was quietly snoring next to me. I had to poke him awake thirty seconds before the end of the break, because the presenters were shouting at him about what was coming next.

After the adrenaline rush of being on air, you then had to make your way home. At the end of the shift, your whole body would ache. You then had to summon up the energy to battle the commuters. Walking to Waterloo station in the opposite direction to everyone else at nine in the morning is hard work. Trying to do it after a twelve-hour night shift, when you are physically and mentally shattered, is torture. You felt like you were playing a computer game trying to avoid being knocked down by aliens coming towards you.

One time, I lost my footing and fell over, landing hard onto my bottom, my bags strewn around me. I didn't have the energy to get up. I just sat there watching the world go by. No one stopped to help me; they just took a wide berth and carried on.

I started to gently weep. At this point a homeless man shuffled past me, his sleeping bag under one arm and his crinkled carrier bag under the other. He bent down and offered me a tissue, but I declined, as I could see it was his last one. He offered his hand to get me up, but his hands were already pretty full with other things, so I thanked him and he shuffled on. It made me realise then that the only person who had stopped to offer help was someone who knew what it was like to be on the floor and everyone ignoring them. Finally, I summoned up the energy to get up and dusted down my clothes, I picked the grit out of my grazed knees and carried on.

When I started doing nights, I used to get the fastest train out of Waterloo to Epsom station where I lived, just to get home as quickly as I could to my bed. However, I soon learned this was pointless, as I often fell asleep on the way home and missed my station stop, ending up further down the line.

The station manager at the following station knew me well. "Fallen asleep again, love?" He would chuckle as I nodded, crossed the platform and waited to go back down the line.

This happened so many times that I decided to take the slower train, which at least terminated at my station. This was before the days of mobile phones with alarms on them, so instead I used to rely on human alarm clocks in the shape of South West train staff. Either the station manager would bang on the window to wake me up, or the guard would walk through checking the train and would lightly tap me on the shoulder to tell me to get off because it was the end of the line.

This time, though, my human alarm clocks were nowhere in sight and the plan had not worked. Not only had no one spotted me asleep in the carriage, but the train had left the station and slipped into the local sidings with me still snoozing inside it.

Five minutes later, I woke up with a start. "We've been a long-time outside Epsom?" I thought to myself. The last thing I could remember was waiting for the signal to turn green outside of the station. Now, looking around the carriage, I realised I was the only one there.

I started to panic. Here I was in an empty train in the railway sidings. Perhaps it was still in service, or maybe it would be there all day. Thoughts flashed through my brain of spending the next eight hours sleeping in the carriage, before wearily heading back into London for my next night shift.

I heard a noise at the end of the carriage and decided to go and investigate. The driver was walking through the carriages, opening and shutting the interconnecting doors until he reached the other end of the train. He jumped when he spotted me.

Having discovered my predicament, the train driver felt sorry for me. He had originally thought I was some young drunk woman back late after a night out, but then he realised I too was a night shift worker and he sympathised with me. I was still an insurance risk, but he now realised I hadn't done it on purpose.

He made another suggestion. "Come and join me in the cab. I could walk you back down the track," he said. "But I am going back down the line in ten minutes. It makes more sense for you to stay here with me. Do you want to join me for a cuppa?" He pulled out his flask from his bag. I took him up on his offer and tried hard not to cry at his kindness. He offered me a digestive biscuit to dunk in my tea.

I am incredibly grateful to people like the train driver who help you in times of need. True to his word ten minutes later, we went back down the line and I got off and thankfully made it home to bed by 10.30–enough time to get some sleep before heading back to work later that day. As a fellow shift worker, he knew very well how tired and vulnerable you felt. I will always remember him and his kindness, sharing his tea with me in his cab.

There are rarely regular hours working on television. As I have told many students over the years who have asked me about how to get a job in TV, if you want a nine to five job Monday to Friday, don't become a TV producer. The job required late nights, early mornings, working Sundays, bank holidays and often very long hours.

When I joined our Features Department on weeks when you had a major programme strand going out, working 70-hour weeks was common. You'd start at four or five in the morning then work throughout the day, before preparing for the next day's broadcast. It was your responsibility to get everything ready for the item you were producing, however long it took.

Years after my experience with the kind train driver, I had just had one of those days. I had been working all day as we were launching our campaign to end loneliness, called *1 million minutes,* the following morning.

The campaign was asking people to pledge as little as thirty minutes of their time to help someone who was lonely. It was called *1 million minutes* because according to the charity Age UK there were over one million elderly people in the UK at the time who never spoke to anyone on the phone or in person in a week. This was incredibly shocking and sad. My editor Neil decided he wanted to launch a campaign to change that by encouraging people to get in contact with and befriend an older lonely person.

We were hoping that we would encourage viewers between them to pledge one million minutes of their time. The first year was a huge success, we far exceeded that total. Now, in its second year, I was really chuffed that we had managed to persuade Dame Joan Collins to launch it for us.

She was due to be joining us on the Good Morning Britain sofa the following morning along with a 92-year-old man called George, who was talking about how lonely he had been until he started going to tea parties organised by the charity 'Contact the Elderly' where he had met other people and had a chance to chat. Having left the office at 10.30pm after a 5.30am start, I had worked seventeen hours straight and I was shattered.

I managed to jump on the last train heading to Epsom. I toyed with the idea of leaving my laptop at work. After all, I would be back at the studios in less than seven hours, but there was still work to be done on the way home, so I took it with me. Having completed what I needed to do, I put it back in my red satchel and tucked it by my side on the train. I then spent the rest of the journey answering emails on my work mobile phone that I hadn't had the chance to look at during the hectic day.

The train arrived at my station and I put on my red anorak and stepped off, wearily heading down the stairs to the ticket office below, through the automatic gates and out onto the street. I jumped into a black cab at the taxi rank and told the driver my address. It was too late to get a bus home.

As the taxi set off round the one-way system, it suddenly dawned on me; I had left my red satchel bag complete with laptop on the train. My heart sank. Not only would I be in serious trouble if I lost the computer, more importantly it contained the briefing notes I needed for Joan Collins. I had to get it back.

"Excuse me," I yelled at the taxi driver, banging on the glass between us as he listened to LBC late night radio. He finally pulled back the screen. "What is it?" he said, annoyed that I had interrupted his late-night radio listening.

"I'm really sorry, could you take me back to the station, please? I've forgotten something."

The driver looked confused, but did as I requested and drove me back round the long one-way system to the station. As it was after 10pm, his meter was clocking up the more expensive evening tariff, so it was already costing me £10, just to come back to where I had started.

I jumped out of the car and ran into the station. The ticket inspector at the automatic gates stopped me. "There's no more trains tonight," he said, blocking me from entering.

"I know that, but I need to get my bag back."

"All lost property goes to Waterloo. It will be logged and you can collect it in two days." He was reeling off a well-rehearsed script. "You just have to describe the item and give them a small fee and if they have it, you will get it back."

"Two days!" I cried at him. "It's got all my briefs in it and I have Joan Collins and a lonely old man called George coming into the studio in just six hours and I need my laptop to speak to her. Please can I go onto the platform and just try?" I pleaded.

He wrinkled his forehead and looked back at me, not quite sure what to say next.

"I have a plan," I continued, recalling my trip into the railway sidings all those years before.

"A plan to do what?" he said, looking at me suspiciously. I could see he wasn't quite sure if I was a potential terrorist disguised in a red anorak, or just plain bonkers.

"I know the train I was on terminated here at the station, so it's probably gone into the railway sidings. It must be coming back down the line to head back to the train terminus. As it stops at the platform, I could jump on the train and retrieve my bag?" I said, pleased at my own ingenuity.

He looked unimpressed by my enthusiasm.

He stood for a moment and thought about it. I could see he was interested in the Joan Collins part of the story, but he obviously didn't have a clue what my laptop had to do with her and a 92-year-old lonely man called George.

He looked at me standing on the station and he gave in. He could see I was desperate and tired, so he let me through the barriers up onto platform four.

The station manager was sitting in his guard box eating a bag of cheese and onion crisps. He kept looking at the station clock, obviously counting down the minutes until he could leave and go home.

I explained my plan to him.

"That's a great plan, but there is one flaw; the train you are talking about has finished for the night. It's not in service," he said, checking his train schedule pinned inside his guard box. "It's just going straight through the platform and back to the depot at Wimbledon." He continued munching on his crisps.

I sat down on one of the cold, blue iron station seats, deflated. My plan was hopeless. I had no way of getting my bag back.

Then I thought of something. "But it is definitely going through this platform on the station?" I asked him in desperation, clinging to any bit of info that might help me track it down.

"Yes, it is," he confirmed, not sure where this conversation was going.

"When is it due?" I enquired.

He pulled out his timetable and made a few calculations. "If I am not mistaken, it's due back down the line at eleven minutes past midnight."

My mind was whirring away and I spoke my thoughts aloud. "So, if it's coming through the station then...I could wave my coat and get him to stop," I said, pleased with myself for coming up with such a great plan.

"Are you mad?" He looked at me in horror. "This isn't a scene from The Railway Children. You can't just go around flagging down trains. It's not a taxi service. Train drivers don't just stop because of people standing on platforms waving red coats at them."

I knew it was a crazy scheme, but until that train came through the station, I had hope. Hope that the train driver may indeed see me and stop. It was now five to midnight, so I just sat back down on the cold blue iron seat on the empty platform and waited. It was worth a shot. I took my red anorak off, ready to do the waving.

It was a cold November night, and the wind whistled along the platform, making the advertising hoarding boards rattle.

I could feel the cold seat beneath my bottom. I wrapped my coat around my legs and tucked the coat arms under my trousers to try and warm them up.

I too had a bag of cheese and onion crisps in my bag, which I hadn't had a chance to eat. I opened the packet and started eating them. I offered some to the station manager.

"They are my favourite crisps," I said, trying to keep him in conversation, but he was now staring at his phone. Hoping I would stop talking and he could go home.

At midnight, the station manager collected up his belongings and made for the exit. His shift was over. I remained sitting on the platform.

He was halfway down the stairs when he turned and walked back up again.

"If you're going to stop that train, we'll need to flag it down further up the platform, otherwise it won't stop in time," he said. "I'll go to the end of the platform and you can stay in the middle. You can then be ready to run along and explain to the train driver what the hell is going on."

I couldn't help it. I gave the station manager a big hug. "Thank you," I said. "I really do appreciate it."

Eleven minutes later, right on cue, the misty lights of the train appeared in the distance. Thankfully, as it was going through the platform it wasn't going very quickly and yes, it was like a scene from The Railway Children, but instead of big knickers I was waving my red coat at one end of the platform and the station manager–who had also taken off his jacket–was furiously waving it at the other. The train driver spotted the manager and I heard the screeching brakes of the train as it slowly came to a halt just in time so as not to overshoot the platform.

I ran to the driver's cab. He pulled down the cab window and looked perplexed.

"What the hell is going on?" he exclaimed.

"I'm really sorry but I've had a long day and I left my laptop bag on the train and I really need it because I've got to get up and use it in less than five hours to brief Joan Collins and I really can't do without it, so can I please go and check on the train. I was in the last carriage and it's a red satchel." I garbled without drawing breath.

"A red one like this?" he said, producing my satchel from inside the cab. I felt small, warm tear droplets run down my cheeks. I really couldn't quite believe it. My plan had worked.

"Thank you, thank you," I said. I was so relieved that I leant over and kissed him through the cab window, planting a big sloppy smacker on his cheek.

"You are my knight in shining armour," I told him. My face was now bright red and beaming from ear to ear.

"I'm not sure about shining armour," he replied. "But maybe a knight in a shiny train cab." He laughed. "I'm off home now," he said. "And I think you should be too." He closed the window, and slowly eased the train out of the station, waving as he went.

Meanwhile, the ticket inspector was still sitting at the gates. He too had stayed late on his shift to see what would happen to this crazy red-anorak-clad woman.

"You got your laptop then?" he said, smiling. "Make sure Joan Collins gets her knickers back," he added, picking up his belongings and making for the exit.

I didn't see the connection. What had Joan Collins' knickers got to do with it? Until it dawned on me. He was talking about the briefs. I started to try and explain that they were actually notes to brief her, not a pair of scanty lace panties, but he wasn't listening.

"Tell her if she's ever lonely I'll happily take her out for dinner." He smiled. I didn't have the energy to explain to him that she was neither lonely nor missing any underwear.

"I'll let her know," I said and walked out to the taxi rank where I had been forty-five minutes earlier.

Outside was the same taxi and driver who was still listening to LBC.

"You again," said the taxi driver. "Where do you want to go this time, another trip around the one-way system?"

Clutching my red satchel, I said, "No. This time I am going home...even if it is for only a few hours."

He set off round the now empty streets of Epsom and I promptly fell asleep in his cab. Ten minutes later I heard a loud tapping on the glass dividing plate of the cab. I woke up with a start. I had done it again. I had fallen asleep on public transport.

I now always use my phone as my alarm clock to get me up and stop me from ending up in more railway sidings. However, I still never totally trust technology, so I make sure I have back up Human Alarm Clocks, whether it is a railway worker, a work colleague or my husband.

I owe a lot to them. Who knows where else I would have ended up without them.

5

A LIGHTER SHADE OF BROWN

The director tapped the Dulux paint chart lightly on the desk in front of him. He placed it beside his new cup of tea.

I looked nervously towards him. He liked his tea a certain shade of brown. Cuddlepot, New Penny or Buffalo Bill shades were all acceptable, but anything lighter than Recycled or anything darker than Coconut Husk and you would have to chuck it away and start again.

But the colour of his tea was the least of my problems that morning. I was worried that I was about to lose my job, after offending a member of one of Britain's most famous young bands at the time–Westlife.

And it was all thanks to something as innocent as a cup of tea.

"Have you seen the runner?" whispered Ingrid, the PA sitting next to me in our TV gallery. "It's almost eight o'clock and there's no sign of the director's cup of tea," she said. "He's getting very grumpy." She raised her eyebrows and went back to her stopwatch.

PA is short for production assistant. Their job is vital. Every item on a live show has an allocated number of minutes, including the ad breaks, and the PA's job is to time everything and let people know when it is time to move onto the next item. On *GMTV*, if one item went over time, then others had to be cut so that we could get to the news bulletins on the hour and half hour and ultimately finish the show on time to hand over to Lorraine Kelly.

That morning, I remember we were in an ad break. The studio was half-empty as lots of people had run to the toilet–the only time they could get away from their desks during a busy three-and-half-hour show. Every other ad break so far had been taken up with the hot young Irish band rehearsing their performance.

Outside the building, hundreds of teenage fans had turned up to try to get a glimpse of them.

Not surprisingly, like most musical acts we had, the members of Westlife did not want to come in at five o' clock in the morning to rehearse their musical number before the show. Instead, the crew and the band had to make do with squeezing camera, sound and dance rehearsals into the ad breaks. Often, if the break was short, the director would have to cut the rehearsal off halfway through the song and pick it up again at the next break.

Sometimes, they never had a chance to rehearse the whole track, so the directors had to work on the hoof. The camera operators would offer up shots and the director would just select the best one. For shows like Graham Norton and Jonathan Ross, the team had a whole day to rehearse music numbers. In Breakfast

TV, it was not so much as 'Flying without Wings' as flying by the seat of your pants.

This morning, though, we had managed a full rehearsal and it had gone well. I hadn't seen it myself, as I was in the green room trying to get some extra information out of one of our other guests, but apparently the boys knew their routine inside out, and for ease they were singing along to a backing track, so no issues with trying to balance their voices against any noisy live instruments.

In the gallery, however, the director was not happy. He was a creature of habit. Every morning, in the same ad break, he expected the runner–TV's office junior–to deliver him a cup of tea. This was not any old cup of tea though, it had to be an exact shade of brown.

Two and a half hours of live television is thirsty work. Most of the crew in the gallery just took the tea or coffee as they found it, but this director was a stickler for the colour. Too milky and it went cold, too strong and he refused to drink it. His shade of tea colour was a huge talking point. When the new runners learned their job, everyone warned them about this particular director and his particular way of taking his tea.

One former runner Christina even brought in a Dulux paint chart with different shades of brown on it – which she presented to him as a joke. The director absolutely loved it, however, and it now sat on his desk in the gallery waiting to judge his daily cuppa.

This particular ad break had finished and there was still no sign of the tea for either him or anyone else in the gallery. Now a senior producer, so my job was to sit and work alongside the overnight programme editor in the gallery and help them to write and rewrite the running order, depending on what was happening.

"What do you have to do to get a drink around here?" the director piped up.

"You know what," I said to Ingrid the PA, "things are running pretty smoothly here, so I'll go and look for the runner."

Now we always had five different runners working with us at any one time, all on a rotating roster. Runners did not stay in their jobs for long, normally around six months. The hours were long, including nights, and, unlike the rest of us that did those hours, the pay was terrible. However, for many, it was their first step into television and saw them go on to do some amazing jobs. Georgie Thompson–Sky presenter and wife of Sir Ben Ainslie–started as a runner, as did Dermot O Leary and top TV executives like Dominic Bird and Ruby Kuraishe.

I was never a TV runner, but I had started in a similar role at LBC radio, working alongside the likes of BBC newsreader Clive Myrie, who was also at the beginning of his career. I learned very quickly that the way to get on was to make a good cup of tea or coffee. I used to wander round the newsroom at hourly intervals asking if anyone wanted a brew. Not only did I get to know their drink orders by heart, but they also got to know me, so later called upon me to help them with more interesting tasks like tracking down guests or interviewing people.

The problem with runners was you had just worked out who they were and to start remembering all their names and they were gone. This was one such time. The runners had all just changed, so we had new recruits and I did not have a clue who was doing the job that morning.

Apart from making the refreshments, they were also responsible for organising all the car bookings and printing out the running orders and scripts for all the presenters and crew. Their busiest time was between 5am and 8am.

If they were not making tea, you could always find them by the huge photocopying machine, printing out hundreds of pages of scripts. Every time it was updated it would appear on different coloured paper.

I walked outside the gallery, in search of our latest office junior. I saw a young man asleep, resting his thick dark-haired head against the coffee machine. "Poor thing," I thought, "he's just started night shifts and he's knackered."

I gave the sleepy young man a gentle tap on the shoulder. He woke up with a start.

"Excuse me, do you think you can make our director his tea? He's been waiting for it for twenty minutes now, and he's really not happy." I pointed towards the gallery and at the tea and coffee machine beside him.

The young runner looked at me, confused. "I'm really sorry," he said. "I don't know how to operate the machine."

To put it mildly, I was flabbergasted. Here was a new runner and he didn't know one of the main parts of the job. I repeat, he was a runner and he did not know how to make tea! Surely someone had taught him how to do that? The new recruits all had a week's training before going solo, and making the drinks for everyone in the gallery was top of the list.

"You really are not going to get very far if you don't know how to do that one basic task," I said curtly.

I tried to show the lazy runner how it was done. "All you do is select the type of tea or coffee you want, put it in the machine and wait for the tea to come out the other end. You see, it's very simple."

Rather than follow what I was doing, he just looked at me oddly. I hadn't even reached the part where we added the milk, when he got up and walked away from me.

"How utterly rude," I thought. Words would need to be had with this young man and his supervisor, but it would have to wait. We still had half a show to produce. I went back to the gallery to give the director his tea.

In the next ad break, we had to rehearse Westlife again before they performed in the 8.20 slot–one of our normal showbiz slots.

Ingrid pulled me to one side. "Sorry to do this to you, but the director's tea has gone cold, before he could drink it. Can you make him another one?" she said apologetically.

I was really going to have to find this runner and have a word with him. I had better things to do that morning than do his job as well as mine.

As I walked back out of the gallery, the autocue operator–a young woman called Apples–tapped me on the shoulder and enquired. "What did you ask him?"

"Who do you mean? Who are you talking about?"

She pointed to where the young man had been sitting fifteen minutes before.

"Do you mean the young runner half-asleep on his shift?" I scoffed. "I asked him to make tea but he didn't know how to do it. He's not going to get far if he can't operate the tea or coffee machine."

"That wasn't a runner," she giggled. "That was Shane from Westlife." She spun me around to show me the young, dark-haired lad I'd asked to make tea, currently prancing around with the rest of the band to a backing track in the studio.

My mouth went dry and I felt bile come up into my mouth. I thought I was going to be sick. How was I going to get out of this one? This guy was part of one of the most sought-after pop bands in the UK and I had mistaken him for a runner!

While some celebrities are lovely, others can be ogres. The last thing any producer should do is upset them just before they are supposed to be performing live on air. My head started spinning. It was safe to say I could lose my job over this.

It turned out Shane had been sitting outside waiting to get into make-up, as there were five members of the band and only two make-up artists that morning. Being a woman in my thirties, who no longer tuned in every week to Top of the Pops, I had heard of the band Westlife, but I had no idea what they looked like.

I rushed out of the back of the gallery again and sent a grovel-ling apology to his manager via our entertainment producer Amy. I could see my career in television coming to a very abrupt halt.

While I waited for his response, I tried to calm my nerves by making the director his cup of tea, to what I thought was a Buffalo Bill shade of brown.

Unfortunately, my effort did not pass the grade and he rejected it. I really didn't care. At this point, his tea was the least of my worries.

Thankfully, Shane from Westlife saw the funny side of my error. Amy explained the situation to him and I kept my job, but from that day on, I always tried to keep abreast of new bands and celebrities, to avoid any other unfortunate tea-making incidents.

I have met quite a few stars since who would have been less forgiving. I was lucky, otherwise my career on breakfast TV could have easily been toast.

6

WHO'S YOUR DADDY?

When I was growing up, people often asked me what I wanted to do. At the age of eleven, I remember most of my friends wanted to be a ballerina or an air hostess. I, however, was adamant that I wanted to be a police detective.

I'm not sure where I got that idea from, perhaps it was from watching detective and police programmes on TV. I loved Charlie's Angels. Being blonde, I always fancied myself as Farrah Fawcett's character Jill Munroe—with the flicked blonde hair and sharp trouser suit. Or if I needed a British equivalent, I could always be Inspector Jean Darblay in Juliet Bravo, as I always liked the idea of wearing a hat in my job–I always have had a thing for hats.

It was probably down to my love of reading detective stories. I was an avid reader and my Nanny Joan had introduced me to Agatha Christie when I was ten. If I wasn't reading her books, I was watching her stories on TV, or, whenever we could, my Nan would take us along to the local theatre to watch one of her plays. I actually preferred Hercule Poirot to Miss Marple–and I definitely didn't look anything like him–nonetheless, solving a mystery always fascinated me.

By the time I turned sixteen, I'd definitely gone off the idea–the thought of having to wrestle with a drunken youth covered in sick or come across a blood-spattered crime scene was definitely not my cup of tea. I have always been a bit squeamish so I decided to be a journalist instead. Kate Adie had something to do with that, but the idea of solving a story or looking for clues never really left me.

As a journalist or TV producer you often have to play detective. Trying to track someone down, using all your investigative skills to find and secure an interview with them as quickly as possible before your TV rivals on the BBC or *This Morning* got their hands on them–I quite enjoyed that part of the job. I never actually thought I would be able to put those skills to the test on a real live police case.

That all changed when I went to Norwich.

It was the morning meeting at work, where all the producers pitch stories and the editor decides which ones will make it into the following morning's show.

Despite being two and a half hours long, our show actually only had room for fifty minutes of full programme items. By the time you had done the news bulletin, the local news, the weather and the ad breaks, and all the teases into those items, there was just enough space for ten different stories, or less, if it was a big story.

They could be a mixture of breaking news stories, feature or human-interest items and entertainment. On some days there were so many stories, you were fighting to get your item on the show. On other days, the news was so thin that you were scratching around trying to find something to fill the slots.

The nine o'clock planning meeting on this particular morning was dire. Apart from a couple of dull Government announcements the following day, there was nothing on the planning list that grabbed anyone's interest. The editor, Gerry, told the different teams that they needed to go away and find something more interesting.

By the early afternoon meeting, things hadn't improved. We had a guest for the showbiz slot–Mark Wingett, who played DC Jim Carver in The Bill–but there weren't any good stories and no prospect of any.

"We need a good human-interest medical story," said Gerry. "Something for Dr Hilary to get his teeth into."

Silence followed. As we all sat in the meeting, he started trawling the ITV regional news lists to see if they had something suitable.

"That's it!" he said, pointing at the picture of a police officer holding a newborn baby.

The headline read 'Norfolk Police urge mother of abandoned baby to come forward'.

"Tomorrow morning, I want Dr Hilary live from the hospital with this baby," he said. "There's nothing like a handsome TV doctor and a newborn baby to help the ratings."

From our input team, Ros, a bubbly woman with red curly hair, hit the phones trying to speak to the police team in charge of the case. On the output team, we were responsible for getting some video or pictures to illustrate the story. So, just half an hour later, I set off to East Anglia with my cameraman to get shots of the place where the baby had been found and to inter-view Norfolk Police.

Getting out of London took ages with the traffic. By the time we arrived in deepest Norfolk it was 4pm. It was November and soon it would be dark, so we decided to do the outside filming first.

It took us a while to find the first location–where the baby was found. It was in a sleepy hamlet, down a quiet country lane about eight miles from Norwich. There was no one around. The house where the baby had been found on the doorstep was a large, four-bedroom detached house with a stylish thatched roof. It was on its own in the middle of nowhere, with a neatly trimmed hedge and a sweeping driveway.

The police were supposed to be meeting us there, but they hadn't arrived yet, so I instructed my cameraman to start filming.

I went inside the gate and up to the front door of the house and rang the bell. No one answered. There was no car in the drive and no signs of life. The curtains had been half-drawn, but looking in through the windows, there was definitely no one at home. Without their permission to film, we could not enter the property, so my cameraman used a long lens to get shots of the house and the porch, where the baby had been left, from outside the fence.

I had never been involved in a story with abandoned babies before, but the location struck me as odd. If I was a mother abandoning my baby, I thought, I would definitely make sure to leave it in a busy place where it would be found easily. By a bus stop on a busy main road or in a shopping area. If I didn't want the baby to be discovered, I would have left it in a ditch or a wood or something. This location didn't fit into either category.

On the doorstep of a fancy house in the middle of nowhere? To me it seemed blindingly obvious that the house had something to do with the story.

At this point a police officer arrived.

"How are you getting on with finding the mother?" I asked him.

"Well, we've had a few interesting leads that we are following up, but nothing substantial."

I opened my notepad and took down some notes. I was curious to know what those leads might be.

"Our incident room in the police station has been very busy though," he went on, trying to sound positive.

"Okay, we'll film there after we've finished here," I said. "How's the baby doing?"

"Well," said the officer, "she's being looked after at the hospital. We're hoping that Dr Hilary appealing on television with the baby tomorrow morning will prompt someone to to call who knew the whereabouts of the mother."

"We'll do our best," I replied, hoping that the broadcast might prompt someone to come forward who knew the whereabouts of the mother.

We stood in silence for a few minutes, while my cameraman continued to film in the now fading light.

"I'd be interested to know what those lines of inquiry are?" I said, trying to encourage the officer to spill the beans.

"I'm afraid I am not at liberty to tell you at this moment," he replied, and we stood in silence again.

"Well, my guess is that it's got something to do with this place." I pointed at the large house in front of us with its sweeping drive.

"No mother is going to drive all the way out here without a reason. Maybe the father of the child lives here, and the mother wants him to take responsibility for the baby?" I looked at the officer, trying to see if his face would reveal that this was indeed one of their lines of enquiry.

Instead, something quite different happened. He suddenly seemed preoccupied with a new thought, as though he had had a lightbulb moment and a new idea was just germinating in his head.

Within minutes, he had excused himself and rushed off in the direction of his police vehicle to make a call.

It was all very odd, I thought to myself. Had the police really not thought of this before? The baby had been left on the doorstep four days ago, so I really couldn't believe they hadn't pursued this line of enquiry–but apparently there was no one at the house to enquire with. Evidently the family had left soon after the baby had been discovered.

Having filmed all the footage we could, before it got dark, we followed the police officer back to the police station in Norwich.

"Can you tell me where the incident room is for the missing mother of the baby girl?" I asked the receptionist.

"In there," she said, pointing to a locked door. She picked up the phone, and minutes later a serious-faced policeman with black, bushy eyebrows let us in.

Inside, the room was empty apart from the desk where the bushy-eyebrowed policeman had been sitting. On it was one telephone, one computer and a box of half-eaten Roses chocolates. Brightly coloured sweet wrappers littered the desk.

"This can't be the incident room?" I said jokingly looking at the empty chairs and desks. "Is there another room where everyone is working?"

"No, this is definitely it," said the bushy-browed PC, who had now been joined by the police officer from the house.

"Would you like a cup of tea?" said the officer. I thanked him, but declined.

"I understand that you have been very busy," I said, to which both officers nodded.

"It's been really, really busy," said the police officer. PC Bushy brows nodded his head vigorously in agreement.

"We've had four calls," he said, consulting the notebook on his desk.

"Four calls an hour?" I asked.

They both shook their heads.

"Four calls a day?" I said, thinking their idea of busy was somewhat different to mine.

"No, four calls since we opened the incident room," he said proudly.

I really couldn't believe it. We were on day four of a missing mum investigation and not only was the incident room empty, but there were no ringing phones, or evidence of any activity at all! Trying to make this look like a busy incident room was going to need a bit of set dressing.

"Is there any way we can get a few more people in here to make it look a bit busier?" I asked. "Just for the TV cameras."

"Okay," said PC Bushy brows and off he went in search of some colleagues. They trickled through the door, sat down and tried to look like they were occupied writing notes or answering fake telephone calls, while I interviewed PC Bushy brows.

"Have you got any leads as to the identity of the mystery mother?" I asked. "Or why the baby was left where it was?"

"As it happens, we have," said PC Bushy Brows, getting out his notebook. "In fact, a new lead just came in an hour ago," he continued, "but we're in the early stages of that inquiry. I can't divulge any more at this stage."

Now I am no detective, but it was fairly obvious to me where that new line of enquiry had come from – me! Surely, I wasn't the first person to think that the location the baby had been found in was suspicious, but I obviously was.

I finished the interview and decided that both the incident room pictures and the interview would probably end up on the cutting room floor. We were going to have to make do with Dr Hilary in the hospital with the baby in his arms and the pictures from the location where the baby had been found.

The cameraman headed back to London and I went into the local hospital to see the abandoned baby. The little girl really was very cute–and this was from me, a woman who didn't like babies. She had a mop of jet-black hair and big blue eyes. I was sure that the viewers would love seeing her little scrunched-up face on TV the following morning.

Back at the hotel around 9pm, I called in to the news desk to get an update. I was going to run through the script and the video we were going to use to illustrate the story.

"I've got some good news and some bad news," said Ros, the input producer who I had been working with on the story. "The police have just phoned up to say they have found the mother of the baby. Apparently, she had left the baby on the doorstep of the father's parents' house. It seems he hadn't told them he was a father. The young mother just wanted to prove a point that he was just as responsible for the baby as she was. The mum and the baby have been reunited."

"Yes, that's very good news," I agreed, smiling to myself. I was just about to tell her my part in solving the mystery when I thought I ought to ask about the other piece of news.

"And the bad news?" I asked.

"Gerry is furious. We have had to drop the story and now we have a four-minute slot to fill at 7.40."

At that point I decided it was better to keep quiet about my role in making this happen.

One person's joy is another person's woe.

I also had the unexpected pleasure of staying in a hotel without a 4am start in the morning and had time to actually experience the breakfast.

The following morning, I switched on the TV in my room to see another item in my slot. Fortunately (for us), a Hollywood celebrity had been found drunk behind the wheel. The show was interviewing our showbiz reporter live from LA about the incident.

I had solved a case, but ruined our story.

I think I would have made a good police detective, but I was glad I had decided on a career in television instead. In the future, I decided I would stick to my day job and leave the police to do theirs.

7

GET UP AND MOON

"Wouldn't you prefer to take a picture of my bottom?" asked our presenter Ben Shephard as we stood together in his dressing room. I had to stop for a moment and process what I had just heard. It was only 9.30 in the morning and I had been up since 4.30 and after the adrenaline rush of producing a show you can feel a bit weary. But no, my ears had heard correctly; Ben had just said the word "bottom".

Before we continue, I wish to establish that this is not some horrible 'Me Too' story. It was one of my funniest moments working in TV, but more on that later.

In my early years of working on breakfast television, I had the honour of producing a charity week called *Get Up and Give*. It was *GMTV*'s version of *Children in Need* or *Comic Relief*, but on a much smaller scale. It involved a weeklong telethon where viewers could phone in and pledge money to one of the five smaller charities, we had chosen to represent that year.

Through this work, I had met some well-known celebrities who supported these charities.

Once, I travelled to Herefordshire and found myself sitting in the famous garden of Monty Don–who later became the main presenter on *Gardeners' World*. The sun was shining and he poured us pink lemonade as he told us why he supported the gardening charity Thrive.

It was difficult to believe, sitting in this beautiful location, that this was a man who suffered from depression. Gardening, he said, helped him with his illness, so much so that he now blocked out at least a day in his diary each week just to work in the garden to improve his mental health.

Another time, as part of *Get Up and Give*, we did a week's worth of broadcasts live from the Millennium Dome–now known as the O2 Arena in London–where amongst the appeal films which showed some of the personal stories from the charities we were supporting, we also had pop bands performing their latest tunes.

That year we had well-known performers like Ronan Keating, Five and Heather Small, but our showbiz producer David kept raving about a young female group from America. I had to be honest, I had never heard of them, so much so that I had no qualms at all chatting to them in the ad break before their performance while they quietly waited to go on stage.

I remember thinking how gorgeous they all looked, their hair and nails were incredible, but also what nice, polite girls they were. Minutes later, they were singing and bouncing around the stage with so much energy it was breath-taking to watch.

I remember thinking then; I hoped they would do well. So often in the past, I had seen pop bands come and go through our green room and then disappear into obscurity. I need not have worried. The band was Destiny's Child and I had been standing next to Beyoncé.

Overall, the pop bands who performed for us and the celebrities who supported us were lovely, but there was the occasional horror. The stars who had been around for years were not the problem, it was often the new kids on the block who let their sudden fame go to their heads.

One year we had bands performing on the wharf by the river Thames, outside our studio on the South Bank. My job was to help escort these bands from their dressing rooms to the wharf through a labyrinth of tunnels and corridors. Outside, young fans had gathered to get a glimpse of their idols. One particular young band–who will remain nameless–consisted of several members.

"I just need to take you outside for the menu tease at the top of the hour," I explained.

By now, I knew this didn't involve hunting for bacon sarnies, but getting the band ready to do a live appearance at the top of the show.

"It's in five minutes so we need to get moving," I said, opening the door of the dressing room to wave them out along the corridors and out onto the wharf.

One of the young male members of the band was miserable and sulky. "I'm not going outside, I haven't had any make-up yet," he wailed.

There were so many people that morning, the make-up artists were working flat out to get everyone ready in time.

"Don't worry," I said to the surly singer. "We'll get you through make-up in time for your performance." I gritted my teeth and smiled while ushering them all out of the door.

"I'm not going until I've had some powder and eyeliner," said the moody band member sitting back down in a huff.

"It's outside so you don't need to worry about the studio lights," I explained. I was running out of time, and I really needed to get them all out onto the wharf or they would miss their slot.

"Honestly, it's five seconds of you waving in a wide shot, so I really don't think the viewers are going to notice if you have eyeliner on or not," in a last-ditch attempt to pacify him.

"I'm not going," he said, and turned his back on me.

I think he expected me to run him directly to make-up, but I still had the other band members who were happy to go out and wave to the crowds, so I took them outside and just left him in the dressing room sulking.

The other four emerged from the back of the building and onto the stage surrounded by security. There were hundreds of screaming young fans who had got up especially early and had come into London to greet them.

Meanwhile, just off the stage there was an even bigger band called Mike and the Mechanics. Unlike my miserable young pop star, they were all happily standing there with no make-up on, having their photographs taken with fans and signing autographs. If only this younger guy could learn a thing or two from the older ones, I thought to myself.

On the way back, I took the rest of the younger band members directly to make-up where they had their hair and make-up done with plenty of time to spare before their performance. Everyone except for my grumpy male band member, who I had left in the dressing room.

As far as I was concerned, he may have been a member of one of the hottest bands just then, but he could still develop some manners, particularly towards the backroom staff, i.e. me, who were looking after them. My dad always taught me that you should treat everyone the same, whether they were the cleaner, the security guard or the star. This was one such example where this young man's actions would have consequences.

I took the well-behaved band members back to the dressing room. I will never forget the look on the grumpy pop star's face when they all returned fully made up. Before he could moan anymore, I quietly slipped out of the door and left him sweating for a full thirty minutes. If he wanted make-up now, he was going to have to beg for it. I returned just in time for him to have a quick powder–but no eyeliner–minutes before the band were due on stage.

Years later, I spotted him again, walking along the Strand in London. There were no longer screaming fans to greet him. He was just an ordinary guy walking down the street without any powder or make-up. I hoped he had learned his lesson by then.

Get up and Give wasn't all about the celebrities, however, it was about the people who were being helped through the charities. As I mentioned before, when people found out I worked in television they always asked me what famous people I had met. I would always reply, "Yes, I was lucky enough to meet lots of them, but what I enjoyed most was meeting ordinary people who had done extraordinary things."

Some people didn't like that answer, but it was true. I would have happily spent twice the time with a member of the public who had overcome adversity or achieved something amazing, compared to a spoilt pop star. The contrast between the way some celebrities–like that boyband member–behaved compared to Joe Public was shameful.

Get Up and Give thankfully helped me meet more of the ordinary, nice folk. Whether they were champion fundraisers or people who had overcome huge obstacles in their lives, I never tired of meeting them.

We used to raise millions of pounds a year–nothing in comparison to the juggernauts that were Children in Need and Comic Relief–but the money made a huge difference to the small charities we helped.

We wanted to make sure as much money as possible went to the charities, so we kept our admin costs to the bare minimum. Once my colleague Ali and I had to go and do a live broadcast in Nottingham. Conscious of needing to save money, we booked ourselves into a Travelodge on the outskirts of town and shared a room. We drove up together, arriving around nine at night. The hotel was in the middle of an industrial estate and there was no restaurant or takeaway nearby. So that night we sat on our beds watching ER and eating a Crunchie bar and a Cornish pasty between us, purchased from the hotel's vending machine.

We also never turned down the offer of free help. One year, a woman who worked for the Banana Marketing Board contacted us. "We have two men who dress up in banana suits you can use for your broadcasts," she said.

In normal circumstances, if someone came up to you in the street and offered you two grown men in banana suits, you really would think they had gone bonkers, but for *Get Up and Give* anything went and all help was gratefully received.

They ended up accompanying Richard Arnold, our entertainment presenter, on a golden bus–donated by National Express–around Britain. The tour went well, apart from the day they were in Blackpool.

Richard, the Bananas and an Elvis impersonator were due to be performing on top of the gold double-decker bus, but that day the wind and rain decided to make an appearance.

I can still picture it today, the poor Elvis impersonator bravely holding onto his wig and microphone as he tried to sing "All Shook Up" on the open top bus. Not only could you hardly hear him, but the poor singer could barely stay vertical due to strong south westerly wind coming off the coast. Meanwhile, poor Richard and the now soggy Bananas tried to dance while hanging on for dear life to the sides of the seats, hoping that they wouldn't be blown out of the top of the bus!

There were definitely some fun times on *Get Up and Give*, among them the *GMTV Get Up and Give* Staff Quiz.

Every year we held an internal *GMTV* quiz amongst all the staff from the daytime shows–*GMTV*, This Morning and Lorraine–to help raise some extra money for the five charities.

It was fronted by Richard, who compered the event with a very glamorous and bubbly woman from sales called Gill. The *Get Up and Give* team of Helen, Janet, Ali, Ellie, Ollie and myself were responsible for organising the event, writing all the questions and getting as many people at ITV to participate. It was always a huge hit and was great fun, as well as raising thousands of pounds for our lovely charities.

In addition to the usual rounds on news, sport and entertainment, we also used to have a round specific to *GMTV*. In this particular year, it was my job to come up with the questions for this part of the quiz.

I decided on a picture round called *GMTV* Presenter Body Parts. I knew all the presenters quite well by then, so every morning I would go down to the dressing rooms after the show and ask if I could take a picture of a particular part of their body.

I had pictures of Andrew Castle's elbow, Kate Garraway's ankle, Penny Smith's nose and John Stapleton's ear, but still needed to photograph Ben Shephard, who at this point was presenting our Friday show, Entertainment Today.

I have known Ben for many years now, but he always was, and still is, incredibly approachable and great fun. As well as being a seriously good presenter, he also has a mischievous side.

On one occasion, we were appealing for viewers to take part in our Tough Mother event, where we wanted inspirational women to come and take part with our presenters in a mini version of Tough Mudder, a tough, very muddy assault course that was popular at the time.

Early one morning we had set up a mini assault course on the roof of our studios including some mud to run through, nets to climb under and a cold-water tank. Presenter Julia Bradbury had agreed to take part in the challenge. Kate Garraway and Ben Shephard were presenting the show. Just before the item was due to start, Kate and Ben walked out onto the roof from the studios.

Laura Tobin, our weather presenter, and Julia Bradbury were racing against each other scrambling through the nets, balancing along a raised plank before having to plunge into the very cold tank of water. Laura, being extremely competitive, was the winner. The race over, it was time to thank everyone and end the show. Just as the event finished, Ben grabbed Kate, picked her up and started dangling her over the water tank. Kate screamed, her legs flailing as she tried to avoid the cold open water, so much so that you could clearly see her very large Spanx knickers! The pictures, not surprisingly, went viral.

Years earlier, back in his dressing room, I found myself contemplating the prospect of looking at Ben Shephard's pants. Keen to get the final photo so I could compile the Presenter Body Parts quiz round, I knocked on his door after he had finished Entertainment Today and explained what I needed.

"Could I take a picture of your knee or elbow maybe?" I suggested. "Something that people don't see that often."

"Why don't we do something a bit more unexpected – would you like to take a picture of my bottom? That could confuse people who are playing the game!" he said with a mischievous glint in his eye.

I couldn't deny it. "Well of course I would," I said laughing, "as long as you are happy to do it?"

Ben nodded. "Yes," he said, "we want to try and raise as much money as we can so let's go for it!"

At which point he turned around and dropped his trousers. I was fully expecting to be taking a picture of a pair of boxer shorts, but instead he had taken those down too and Ben's very pert, round bum was staring back at me.

There I was, standing in a room with Ben Shephard mooning at me!

Afterwards I didn't think anyone was going to believe me, when I told them I had a photograph of Ben's bottom and I was right.

On the day of the quiz, not one team got the answer right. Everyone assumed the bottom belonged to Richard Arnold, already known for his cheeky (pardon the pun) antics, but Ben and I knew differently. When many of the women discovered it was Ben's derriere, they offered to donate more money for him to do it again! He declined–we had already raised a lot for the *Get Up and Give* campaign.

For all the long hours and stress of the job, working in Breakfast Television was great fun. I never forgot how lucky I was to have a job like that. I got to see all sorts of things in all sorts of places that others never had a chance to see–including Ben's bottom.

8

DON'T GET YOUR KNICKERS IN A TWIST

"Stop right there. What on earth are you doing with your hands in Beryl's knicker drawer?" the matron of the Cardiff care home shouted at me. It was a very long story, and I was not sure she was going to believe me.

By now, you will be getting the idea that you have to put your hand to everything as a Producer. Doing the hair and make-up for a presenter, when there is no-one else to do it. Making props from anything you can find in the vicinity. Little did I know that days watching *Blue Peter* would come in handy so often. I had not made things out of the show's staple ingredient 'sticky back plastic', but I had made flags for children to wave, Christmas decorations and countless hand-made signs over the years which I would hold out of view of the camera instructing the audience to cheer, wave or just react in some way or another to whatever was going on in front of them.

Rounding up members of the public to act as a rent-a-crowd or interviewing random members of the public for 'vox pops' were all part of the job. In fact, you had to turn your hand to anything to make sure the filming ran smoothly.

This time I was in Wales trying to make a film with a young female nursery worker called Hannah in her workplace on the outskirts of Cardiff.

We had come here under false pretences. In cahoots with her boyfriend and her colleagues, we had told Hannah we were making a film about the work of the nursery, but in fact it was a film just about her that we would show a week later, when her partner surprised her with a Valentine's Day wedding proposal.

The call time was 10am. I arrived fifteen minutes early, but only because I had stayed overnight in a local Premier Inn. I had originally planned to get up at the crack of dawn and jump on a train from London to Cardiff arriving around 9am, but having listened to the *GMTV* weather report the day before, there were forecasts for heavy snow in the west of Britain. I had grabbed my overnight bag – by this time kept in my desk drawer for just such occasions – and jumped on a train from Paddington to the Welsh capital.

I was glad I did. I woke the following morning to see white gloopy blobs of snow sticking to the outside of my window. Peeking through the curtains out on the hotel car park below, I could see everything was covered in snow. The steeple of the local church had a light dusting of snow, like icing sugar on top of a wedding cake and icicles clung to the underside of the nearby park railings.

Two inches of the white stuff had fallen overnight, enveloping the city in a big white blanket. The snow cast an eerie silence over the surrounding streets.

Switching on *GMTV*, I discovered we weren't the only ones with snow. Our weather presenter, Clare Nasir, was standing in a similarly white Gloucestershire field just twenty miles from me, wrapped up in a big puffer jacket and bobble hat. She was telling viewers how the snow was still coming down heavily in the South West and to expect more throughout the day.

Ten minutes later, the local traffic reports confirmed what I had suspected–the roads and intercity train lines had been heavily disrupted. If I had tried to catch the early train from London to Cardiff, I would not have made it.

I would normally have taken the bus or a taxi to our location, but the streets were snarled up with cars all trying to navigate the icy streets. Thankfully, I worked out it would take me just twenty minutes to walk to the nursery, so I set off early, navigating the icy pavements and I arrived with time to spare.

The crew however, were not so lucky. I soon discovered that they were filming with Clare on the live weather broadcast in Gloucestershire. Having finished at 8.30, they set off to meet me in Cardiff. They were trying to cross into Wales using the Severn crossing bridge. The snow and ice had reduced the bridge to one lane each way and there were long tailbacks.

It was annoying that my cameraman was late, but it was not his fault. The production manager who had booked him had calculated that the journey would only take an hour, but this did not take into consideration any delays due to inclement weather and the subsequent traffic jams.

We were due to be filming with the nursery nurse at 10am, but at 10.30 the cameraman had still not arrived.

The nursery staff and Hannah, our unsuspecting fiancée to be, were all really excited about the prospect of being filmed and had all turned up with their best clothes on. Several had obviously made special trips to the hairdressers so they would look their best for filming.

The nursery had also been given a special spruce up. There were fresh new finger paintings on the wall, and every toy had been tidied away into neat coloured stacked plastic boxes. The children all sat cross legged on a bright yellow carpet, waiting for us to start the filming.

But having been sitting there for half an hour, the children were getting irritable and had started fidgeting, tugging at their clothes and buttons and rolling around in their neatly pressed clothes. The staff were trying to get them to sing nursery rhymes, but having gone through the normal repertoire they were finding it hard to keep them still.

With still no sign of the crew, I told the nursery staff to go back to their normal activities with the children until the crew arrived and we could start.

Without the crew all I could do was tell them what we planned to do when they arrived. Getting some B roll of the children- some general video shots of them- with Hannah and then doing an interview with her. Having run through all the questions, I had nothing left to tell them.

I looked at the clown clock on the wall which now had the first balloon hand half way round the cloth face. I sighed, feeling helpless.

To my relief, the cameraman arrived ten minutes later, but he was in a bad mood. By this time, he had been up since 4am and was not happy that he had been sent on another job after the live broadcast.

"How was the live weather broadcast with Clare?" I said, trying to sound chirpy. "I loved the bit at the end where the children all threw snowballs at her. It looked like great fun."

"No, it wasn't," snapped the cameraman. "After throwing snowballs at Clare, the kids decided to throw snowballs at the camera and me." he grumbled. "The snowballs melted on the camera and now it's stopped working." He shook his head from side to side and made a big huffing sound.

Cameras, as you probably might guess, like any other piece of electrical equipment, do not react too well to getting wet.

"We're going to have to hire another camera," he said. "Otherwise, there's nothing we can do here. My hands are also numb with the cold," he added irritably as he plonked himself on a small children's chair in the corridor, resting the camera on the tiny table beside him.

He phoned Carol, one of our production managers, to ask her to look into hiring one.

I meanwhile tried to cheer him up by bringing him a hot cup of black coffee. He sat there on the tiny chair, warming his hands around the cup.

Waiting for Carol to call back, I had to make small talk with the nursery staff. As a producer I had quickly learnt the art of being able to talk to anyone about anything.

Aside from occasions like this when equipment wasn't working, it often took camera crews time to set up their cameras, light and sound for interviews, so in the meantime you had to chat to the person being interviewed. Often it was people who were nervous, and had never been filmed before so it was a good opportunity to try and put them at ease.

There were always a few staples that could get the conversation going.

I had started by asking about the weather, always a good and safe starter topic for anyone living in Britain. What a surprise the weather had been? How had they got there that morning? How were the children looking forward to playing out in the snow etc. We segued through to what the children were having for lunch, through to a conversation on the best restaurants to eat at in town–if I had the chance to try one. Italian, was the answer, due to the large Italian community that had settled there after the war.

All the time, though, I was waiting for Carol to call back from the office about hiring a camera.

Ten long minutes passed before the cameraman took the call. The news was not good. Whether it was due to the snow or just because of the location, we were out of luck.

"There are no cameras available within a fifty-mile radius," he said. "We're going to have to cancel the shoot." He started to pack up his equipment and headed for the door.

I looked at him in horror. Not only would I have all the hassle of coming back to film another day, I also had twenty expectant toddlers and nursery nurses waiting for their five minutes of fame.

"We can't cancel the shoot," I said. "The nursery will be so disappointed."

"Surely there must be something else we can try?" I pleaded.

He stopped and thought about it.

"I need something to dry the camera out," he demanded. "Otherwise, we're not shooting anything today."

I looked around to find something that might help.

"There's a radiator here, can you not just place it on the shelf above that for ten minutes?" I suggested.

"I hardly think a radiator will do the job," he said gruffly. "There's been half a dozen snowballs thrown at this camera. The lens keeps steaming up, lord knows what other damage it has done to the camera."

"What do you suggest then?" I said, trying to put the ball in his court. I actually thought my radiator idea was a good one, and he was just being obstructive for the sake of it.

He looked at me, and looked through the nursery window. Several of the children waved back at him. His paternal side got the better of him.

"Ok," he said. "I need a hairdryer. If you can find me a hairdryer, I could try blowing it on the camera at a low setting, it might just work." He sat back down again, nursing his coffee.

Having come up with his idea seemed to be enough for him. He obviously had no intention of actually looking for one.

As usual, it was up to me as the producer to try and find one. I walked back into the nursery.

"I'm really sorry for the delay, but we have a technical problem with the camera," I explained. "Strange request for you, but do you by any chance know, anyone who has a hairdryer here?"

The answer from Hannah was not promising.

"We can provide you with as much play dough, building bricks and nappies as you like, but no hairdryers I'm afraid."

Seeing the deflated look on my face she made another suggestion.

"There might be a toy hairdryer in one of the toy boxes?" she suggested helpfully. "I know it definitely blows out some kind of air, but I'm not sure how powerful it is."

At this point any waft of air blowing anywhere nearby was better than none at all. She and I began searching.

I started to open up the neatly packed boxes. I found crayons, coloured paper, tiny rounded scissors, blue and yellow plastic cups and saucers, and every kind of doll you could imagine, but no toy hairdressing equipment.

By now we were running an hour late. I ran into the toilets to see if there were any fancy hand dryers that might do the job, but sadly they were fitted with rolling hand towels.

I went back to find my colleague, who was now sitting there playing a game on his phone. "Any luck?" he said.

I shook my head sadly.

"I need to be back home by one," said the cameraman. "My shift finishes then. Unless you find a hairdryer shortly, I'm off, as it's at least an hour's drive."

It was eleven o'clock, time was running out. I needed to get a hairdryer and get one quickly.

"Think Michelle," I muttered to myself. Having exhausted all the options inside the nursery I walked out onto the cold snowy pavement.

I was in the outskirts of Cardiff, in the middle of a housing estate. There was no sign of a hairdressing salon or any parade of shops that might sell a hairdryer. Where was I going to get one from at such short notice?

Across the road a taxi pulled up and out stepped a nurse. She helped an elderly woman out of the car and into a wheelchair and pushed her to the front door of a building. Pressing some numbers on a keypad, she opened it and they both went in.

I guessed this must be the entrance to some kind of care home. This place was my only hope. I walked across the road and buzzed the intercom. The security wasn't great, as without speaking to anyone the door buzzed and I was able to walk straight in.

I soon found myself wandering the corridors in search of a member of staff. I found a friendly nurse called Gwen in her plastic blue apron and rubber gloves. I asked my unusual request.

"Do any of your residents have a hairdryer I could borrow? We need one to help dry out our camera, without it I'll have lots of upset children who were all excited about being on TV, not to mention my whole day and trip up to Wales will be wasted."

The nurse looked at me with puzzlement on her face. "I'm really sorry," she said. "We have a mobile hairdresser who comes around twice a week to do our residents' hair. They all have shampoo and sets nowadays, so I don't think they need hairdryers anymore."

I thanked her for her help, but I think she could see from the look on my face how desperate I was.

She took pity on me. "Come with me, I've got a feeling Beryl might have a hairdryer in her bedside chest of drawers," she said and off we went towards Beryl's bedroom.

The nurse knocked on her door before opening it slowly. Beryl was quietly snoozing in her chair watching *Homes Under the Hammer*.

"I think she keeps it in here," said the nurse, pointing to a chest of drawers. "Take a look in there. I'll be back in a moment." She headed off down the corridor to answer another resident's bell.

I was in 92-year-old Beryl's bedroom searching in her underwear drawer for a hairdryer, when the Matron appeared.

"Stop right there. What on earth are you doing with your hands in Beryl's knickers drawer?" the Matron shouted at me.

I had to admit, it did look very fishy from her perspective. Here was a strange woman, rummaging through an old woman's chest of drawers.

I tried to explain, waving my *GMTV* badge at her, but my tales of a grumpy cameraman and a wet camera were holding no sway with Matron. She took me by the arm and frog-marched me out of the care home.

"If I ever catch you in any resident's room again, I'll report you to the police," she said, slamming the door and leaving me back out in the cold.

Not only did I still have no hair dryer, but I had narrowly escaped being arrested for knicker theft.

I had run out of options. I would have to go back to the nursery and tell them it was all off, as I had failed to help fix the camera.

Inside, the tiny table and chairs where the cameraman had been sitting was empty. Instead, I found he had started filming without me.

Hannah and the children were playing quietly while he filmed them. His now defunct camera had sprung back into life.

"How did that happen?" I asked.

"Sitting it on a radiator for ten minutes worked a treat." He smiled and carried on with the shoot.

While on the one hand I was hugely relieved we had started filming, on the other I was absolutely livid. Not only had he completely pooh poohed my idea, but he had then sent me on a wild goose chase rummaging through play dough, toilet blocks and care homes, looking for a hairdryer which we hadn't even needed.

I would happily have told him exactly what I thought of him, but he was too busy shooting, and my choice of words would not have gone down well with the children.

An hour later, the shoot finished and it was time to go home. I was fully expecting the police to appear at the door with a matron in tow, but fortunately, I think the kind nurse had explained the situation and come to my defence.

I never did find out if Beryl had a hairdryer, but I did discover she had some very nice scented soap amongst her undies. No use for a broken wet camera, but who knows when it could come in handy for something else.

Little did I know it would be the first of many *brief* encounters in my job.

9

SOOT AND SONGS

"They are either going to love it or more likely they'll hate us," I said to my presenter Kate Garraway standing in a *wharenui* (carved Māori meeting house) in Auckland, New Zealand. There was no turning back now, but my hunch was, as soon as we launched into our song, we were going to have to make a run for it.

This was my first 'foreign'–as we called it in the office–an opportunity to travel abroad for work–and I really didn't want to cause a major diplomatic incident just two days into the trip.

It was November 2002 and presenter Kate Garraway and I had been sent to New Zealand to film a series of holiday reports called Great Escapes.

Kate had been selected for the trip about two months before-hand. Ten days before the trip, my boss Karen called me into her office.

"I wonder if you can do me a big favour?" she asked. "As you know, Jeremy was going to produce Kate in New Zealand."

I nodded.

I did indeed know about it. I had sat next to my colleague Jeremy, green with envy as he talked about jetting off to the sunshine of New Zealand, while I was trying to set up filming in the coldest place in Britain at the time, Braemar, deep in the Cairngorms of Scotland.

While he was setting up for Kate and himself to go bungee jumping and riding jet boats around Queenstown in the South Island, I was trying to work out how on earth I was going to get myself and crew to deepest, darkest Scotland in the depths of winter for our annual Old and Cold campaign–highlighting the plight of old people in Britain who couldn't afford their heating bills.

Karen continued: "Unfortunately Jeremy can no longer do the shoot, so I wondered if you would mind going?"

Would I mind going? Would I mind going? Outside, I tried to keep a serious straight face as I listened carefully to Karen's request. Inside, I was doing the 'Macarena'. I tried not to sound too enthusiastic with my response.

I would have been happy with a trip to Spain, France, hell, even Guernsey. New Zealand was something else entirely.

"Well of course Karen, I have lots of work to do, but if it would help you out, of course I would do it," I said, scribbling a few notes in my notebook. One of which was "Yippee!"

While I was looking forward to going to Braemar–a place I had never visited–I would happily swap a winter shoot in the coldest place in Britain for summer in a warm antipodean isle. Braemar would have to wait.

As the day for departure drew closer, I don't think either Kate or I could believe we were actually going.

Filmed in November and then broadcast in January, the aim was to show New Zealand as a holiday destination and, also to bring a bit of sunshine into peoples' lives on a cold and dreary winter morning.

Our trip was arranged and hosted by Tourism New Zealand. Kate and I arrived in Auckland and met up with our Australian camera crew and our local guide–journalist and broadcaster, Greg Ward. Greg was brilliant, making sure we had all the information we needed, and doing everything he could to make sure the trip ran smoothly. He was extremely professional, but also good fun.

The team had put together an amazing itinerary, involving climbing the Sky Tower, chariot racing and helicopter rides in Auckland and wine tasting and sheep shearing in Martinborough, bungee jumping and jet boating in Queenstown and experiencing some of the country's cultural heritage too.

Being welcomed by Māori onto a *marae* (traditional meeting ground) was one of our cultural highlights. One of our historical highlights was filming on the TSS Earnslaw, a 19th century coal-fired paddle steamer that took tourists across Lake Wakatipu in Queenstown, still one of the most stunning places I have ever been to in the world.

Cast your mind back almost twenty years and although the internet was just getting going, social media was non-existent, so in planning the trip we had to rely on the expertise of Tourism NZ and guidebooks to pick the best things to film.

When one of the guide books suggested the old paddle steamer, the TSS Earnslaw, my mind went back to several years earlier when I had been standing in a bar with my husband in the Sydney Docks, watching the 2000 Olympics. We had planned a trip of a lifetime and had managed to get tickets for several events for the games, but in between events, we were taking in the atmosphere and people from all around the world crowded onto the streets of Sydney.

One night in a bar, we got chatting to a guy from New Zealand. He had a wrinkled, weather-worn face and the biggest biceps I had ever seen, the size of small melons, under his tee shirt. When we asked him about himself, he told us that he was from Queenstown, New Zealand and he too had come to Sydney to soak up the Olympic atmosphere.

Standing in a packed, lively and noisy Sydney pub with the Olympics showing on TVs all around, I always remember him telling me.

"I have the best job in the world. Not only am I part of history, I have the most amazing view out of the window."

When I asked him what he did, He said he worked as a coal-stoker on a 19th century coal-fired paddle steamer in Queenstown.

Therefore, when I knew we were going to that location, and the opportunity arose to film on that very ship, I thought he would be a great person to interview. Not only could we chat to him about his life working on board this historic ship, but we could also get some great shots of him and Kate stoking the coal into the furnaces below deck. So, while in London preparing for the trip, I asked Tourism NZ if they could track him down.

Two weeks later, the tourist board came back to me and told me they had found him. He was still working on the ship and he had told them he would be happy to appear on camera.

So, one sunny November day on the banks of Lake Wakatipu, Kate, the crew and I climbed aboard the TSS Earnslaw. He was there to meet us.

"Hi, " I said. "Pleased to meet you again and thanks so much for agreeing to film with us."

I shook his greasy and soot-covered hand. I talked to him about meeting in the Sydney pub, which it soon became obvious he clearly did not recall. I think he might have had a few pints by that point. Nonetheless, he was obviously chuffed that I had remembered him from several years before.

While the camera crew were getting ready to film, he pulled me to one side. "Hey," he said in his broad nasally Kiwi accent. "What time are we meeting for a drink later?"

The engines were now turning and the boat had set sail across the lake. I thought I had misheard him. I just smiled and ushered him down to the bottom of the ship where Kate and the crew were waiting.

He tried again, shouting louder. "What time are we going out on our date later?" he said and winked at me. I really did not know what to say in return. I had no idea what he was talking about. What date and when had I agreed to that? There was obviously some misunderstanding.

Now I was in a tricky situation. I did not want to upset him before filming, but there was clearly no way I was planning to go on a date with him. I tried to avoid responding to his question, so instead changed the subject and suggested we start the filming.

Down into the bowels of the ship we went with Kate and my potential date for the night, preparing to feed this historic ship with coal to keep the engines going.

Midway through the filming, it dawned on me: he had obviously told all his mates that this English woman had tracked him down from half way across the world. After all, it is not everyday someone looks you up in your hometown after meeting at a bar two years previously, and brings a film crew to your doorstep.

The interview carried on. We got some fantastic shots of Kate shovelling the coal next to him into the hot furnaces. By the end of the filming, they were both covered head to foot in soot.

All the time I was worrying about how I was going to get out of this awkward situation. I did not want to offend him–he had obviously been telling his mates about it for weeks–but neither did I want to go on a date with him. One, I was married and two, he was definitely no oil painting–or in this case a charcoal drawing.

I asked Kate what I should do.

"Why don't we just all come along for the drink? That way you're not offending him and you're not getting yourself into a tight spot," she suggested.

Good idea, I thought, and I went over to tell him. I thanked him for allowing us to film him and got him to sign a release form–a form which said he was happy to be filmed.

"When shall we meet for that drink then?" he asked in his Kiwi drawl. I was about to tell him a time and place we could all meet, when he added. "When we do catch up later can you do something to yourself, because you're looking a bit rough at the moment!"

Now for people who know me, I am not one for wearing much make-up or having manicured nails and perfect hair, but even I thought this was a bit rich. Here was a man with a face like a prune, covered head to foot in soot, who was telling *me* I was the one who looked rough!

Needless to say, we did not go for a drink or any other form of date that night, either with or without Kate or the camera crew in tow.

That afternoon was also when I first experienced Kate's hair, or the secrets of Kate's hair. As a producer, you are responsible for doing all you can to make sure things run smoothly and that the presenter has all they need to do their job, whether it's providing them with scripts or briefs, arranging their accommodation or travel, or arranging their hair and make-up.

With female presenters, you often have to factor this into filming shoots. On this shoot, we did not have a hairdresser or make-up artist with us, so we had to rely on Kate to do her own hair and make-up. This obviously took time, so we had to factor it into the schedule.

Every day Kate would ask for her call time–the time we needed to start filming–and then have to work backwards to what time she had to get up to get herself 'camera ready' as we called it in the trade.

Having spent the morning shovelling coal into a hot furnace, she desperately needed a shower and to wash her hair. When we returned to the hotel mid-afternoon, she asked me what time we needed to leave for the next filming segment.

"Well, we have to get the gondola up the mountain at 6pm and the time is 3pm now, so we'll leave here at about 5.30," I told her.

"Great," she said. "Plenty of time to get ready."

An hour later I had a call from Greg: "I've just heard that a large coach party is arriving at 5.30, so we need to get up the mountain earlier, otherwise we'll get stuck in a massive queue behind them."

"No problem," I said, "I'll tell Kate and we'll be ready by 4.45."

I phoned Kate with the news. Now I have relatively thin hair that can be blow-dried in ten minutes max. Kate was quite the opposite. Her hair was, and still is, so thick and wiry that you can stand a brush up in it all by itself. It also took over an hour to tease the curls out of it and make it straight.

"There's no way I'll be ready by then," she shrieked. "Can't we put the call time back a bit?"

I explained the problem. "We need to go earlier or we'll get stuck behind the coach party and we could miss the sunset."

"Okay," said Kate. "We'll have to improvise." When I collected her fifteen minutes later, that's exactly what she had done. While the front part of her hair was blow-dried and straight, the back was a wet frizzy mess.

"We'll just have to make sure the cameraman only shoots me from the front." She giggled.

Looking back at the film, there is a fantastic shot of Kate with the sun in her face. Stunning Lake Wakatipu shone behind her; we even took some photos which later turned up in OK! Magazine, but little did the viewers or readers suspect that while she had perfectly groomed hair at the front, the back looked like a giant, blonde *Brillo* pad!

Since then, Kate has discovered the magic of Brazilian straightening for her hair, but I now always know that we still have to factor in extra drying time for her locks.

Back to our Māori meeting house and we found ourselves in another awkward situation.

Greg had explained to us that we could film outside the beautifully-carved meeting house. We had just been told that filming would not be allowed inside the building. This was not in our original plan; we would have loved to film the ornate interior, but we did not want to offend our hosts. In hindsight, thank goodness we didn't.

Before we entered the meeting house for speeches, Greg explained the basic *marae* etiquette, known as *tikanga*. First, we would have to remove our shoes and leave them outside. Once inside, there would be traditional seating arrangements: men on one side, and women (including Kate and I) on the other. In keeping with custom, local *kaumātua* (elders) would be the first to speak. Then someone from our group would be expected to say a few words on behalf of the visitors. Greg offered to speak on our behalf, which we were perfectly happy for him to do.

We all walked inside and took our seats. One of the elders then rose to address us in Māori. I did not know what he was saying, but I assumed it was words of welcome from the local *iwi* (tribe). When he sat down, all the women around us stood and responded with a beautiful *waiata* (song). A second elder rose to speak. Once again, the women responded with song and so it continued until it was the turn of the visitors.

Greg got to his feet and started his speech. I was enjoying his words when the *kuia* (female elder) sitting next to me leant over with some startling news: "Don't forget, after this you and Kate need to stand and sing." She smiled and returned to listening to Greg.

"I beg your pardon," I whispered back. "You want us to sing?"

The woman nodded, "It is a tradition."

Now I had known Kate for several years by that point; we had eaten together, travelled together, drunk wine together, but at no point had we ever sung together. I didn't even know if we knew any of the same songs, but I calmly leant over to Kate and explained the situation.

"After Greg has finished, we need to get up and sing. What songs do you know?" I whispered.

"God Save the Queen," Kate suggested.

While agreeing we both knew the words, I also pointed out that this might not go down too well, as Māori had lost thousands of lives during decades of battles with British colonists in the mid-19th century. "If we sing that, Kate, they'll be offended, and things could get really awkward."

"Good point," said Kate. "Let's think of something else."

"'Dancing Queen,'" she suggested. Once again, we both knew the words but I was not sure how appropriate this ABBA classic would be in such a solemn setting.

"How about Baa Baa Black Sheep?" she suggested, "there's lots of sheep in New Zealand." She laughed. Even she knew this was not very appropriate for the occasion.

We racked our brains to think of any other song we both knew, with either one or other of us not knowing the words or not being sure of them. All the time we knew that at some point

Greg was going to stop talking and sit down and we would need to get up and sing.

We were still in heated whispered discussion when Greg concluded his speech and sat down. Everyone was waiting for us; the woman next to me encouraged Kate and me to get to our feet. "It's got to be the National Anthem then," I whispered. "They are either going to love it or, more likely, they'll hate us."

There was no going back. If they were offended, we were going to have to make a run for it.

With warbling voices, out of key, Kate and I launched into the British national anthem. It was a surreal feeling, standing in a sacred and historic Māori meeting place, singing as though we were representing the Queen at some official event.

At first, it was just two of us with shrill voices singing under the brightly painted rafters. But after the first three lines our wonderful hosts joined in. I felt tears prick my eyes and a wave of emotion came over me. Whatever the British Empire had done to these people in the past, whatever this song represented, they were now welcoming us into their home and respecting our culture and heritage, just as we were respecting theirs. It was a very special moment. It also meant that their beautiful voices drowned out our tuneless ones, which was no bad thing.

Since then, I have had to sing in all sorts of places, from joining in with colourfully dressed women in Mozambique to more sombre World War II commemoration events, but I will never forget the feelings of sheer terror and panic as Kate and I stood up to sing in that Māori meeting house.

Needless to say, I've now increased my repertoire.

10

LOST IN TRANSLATION

All I could think was that I had to keep the drug addict and the dirty needle in his hand away from my correspondent and the live broadcast that was just about to start around the other side of the coach.

"Tell me," I said, trying to look interested. "How many times do you like to shoot up a day?"

Alan the junkie looked genuinely happy that I wanted to know. "Well," he said in a soft Geordie accent, "it depends how good the gear is." He then proceeded to tell what he got from which dealer and the merits of snorting versus injecting the heroin. I nodded and tried to look impressed, but really, I was not listening to a word he was saying.

One of the best things about working on breakfast telly was I saw many parts of Britain I had never seen before. My knowledge of the geography of Britain improved dramatically. Living in the south of England, and having spent most of my summer holidays either in Spain or on the South Coast, I had never been to places in the north like Newcastle, Glasgow, Leeds, Bradford, Warrington or Sheffield. Thanks to my job, I saw these and many other parts of the British Isles. In some cases, I even had the chance to have a quick whizz around the town or city to check out their local attractions.

After twenty years in television, I have now been to Newcastle on many occasions, but one of my earliest jaunts there was in May 1999. Working as a Producer on our News Output desk, I had to organise and help to produce a live broadcast with our then-chief correspondent Martin Frizell.

It was a day in early May, before the football FA Cup final, and our Managing editor Peter McHugh wanted to do a live broadcast with a group of Newcastle football fans who were travelling down to Wembley for the match.

My job was to head up to Tyneside, recce the location at the National Express coach station which was opposite the club's football ground St James Park and find out what coaches were heading down to London with football fans between 7.00 and 7.30 the following morning, when we were going to be doing our live broadcast.

Having spoken to the very helpful coach station manager, at Thursday lunchtime, I hopped on a train to Newcastle to sort things out for the Friday morning broadcast. Martin, our correspondent, would be driving up by car very early the following morning.

The first thing that surprised me about the whole experience was the journey. The train went from King's Cross to Newcastle in less than three hours. It was almost three hundred miles from London and took at least five hours to drive. Sometimes with London traffic, it could take you longer to get to the South Coast by car, just seventy miles away.

The next thing that amazed me was how friendly everyone was. Having grown up living and working near London, I was not used to taxi drivers and random people just striking up a conversation and being super helpful. In London, you might get a talkative cabbie prepared to give you his views on the world in general, but you would never see a black taxi driver getting out of his cab to open the door for you, let alone actually helping you get the luggage into the vehicle.

Here they did all three. The taxi driver who picked me up was so chatty, he had given me his life story before we'd even left the train station taxi rank. The problem was, I could only understand every other word he was saying. I just smiled and nodded politely.

The problems began when he started asking me questions.

"Reet there lassie. Are you here lang, did you stay for the neet?"

This was all gobbledygook to me, but I was going to have to make a stab at an answer.

I assumed neet was some form of food, like neeps and tatties, so I tried to sound interested.

"No, I haven't tried them, but I'd like to," I said back.

The taxi driver turned around and looked at me oddly. He tried again.

"Do ye know this toon at all?" he said, waving his arms around widely.

Barry Manilow was playing on the radio, so I felt relieved. Yes, I did know this tune, so I told the taxi driver so.

"Yes, I have heard this song before; do you like it?" I said, hedging my bets.

The taxi driver looked at me even more strangely, this was obviously the wrong answer and I could see he was now worried he had picked up a crazy lunatic who was just talking nonsense.

Being a friendly chap, he gave me the benefit of the doubt. "No, Pet, have you been to this toon before, have you visited Newcastle before?"

I suddenly realised that toon was the word for town...it was now making sense.

"No, it's my first time," I said. He seemed pleased with this answer.

"And whaddya think about it. Da ya like it?" he said.

I was going to tell him all about my journey so far, but thought better of it.

"It's great," I said.

He tried one more question, but it was hopeless. I had no idea what he was saying so he just gave up and turned up the volume on his car radio and started whistling along to Copacabana, until the taxi arrived at St James' Park.

The coach park was opposite Newcastle's football ground and was to be the location of our live broadcast. I was greeted by the coach station supervisor, who was also super nice.

He assured me that there would be plenty of fans on the early buses, but he had no idea how many until they turned up. He said there were three coaches going the following morning. One at ten past seven, one at twenty past and one at half past and they were all fully booked. It was obvious we would have plenty of people to choose from to interview.

Having taken down some telephone contact numbers for the morning, I went back to my hotel and phoned into the office to plan the next day's broadcast.

I was staying at a very nice four-star hotel, overlooking the Tyne. As I discovered in the years to come, staying in posh hotels was all very well, but for producers like myself they are a waste of money. They could have spas, gyms and the best breakfasts in the world, but you never had the chance to experience them.

You were often so busy working on scripts the night before or setting up guests, the chances of getting to the gym were pretty minimal, and you usually left the hotel way before breakfast started. If you were super lucky, your live broadcast would be over before breakfast had finished and you could nip back to the hotel to get a quick snack at the buffet. Often, though, it was straight back on the train with all the meagre offerings of a railway onboard shop.

I may not have had time for a full tour of the city that evening, but I did think I should at least walk beside the famous river Tyne. If one thing shows you up as a southerner, it is your clothing in such situations. It was cool for the time of year, just seven or eight degrees centigrade, and there was a stiff cold breeze coming off the water. I was wearing jeans and a puffer jacket with my hood up to protect me against the prevailing wind. Everyone else was dressed as though it was the middle of summer.

The men all had short-sleeved t-shirts on, and jeans. The girls all had skimpy tops, miniskirts and stiletto heels. I could not believe it. There I was freezing cold and they looked like they were heading out for a night in hot and balmy Benidorm. I lasted just twenty minutes before heading back to the hotel to check in and to get some room service before going to bed.

I asked the front receptionist about ordering room service.

"There's a moo in the room. Coal down tus when ya ready tall order," she said loudly in her strong Geordie accent. Well, that is what I thought I heard. I tried to work out if there really would be a cow in the room, or perhaps she was offering burgers cooked on coal and getting any of this would be a tall order.

I stared at her blankly and asked her to repeat it again. After several attempts, I worked out what she was actually saying. "There's a menu in the room, call down to us when you are ready to order," she said and waved my card key at me pointing towards the lift. "Yurt on the furs floor," she added.

Having gathered up my belongings, I didn't have the heart to ask her again, and assumed that I wouldn't be sleeping in a tent or yurt or anything similar and there would be no furs or animals involved. Instead, I just headed to the lift anyway, where I looked at my key and worked out I was indeed on the first, not the furs floor.

Having found my room and sorted myself out after twenty minutes, I looked at the menu. There was a limited choice; you could either have fish and chips, a pie I did not fancy, or pizza. I decided on a pizza and picked up the phone to order.

"Helloooo Room Twenty-two," said the woman I had just spoken to at reception.

I assumed the room number had just flashed up on the phone screen.

"That's good you have a system that recognises the number," I said.

"No," she said. "I knew tit were you, coz you're the only one from down South int otel."

This was the first time ever I had been singled out for my southern accent, now I knew how other people felt.

"Oh, I see. Can I order a pizza please?" I said, now very conscious of my 'down south' enunciation..

"Some peas and cheese? We don't have any peas and cheese on the room service menu."

I tried again. "Can I have a pizza please," I said, slowing down my delivery and emphasising every syllable.

"No need ta be rude," she said. "I'm not deaf you know."

I could feel her hostility down the phone.

"Woot you like some warter?"

This I understood. I did indeed want water. "Yes please," I replied.

"Would you like zzzzz or gaz?"

Once again, I had no idea what she was talking about. She repeated it again.

"Do you want zzzzz or gas?"

I did not dare ask her to repeat it for the third time, so I took a punt that she was asking me if I wanted fizzy or still water.

"Can I have some fizzy water please," I said.

"Ya what?" she asked. By now, she was getting annoyed with both my accent and my inability to understand her own. She decided to try my method of speaking very slowly. "No love, do you want a bottle or a glaaass?"

By now, I was feeling incredibly stupid, and settled for a glaaass of water.

The following morning, I got up at 4.30am and met the crew at 5am at the location. At that time, we had to find a place to park the satellite truck so it did not get in the way of the coaches and was pointed at the southern sky, so the dish could see our satellite and transmit the picture back to our studio in London. We also had to lay out cables that connected the camera to the truck without risk of a passing coach running over them or a passenger tripping over them.

Having achieved this, I phoned our offices in London to get the latest news on the timings for our broadcast. Rather than the ten past seven slot, we were now at twenty past seven. The programme item at ten past seven was the item reserved for the freshest news story, and something new had happened overnight so we were now in the 7.20 slot. This would not be a problem; it just meant I had to pick the coach that would still be there at 7.20, in other words, the 7.30 coach.

At six o'clock the sun was just rising. Martin, our correspondent, arrived having just driven all the way from London. I explained what was going to happen and asked him if he needed anything.

"A local paper would be good," he said. "I like to find out what people around here are saying about Newcastle's trip to Wembley."

I ran off and bought one for him from the local shop. He went off to find a spot to sit and go through his notes.

Meanwhile, people had started arriving. There were indeed plenty of football fans, but there were also many elderly grannies, who were just off to visit their families down south for the weekend. As the two groups mingled, I started to speak to the travelling football fans to find one or two groups with good stories we could interview.

There was no shortage of good tales to tell. A family of three generations who were all travelling down to watch the match together, a couple who had cancelled their wedding so they could be there, a father and son who had been saving up his pocket money all year for just such a trip. As the segment in the show was only four minutes, I thought we would have no problem filling it up with interesting anecdotes.

The next thing was to work out which was the coach leaving at half past seven. There were three coaches lined up in the coach park in front of me.

"Excuse me," I said to the super helpful coach station supervisor. "Which coach is the 7.30?" He screwed up his face, checked his clipboard and pointed at the coach closest to me.

"Thank you," I said and waved at my crew to come over and start setting up for the broadcast.

Fortunately, one of the groups I had spoken to were going to be on this coach. Unfortunately, at that hour in the morning, only one of them was wearing his Newcastle United football shirt.

I didn't think there was a hope in hell's chance of them changing into them in a cold windy coach park, but it was worth a shot.

"Do you guys have your football shirts with you?" I asked. They all nodded.

"Is there any chance you guys might be able to put on your tops now?"

"Of course, lass!" they replied and promptly started stripping off in front of me.

There were clothes and bags everywhere, onlookers started whistling and cheering them on. Once again, the weather did not seem to affect them in the slightest. They stood around bare chested, laughing and chatting, before finally putting on their Newcastle football strip.

I knew that if I had asked a group of Spurs fans to do this, I would have had no chance, but the Toon Army were definitely living up to their reputation. Super hardcore when it came to the weather and also like the rest of the Tyneside population super friendly.

I found the camera crew and got them to board the coach to check for sound and lighting.

It was ten past seven by this time and the half-full coach had the Geordie grannies all sitting at the front and all the football fans I had selected at the back.

"We've got a problem," said our cameraman. "I can't get the camera to the back of the coach, so you need to move the football fans we're interviewing to the front."

This was not going to be easy. The old women, while friendly enough, were not giving up their front row seats for anyone, particularly not rowdy blokes in football strips. Likewise, the guys at the back, really had no desire to sit at the front of the coach under the watchful eye of the coach driver.

With the time ticking by, I made them a promise. If they moved around for me, I would buy them all bacon butties to take on their journey. They agreed and, with this, chaos followed as they all moved. The grannies pushed past the football fans to sit in the back and vice versa. We were ready to go.

By now, it was quarter past seven so I went to find Martin to brief him on who and where he would be interviewing people on the coach. I found him still reading the local paper. I heard a coach engine start up and looked up in horror. My 7.30 coach had just closed the doors and driven off, complete with football fans in the front and the grannies in the back. I started running after the coach and banging on the side to try to flag it down, but it was too late. They were gone.

I ran over to the coach station supervisor's office in a panic. "I thought that was the 7.30 coach?"

"No, pet," he smiled. "That was the twenty past seven, the half past is over there." He pointed at the coach in a different parking bay.

"But I thought you said this one was the 7.30 coach!" I said, angrily pointing at the now empty coach parking spot.

"Oh pet, I thought you said seven *twenty* not seven *thirty*. I'm sorry, I really couldn't understand your accent."

It was the first time I had ever thought I had a strong southern home counties accent, but obviously I did and there was nothing I could do about it–or the coach that was now heading down the A1 to London.

I was now in trouble; the fact that the station supervisor had not understood my southern words meant that with just five minutes to go until the broadcast, I was going to have to start all over again.

I found some more people to interview, and had to ask the grannies and the football fans to swap over once again at breakneck speed and change into their football tops. We were ready to go with just minutes to spare.

Out of breath from all the running around, I quickly briefed Martin about who he would be interviewing and where they would be sitting and what they would say. There was no room for me on the coach, so the plan was that Martin would start outside, say a few words and then board the bus with the camera and soundman following him. I would just stay behind, keeping an eye on the cables linking us to the truck. Cable-bashing, as it's called in the trade, is an important part of the job when you're moving around. If the cables had got stuck or wrapped around anything, or even tripped someone up, then we could have lost the whole broadcast.

With just one minute to go until the broadcast, Martin was standing outside the coach waiting for his cue from the studio when I spotted a young man behind him who was off his face on drugs. More worryingly, he was waving a large dirty needle in the air and was making a beeline for my correspondent's back.

Without thinking, I ran behind my correspondent to head him off. Martin had his earpiece in, listening for his cue from the studio, and was oblivious to the scene going on behind him. I politely asked the young man to move back behind the coach, as we were about to broadcast.

The junkie stopped dead in his tracks, looked at me, looked at Martin and the camera and responded with a few choice expletives about why he wanted to be on camera rather than the "f**king shite" reporter. Thinking on my feet, I tried a different tack. I told him that his interview would be next, but I had to ask him some research questions first. As I spoke to him, I slowly moved him around the back of the coach.

By now the proper broadcast itself had started, but I didn't see or hear any of it, instead I was doing my best to keep the needle-waving junkie out of sight and, more importantly, trying to keep an eye on where that needle was heading–in particular not into the back of mine or Martin's neck.

The drug addict, whose name was Alan, seemed genuinely pleased I was taking an interest in him. From what I actually remember he had two favourite dealers, but one of them had just upped his prices and he was not happy. Alan had spent a life in care, and told me he was a promising footballer himself and had tried out for Darlington, but things hadn't worked out.

He had reached sixteen and came out of a foster home and onto the streets. In other circumstances, I would have loved to sit down with poor Alan and hear his story, but this was not the time. He even offered to share his heroin with me, yet another example of a friendly northerner, which I thought was very nice of him. I politely declined.

After four minutes, the broadcast was over and Martin and the crew were walking away from the coach. I did not have to mind Alan anymore, but I felt sorry for him. I offered him a cup of tea and a bacon roll. After all, I had ordered tons of them for all the people on the coach, so why not Alan? However, by the time I came back with them, he had disappeared.

Martin had, too. After a 2am start, he had jumped in his car and headed back home to London. I never had the chance to tell him what had gone on behind him. I meant to bring it up on several occasions, but never got around to it.

Newcastle lost 2-0 to Manchester United, but I will never forget the friendly people I met in Newcastle, both then and later in my career. Even Alan the junkie was friendly and, in spite of everything, he seemed to be able to understand my southern accent perfectly.

Perhaps it had something to do with him being totally off his face!

11

KEEP IT IN THE FAMILY

"I thought you said it wouldn't wake up the neighbours?" my husband Ian complained. "That noise will rouse the whole street."

It was five o'clock in the morning and I had a broadcast links truck outside the house. *My* house. And it was there to film *me*. He was definitely not happy about the situation, and to be fair I couldn't say I was either.

I have never had any desire whatsoever to be on screen. In fact, I have spent my life actively trying to stay behind the cameras. I am more than happy to set up stories, write scripts, produce and direct videos and live broadcasts, but I have never had any aspiration to be a presenter or any desire to be interviewed for that matter.

As a producer, you were always getting roped into doing things. Sometimes you just needed to be in the background as part of a cheering crowd, on other occasions you were required to provide some much-needed library shots for story topics that came up on a regular basis.

I remember one poor colleague who came to work one day with a stinking cold. His nose was running and his eyes looked red and heavy. Despite looking and feeling dreadful, rather than getting any sympathy, he was immediately pounced upon by another producer who wanted to film him.

She was doing a story about the rise in flu cases that winter and her item would be debating whether it was wise to come in to work with a cold or not. A controversial topic in current times, but something we all regularly did pre-COVID.

Having looked in our video library, she realised the pictures we had were ancient. Library pictures, or *stock shots* as they are known in the trade, are bits of video of all manner of things, used to illustrate a story.

They were a TV producer's friend, but they were the bane of the video librarian's job. Every time you did a banking story, for example, you had to ask the library producer for generic shots to use. Inevitably the high street bank signs appeared. When you did an education story, the same anonymous footsteps of children going up and down the stairs were used. We all needed them, and someone had to film them, but they were always somehow at the bottom of your list when *you* went out filming.

This time, the library pictures of someone with a cold were at least five years old and featured a very sweet elderly woman blowing her nose with her lace hanky.

The problem was that while we had permission from the woman to film her, we now had no idea whether she was still alive. So as not to offend her family in case she wasn't, we really needed some new footage.

The producer filming the flu story grabbed a film crew and promptly filmed the other poor producer sitting at his desk coughing, blowing his nose and looking dreadful.

Despite reluctantly agreeing to it, I think he later regretted it. For years afterwards, whenever there was a news story about colds and coughs, out came the pictures of him with a red hooter looking terrible.

Wary of this ever happening to me, I had done a good job of avoiding being on screen–until that fateful morning.

Having a broadcast satellite truck in your street definitely causes a stir whatever time of the day it happens. People always want to know what excitement is going on, but it's less popular in the wee small hours of the morning when the din is waking up the whole street. To be accurate, I had a broadcast links truck outside our house. Unlike a satellite truck, which has a large dish on top of it, this one was a van with a large antenna, which needed to be extended up to ten metres into the air in order to be able to see and send a microwave link to a broadcast mast on top of the BT Tower in London.

Now satellite trucks do make a bit of noise, particularly if they are using a generator, but microwave links, I discovered, were even noisier.

It was there because I was going to be interviewed in my home that morning, even though I had tried everything in my power to avoid it.

It had all started eighteen hours before when we had had our daily morning meeting to decide what would be on the show the next day. The news editor Pete had prepared a list of all the potential stories and then pitched them, letting our gruff managing editor Peter McHugh decide which ones should make it into the show. One of the stories he was pitching was about the mis-selling of endowment mortgages.

I had immediately become interested, as this was something that affected me. When we had bought our first flat together, Ian and I had been sold an endowment mortgage. They were incredibly popular at the time. Unlike repayment mortgages, where you pay back money directly off your mortgage, these products saw you put money into a fund, which theoretically grew in size so you had enough to pay off your mortgage at the end.

The reality was very different. It had come to light that finance and insurance companies had wildly exaggerated the interest and growth you would receive on your investment, and there was no way the money at the end of your twenty-five year term would cover even half of what you had to pay back. We were currently almost halfway through our mortgage term and we had accumulated less than twenty per cent of the money needed to cover the loan. Like many homeowners, we were really worried.

Millions of these endowment mortgages had been mis-sold to customers, without explaining the risk of this. We were one of those customers. Now here we were in the 9am meeting and Peter was giving Pete a hard time about the story.

"Why should we be doing this?" he grunted, adjusting the braces on his chest. "I've never heard about it before. Next!" He was already looking at the next potential item on the list. Pete was not letting him give the item up so quickly, however. "I really think we should be doing it," he said. "It affects a lot of people."

"How many people?" demanded Peter.

Pete started going through his notes. "About one million homeowners."

"Okay, now I'm interested," said Peter. "But we need a case study. It might affect a million people, but if we don't have someone to be interviewed on the show tomorrow morning, the story is dead in the water."

Pete shuffled on the spot.

"Have you got a case study?" he interrogated him.

"Actually, I have," he replied.

"Who?" said Peter.

Pete turned and pointed at me. "Michelle here, she's a victim."

He was pleased that he had an answer to Peter's gruff line of enquiry.

I nodded my head vigorously, trying to help him back up his story and get it onto the air.

"Right," said Peter, looking up and pointing his index finger at me.

"I want to come live from your house tomorrow morning and you can tell us all about it."

"I really don't think you do," I replied. "I'm a producer. I work on the show. Surely, it's better to find a *normal* member of the public rather than me."

"I don't care who it is," he said, "it can be Michelle or someone else, but just find me a case study."

Now bored with this story, he moved on to the next one on the list.

My heart sank. Not only did I *not* want to be live on Breakfast TV the following morning, I knew my husband wouldn't be too keen on it either.

After leaving the meeting, Pete took me to one side. "Thanks for backing me up there," he said, "but don't worry, I am sure we'll find another victim before the end of the day."

I did feel slightly relieved at these comments, but as the day went on, they still hadn't found anyone else. By six o'clock, both the item and myself were still in the rundown. Things were getting serious - the production manager, Raj, was now asking me for details of my address and where they could park the truck.

I decided I needed to break the news to Ian.

He had just got in from work so I gave him a call.

"How was your day?" I started, hoping that he was in a good mood.

"Fine," he said, "and yours?"

"Fine," I said. "Well, actually, not quite so good. You will never guess what happened in the office today?"

"What?" he asked suspiciously. "Where are they sending you this time?" He was used to me by now, always disappearing off somewhere to film or produce something at short notice.

"Actually nowhere," I said.

Now he was confused. "So, what's up then?"

I took a deep breath and broke the news to him.

"I hope you don't mind, we've got a TV crew coming to our house tomorrow morning. They are going to interview us about being mis-sold an endowment mortgage."

"You have *got* to be kidding me." As you can no doubt guess from his reaction, he wanted to be on TV even less than me!

"I'm really sorry. I've tried all day to get out of it, but I can't. They're interviewing us at 6.50 and 7.50 tomorrow morning."

"Oh no they're not," he said. "They can interview *you*, but *I'm* not going on camera. Also, I need to leave for work at 6.45 and I can't be late as we have a big delivery coming."

"Okay," I agreed. After all, it wasn't his fault. It was my big mouth that had got me into it, so I had to deal with the consequences.

"Can you do me a favour though and park your car outside the house, as we need a space for the satellite truck?"

Parking was an issue on our street, so it was essential to have a space near enough to the house so they could run the cables from the truck.

"What about the neighbours?" said Ian.

"Don't worry," I said, trying to reassure him. "They will be very quiet. You will hardly know we are there." He didn't sound convinced, but agreed to help.

"No problem. I can do that," he said. "I'll also try to tidy up the house a bit since you won't be home until midnight," he added helpfully. I was on an 10am to 10pm shift, but I was often late home.

This was the first of many times when my husband came to my rescue. He may not have been officially employed by *GMTV*, but he has been my unofficial Assistant Producer or support act on more times than I can count.

Once, I was doing a live report from a children's hospice on Christmas Eve. We were going to create a surprise Winter Wonderland for the children, complete with snow, reindeer and of course Father Christmas. I had booked Santa, I had booked the animals and fake snow, but three days before the broadcast, I suddenly realised I had nowhere for Father Christmas to sit. I needed a sleigh. Trying to find one was not going to be easy. Any decent sleighs, as you can imagine, are in peak demand at this time of the year. The ones used for Rotary Club displays were all in use, and the rest were in garden centres and Christmas grottos across the UK.

I phoned Ian and told him my predicament.

"We've got some chippies on site"–carpenters to you and me– "I'll ask them if they can knock up a sleigh for you," he said helpfully.

I thought this was a great idea, but I was on a deadline and I needed it within two days. It was already the 21st of December. and the live broadcast was on Christmas Eve, the 24th.

Within an hour, he had sent me a sketch. "Is that what you had in mind?"

I was no expert on sleighs, but it had a sloping front, a seat for Father Christmas and two curved wings on either side. "That looks great!"

"Okay, we're on it," he said.

Within four hours, the chippies had cut and built the sleigh using plywood and a few nails and screws. Ian sent me a picture.

"What colour do you want?" he asked.

Not having made any sleighs before, I decided to go for red, a good Christmas colour (and also my favourite).

The following morning the sleigh had been painted and was ready to be collected. My next job was getting it to our offices on the Southbank in London. I asked Michelle, our transport coordinator, if she could help.

"What are we collecting and where are we delivering it to?" she asked me, poised and ready to type the details into her transport request system.

"Well, it's a red sleigh and it needs to come from a building site in West London and brought here to the studios."

I waited for her reaction but Michelle did not bat an eyelid. In her job, she'd collected all sorts of props, from clothes, inflatable toys and even grand pianos, so a red sleigh was pretty par for the course at this time of the year.

"Where are we putting it when it arrives?" she asked.

Now that was something I hadn't thought about. You would think that a TV studio would have plenty of space to store props, but there were so many shows using the building that unless the show was regular it was impossible to keep anything on site. Often our desks on the fourth floor were filled with t-shirts, flags and Christmas decorations because there was no space anywhere else.

A sleigh, however, was too big to go inside our offices, so I had to get my thinking cap on.

"How about the underground car park? We could put it in one of the *GMTV* car parking spaces," I said hopefully. "I'll ask security to book it in."

I went downstairs to see security. "What's the number plate of the vehicle?" Gary - one of our security team asked.

"It doesn't have one," I replied. "It's a sleigh."

Gary thought I was pulling his leg. "Seriously, what's the make and reg of the car?"

"'It's a red vehicle for Santa and I need to leave it here overnight before we transport it down to West Sussex to a children's hospice."

"Okay," he said. "But make sure it's gone by the morning."

He winked. "'We don't want Father Christmas to not have any transport, do we?"

He laughed at his own joke.

I was so busy organising the rest of the live broadcast that I never got to check on the sleigh that night, but the following day Ray, our driver, arrived in his van to transport the sleigh down to West Sussex.

When we entered the car park, there amongst the Mercedes and Jaguar cars owned by the *GMTV* bosses was a red sleigh sitting in its own parking bay.

Ray and our production manager David loaded the red sleigh onto the truck along with a huge pile of fake Christmas trees and decorations that we would use to create the Winter Wonderland and set off for West Sussex, while I finished up in the office.

At one o'clock, my researcher Aaron and I jumped on the train down to Chichester. We arrived at about 3pm and took a taxi to the hospice, where we met some of the families who would be on the live broadcast the following day.

Everyone thinks these homes are such sad places, but children's hospices are lovely. They are warm, friendly locations that care for children with life-limiting illnesses and give their families somewhere to relax and enjoy their time, knowing that their sick child is being well looked-after.

This one was just the same. The parents there were so excited that we were coming, and knew the children would love it. Ray had arrived with the props and the trees and we set to work secretly decorating them, helped by many of the parents. The children were none the wiser. This was going to be a magical surprise for them. The sleigh had to remain in the van, however, as it was too big to store inside without being seen.

Meanwhile on the news, we were getting reports of snow hitting the Midlands and Northwest of the UK.

I had a call from the driver of the fake snow company.

"We're really sorry, but we are stuck on the M4 in a three-mile tailback caused by the snow," he said. "There's no way we'll make it to Sussex tonight. I am afraid we are going to have to cancel."

You really couldn't make this up. My fake snow had been sabotaged by actual snow!

Then came a call from the animal handler who was providing the reindeer.

"Ralph our reindeer is sick, so we can't bring him tomorrow."

My live broadcast and magical 'winter wonderland' appeared to be falling apart before my eyes.

One of the hospice staff overheard my call and asked what was wrong.

"I can't get you snow or a real reindeer," she said, "but my friend has a miniature pony called Harry. Perhaps we can find some antlers from a local party shop and stick them on him?"

It was not what I originally had in mind, but a pony posing as a reindeer was better than no reindeer at all. "If they can get Harry the miniature pony there in the morning, he's booked."

Within an hour, another local firm had come to our rescue with some fake snow to make the Winter Wonderland. By nine o'clock that evening everything was set up for the next day. The trees were all dressed and ready and we decided it was time to go back to our Premier Inn and get some sleep before the morning.

The problem was there were four of us–Ray, David, Aaron and myself–and only three spaces in the front of the van. One of us was going to have to sit in the sleigh, in the dark, in the back for the fifteen-minute journey along the A27.

My young researcher Aaron bravely offered to do it. "It will be fine. What a great experience–I've never sat in a sleigh before." He joked and climbed in and we set off back to the hotel.

We arrived and opened the van door. Inside was a terrified researcher who was decidedly green and looked like he was about to be sick in the sleigh.

"That was one of the scariest moments of my life! Worse than any roller coaster rides I've ever been on. It was so dark in there, and in that sleigh, you felt every bump in the road. I felt like I was being kidnapped!" he said, scrambling out into the car park as quickly as he could.

Who knew a ride in a Santa sleigh could be so traumatic?

The following morning was magical: there were lights and lots of beautifully decorated trees, there was Harry the miniature pony with fake antlers posing as a reindeer, there was fake snow, and of course, a newly-painted red sleigh provided by my husband and his team of carpenters for Father Christmas to sit in. The children and their parents loved it. The kids were so taken with the sleigh in fact that we left it there for the hospice to keep.

This was one time when my husband had been more than happy to help–unlike when we had a noisy links truck outside the house, preparing for a live broadcast where I would be telling our mortgage woes to the world. We had woken up the whole street with the noise of the antenna cranking into action. It edged up into the sky like a new plant shoot springing into life, albeit a very noisy one.

"I thought you said it wasn't going to be noisy," Ian said.

To be honest, I hadn't expected it to be this loud either, but then I had never had a links truck parked in our quiet street before. I pleaded with my husband to be part of the broadcast.

"It will just be one question," I said. "It would be great if you could join me."

Not only would he not take part in the broadcast, he was terrified of even coming down the stairs. Worried that he would accidentally end up on camera, he stayed put in our bedroom.

So, it was just me, in the kitchen with the camera crew, and the reporter Keir Simmons.

"It's in the news hour, the first hour of the show, so the hit is only three minutes," Keir said. "I'll ask you a couple of questions and you can reply. Don't be nervous."

I nodded, trying to look like I was calm and totally cool with what was about to happen. I was a professional TV producer after all. I really couldn't admit to him that my stomach was doing somersaults.

I had spent years telling interviewees not to be nervous, but now that I was on the receiving end, I realised what a stupid thing it was to say to people. As I was discovering, if you tell someone not to be nervous, it just makes them even more so.

We stood in the kitchen and waited. The bright camera lights flooded the room, dazzling me. I tried to chat to the crew to take my mind off what was about to happen, but it was just making things worse. In our job you spend a lot of time waiting around, ready to spring into life when required.

Meanwhile, my husband had quietly slipped out of the house to go to work. Careful to avoid the crew and the neighbours who had been woken at that early hour.

Five minutes had gone by, and we still hadn't heard word from the gallery that they were coming to us. I could see it was ten to seven already on my kitchen clock and the presenters in the studio were still interviewing the person on the previous item. I didn't have an earpiece, but I could tell from Keir that our item was running late.

Peter, the managing editor, who had ordered me into this terrifying ordeal, was a stickler for making sure viewers got their news exactly on the hour. The result was that if any item ran over time, the last item before the news would be squeezed in length.

We were *that* item.

Keir got a message from the gallery.

"We've just been told that our item has been cut to one minute thirty seconds, so we are going to have to speed things up a bit," he explained to me.

"I'll just ask you one question."

I nodded. In my head, I knew this meant I should just give one shorter answer.

By now, I could feel my chest and neck going bright red. I was hot and flustered.

Keir got the cue from the studio and started talking.

How had I got myself in this pickle? I was in my kitchen doing something I had vowed never to do. I was being interviewed live on TV - and there was no way out.

"Michelle here is one of the victims of the endowment mortgage mis-selling scandal," said Keir, looking into the camera. "Tell me, Michelle, how do you feel about the situation you find yourself in?"

I could hear my kitchen clock ticking, it was now 6:57 and we still had the weather and the menu to get to before the top of the hour, so I knew I had maybe thirty seconds to answer before the studio would be winding us up.

I took a huge breath. I sounded like the suction on my old hoover. It was so loud it could clearly be heard by the microphones Keir and I were wearing. The soundman looked round to see where the noise was coming from.

I then launched into my answer, but instead of just shortening what I was going to say, I responded by trying to desperately cram two prepared answers into one thirty second burst. I was talking so fast that I didn't have time to breathe. I sounded like Pinky and Perky, or a character from Alvin and the Chipmunks.

All the time, I could see Keir and the crew looking back at me in horror.

After I had finished speaking, he thanked me and threw back to the studio, still not quite sure how to react to what he had just witnessed.

He tried to sound positive.

"That was great, Michelle, but..."

I was expecting this. I have used exactly the same words myself, when I've been trying to let a guest know in a gentle way that they were terrible.

"Let me stop you there," I said. "I know exactly what you are going to say. I sounded ridiculous. I just saw that we only had thirty seconds to speak and I panicked."

I reassured him that I would not make the same mistake the second time around.

He smiled, saying "Yes, if you could slow it down a little that would help", and we all laughed.

"I need to slow down a lot, not a little," I corrected him. "You make it look easy, Keir, but it's not as simple as you think, being in front of the camera as an interviewee. Some of us are just meant to be behind the lens," I said, reflecting on what had just happened and why I had been right to try and get out of the interview the day before. My only saving grace was that it was before 7am in the morning and I hoped that not many people were watching.

By the next broadcast I had calmed down and was much better, but from that day on, I always tried to be more considerate to everyone we interviewed and help them calm their nerves.

I have perfected the gentle art of chatting to people before they go on TV about almost anything *apart from* what they are about to do. I have noticed that nurses do the same thing, just before they give you an injection. Just to take your mind off of what is to come.

The reality is that some people have the gift for talking on TV, others do not - and I was definitely in the latter category. I was better at playing tv nurse than tv patient. I confirmed that day something I had known all along, my skills definitely lay behind the camera, not in front of it.

12

I THINK YOU ARE MISTAKEN

"How has it come to this?" I thought, as I stood on London Bridge in the pouring rain, trying to coax down a hysterical young woman who was threatening to jump.

"Please don't do this," I shouted, as she tried to climb onto the wall of the bridge. Tears streamed down her face.

"Why shouldn't I?" she cried. "What do I have to live for?"

The rain was getting harder. Red double-decker buses raced past us on the bridge, their wheels splashing through the puddles on the sides of the road, spraying water across the pavement and onto the backs of my legs, soaking my tights and shoes.

"Harriet please come down, let's go inside somewhere and talk about this," I said, taking her hand. "'You still have plenty to live for.' I had to shout over the traffic and the hammering rain.

It was 10.30 at night. The bridge was empty apart from the odd late-night drunk who staggered merrily across, unaware of the weather or the potential suicide that was taking place nearby. Everyone else had either hopped on the bus, or underground, or into a cab to avoid the dreadful weather.

I would have done the same if it was not for Harriet. She had half-climbed over the wall and was dangling precariously with both legs pointing towards the river and the dark waters below. I had no clue what to do, or how to stop her.

It had all started with an email that had arrived in our main *GMTV* inbox about six months earlier.

I had recently completed a week of broadcasts for Adoption Week, an annual TV event where we encouraged people to consider adopting one of the 3,000 children in the UK who needed a new home. Some of the children's stories were incredibly sad, many coming from homes where they had been neglected and been taken into care. The chance that they might find a new family spurred us on to feature their stories.

This type of feature often led to a flurry of letters from people who had been adopted and desperately wanted to find their birth parents. Remember, this was the 2000s, long before the TV series *Long Lost Family* had first aired.

The email was short and to the point from a young woman I will call Harriet–I have changed her name to protect her. She had written in to tell us how she had fallen pregnant while in the sixth form at school. She said she felt unprepared and too young for motherhood and had been persuaded by her mother not to abort the child, but instead to have the child and then give it up for adoption.

Through an adoption agency, she handed the child over to a wealthy professional couple who were childless. In her email to *GMTV*, she spoke with love and warmth about how she felt she had given that couple a child, and hope. In return, they had said she could write or see the child whenever she wanted.

Having read the email, I immediately thought how lovely it would be for her to share this story with other viewers. To have such a positive tale like this was unusual. For a mother in the UK to give her child away voluntarily was rare.

She had included a mobile number, so I called her. A well-spoken young woman picked up the phone. It was Harriet. She said that she had seen our feature and wanted to share her story, but wanted to do it anonymously. She didn't want to be on television, but agreed that we could use what she had written on our website. She said her new friends at university knew nothing about the child, and her mother had told her to keep it quiet, as she hadn't approved of the fact that Harriet had had a child out of wedlock. Now she just wanted to get on with her life.

Although I was naturally keen to put her on television–this was a heart-warming story after all–I said I understood and would respect her wishes. The web article received lots of good feed-back. I also told her if she ever changed her mind about going public with her story she could get back in contact at any time.

As a rule, I didn't get involved with viewers and their personal lives, but this young woman was different. There was some-thing about her: on the one hand she was incredibly strong and articulate, on the other desperately fragile and vulnerable.

And so, our friendship began. It started simply enough: she asked if it was okay for her to email me to talk about the little girl–Sophie–that she had put up for adoption, as she couldn't talk to anyone else about her. She said she couldn't talk about it at university and her mother didn't want to speak about her either.

She emailed me a picture of Sophie. The little girl–who was almost two–had dark, curly hair and big brown eyes. She spoke of how Sophie's new family sent her monthly updates and how she was growing fast.

Harriet was studying at a university in the north, but I suggested that if she ever had a break from college she could come to London and we could meet up.

A few months later, we met on Primrose Hill and had coffee and cake nearby. We went for a walk in the park and sat on a bench overlooking London where she talked more about Sophie, the things she liked and didn't like, and she showed me a locket she wore around her neck that contained a lock of the little girl's dark, curly hair.

"I'm going to Sophie's second birthday party," she said, twisting the necklace around her nail-bitten fingers as she spoke.

"I've bought her lots of gifts; I really want to spoil her. After all, I am her real mummy, not some pretend one."

She twisted the chain even more, so that it cut slightly into her neck.

I was a little surprised by this news. I was no expert in adoption, but I knew from my TV features that contact between birth parents and their children was tightly controlled, so as to not cause confusion for the child.

"How do Sophie's new parents feel about this?" I asked.

"They are cool with it, we are all cool with it," she said, dropping the necklace and getting up from the bench to leave. I had obviously hit a sensitive subject, so decided to leave it. Even then though, I thought while Harriet might think it was fine, Sophie's new adoptive parents might not have felt the same.

When I texted her a week later to ask her about the party, I received no response. To be honest, I was busy working and she was back to her life at university, so I just left it.

Months later, out of the blue, I received a phone call from Harriet. She was in tears.

"They're taking her away from me. They're moving to Spain. I'll never see her again," she cried down the phone.

I tried to reassure her that she could still write to her and receive emails in return, and I was sure that if the parents allowed it, she could always get on the plane to visit. She seemed to like this idea, but was still pretty upset. She said she wanted to come down to London and meet again.

I met her in a bar near London Bridge. At first, she seemed in good spirits.

"You are right about what you said," she said, taking a large sip of white wine. "I know I was just overreacting. It's just I can't believe they are taking my little girl so far away from me."

She took another large gulp.

"As I said before, it's not like it's Australia, you can easily call her or get on a plane and visit."

Harriet thought about what I had just said and seemed happy with my answer. We then spent the next hour talking about other things. How she was doing and how she had applied to work for an airline as cabin crew once she finished at university.

"That will make it easier for you to visit then," I said. I was trying to put a positive spin on what must have been a difficult situation for her, but it had the opposite effect.

She became angry again. "I can't believe that they are taking my precious daughter away from me." She grabbed her locket again, pulling it tightly. She had now finished two large glasses of wine, and was obviously feeling the effects of them.

I also drunk some wine too. It's probably what gave me the courage to be brutally honest with her.

"Harriet," I said, taking hold of both her hands. I noticed the small birthmark on her trembling right hand like the shape of a tiny heart.

"They are Sophie's parents now, not you, and they can live wherever they like. It might be difficult to hear, but you gave up that right when you put her up for adoption." I looked her straight in the eyes, squeezing both of her hands.

Harriet snatched them away from me. "What the fuck do you know? You've never had a child; you have no idea what it's like to be a mother." She spat the words at me.

I thought that was nasty, but I realised she was upset, so I ignored it.

"I think I'm going to go now," she said, grabbing her bag and running towards the door.

Despite what had happened, my immediate reaction was to go after her. I was half glad I did, and half angry with myself for following her. As I ran after her in the rain onto the bridge, I had no idea she was planning to jump off it. I equally could not believe I could say enough to stop her.

But here I was in this terrible situation, not knowing what to do. In hindsight I should have grabbed a passing member of the public to help me or at least call the police, but at the time the situation felt so delicate, I felt if I was holding onto her life by a thin piece of cotton and one wrong move and it would break. Her legs were dangling over the edge, my words hung in the air. I hoped she felt she had enough to live for.

She turned and looked at me and then at the river. Then with a sad look, she thought for a moment before slowly climbing down.

A wave of relief passed over me like a warm breeze in the cold darkness.

I led her by the hand back towards the south side of the bridge where we sat in a bus shelter until the rain had eased.

With my arm around her, she sobbed and sobbed. Sitting there in the shelter on the bridge, I reflected on how the hell I had found myself in this mess. I was not qualified to deal with this, but I also thought thank goodness someone was there to stop her.

Having coaxed her down off the bridge and into the bus shelter, I didn't really know what to do next. In the bus shelter there was a poster for Samaritans. We walked back to the bar where we had been before to dry off. She called the number and I ordered two coffees to warm us up.

After the fifteen-minute call, she seemed much calmer. I asked her if she wanted to come home with me that night, but she said she was staying with a friend and said she would look after her.

Over the next few weeks, I spoke to Harriet often. I was naturally worried about her. It's not every day you meet someone who has tried to jump off a bridge in front of you, but she just kept telling me she was fine. She told me she had now accepted that her daughter was going to be living abroad and that she needed to move on. I was so busy with work that this was a weight off my mind.

After that, we didn't speak for about six months. I sent her a couple of messages, but she never replied. She had all but disappeared.

Our next contact was a text from her telling me she had graduated and found a job as cabin crew with a well-known airline. I congratulated her and said that now she could get cheap flights to visit Sophie.

When I asked about the child, she described in minute detail how she had already visited the family who were now living in the Andalusian mountains in a house with chickens and a large swimming pool. When I asked to see pictures, she said she'd send me some, but never did.

A few weeks later, she called me again out of the blue. This time it was almost midnight and I was in bed asleep.

"Sophie is dead!" she screamed down the phone. She had obviously been drinking, but then this was hardly surprising. Who wouldn't when they had just found out their daughter had died?

Sophie, Harriet told me, had drowned in a swimming pool accident. The adoptive parents were distraught and in shock about what had happened, but Harriet was inconsolable.

"I should never have given her away, it's all my fault," she sobbed. "I should have protected her. She was my precious child, I trusted her with them and now she's gone!"

After the episode before on the bridge, naturally I was concerned that she was going to try something stupid. I asked her if she had spoken to her mother about this. She said she had, but her mother had not been very sympathetic.

At the time, I felt the mother was being very harsh, but I had no idea about their relationship, as I had never met the woman. I asked Harriet if she could pass on her mum's number and I would speak to her, but Harriet obviously didn't want to give it to me. I talked with her on the phone for a couple of hours, before she said calmly that she wanted to sleep.

All night I didn't sleep a wink, worrying that she had done something to herself. I knew the city she was in, but I had no idea exactly where, so I couldn't even get on a train and go around to her house.

The next morning, I tried calling her, but there was no response. It was still early so she could still be asleep. I followed up the call with a text. An hour later she replied saying she was feeling better. She had spoken with Sophie's adoptive mother and was going to fly out for her funeral.

It was a huge relief to me to know that something had not happened to her. Even then, it struck me how much I knew about her, but also how little.

After her trip, she called me to tell me all about it: the flowers, how she had taken her a cuddly toy for the coffin and so on. She was sad, but happy she had had a chance to say goodbye.

Time went on and our relationship tailed off again. I asked for details of the adoptive parents, so I could send my condolences, but she never sent them. The next correspondence I received from her was another late-night text. This time it was even more tragic.

The mother who had adopted the child had committed suicide. Harriet told me that she had been so distraught at losing her much-longed-for child, she had never recovered and had taken her own life. Rather than being upset at the news, Harriet seemed happy.

"She took my child away from me, so she got what she deserved," she wrote.

I thought she was being harsh and told her so. Again, our text conversation ground to a halt. and I heard nothing from her for months.

Then the following January my husband and I were on a flight back from a winter holiday in Egypt, waiting for take-off.

The seat belt signs had been illuminated, and as I looked up to find the flight attendant waiting to show me the safety drill, there she was. Harriet stood in the aisle in her new cabin crew uniform about five rows in front of me, life jacket and oxygen mask in her hands, waiting to do the safety briefing.

I tried to catch her attention but she was too far away, so after the demonstration I stood up and waved to her

"Harriet, Harriet, it's me, Michelle. How are you?" I waved at her.

To my surprise, she completely ignored me, even though I was sure she had seen me.

"Harriet!" I shouted, loud enough that everyone could hear me, including her.

She turned and looked at me, fear flashed across her face and then she walked in the opposite direction.

I started to doubt myself. Perhaps I was mistaken. Perhaps it wasn't her, but as she moved around the cabin, I recognised her short, cropped hair, her slender fingers with the bitten fingernails and her slim legs that had climbed across the railings of London Bridge, a year before.

At first, I decided to leave it. Perhaps I was mistaken, but the more I looked, the more I knew it was her. She no longer had the locket around her neck, but the heart-shaped birthmark on her right hand was still there.

Midway through the flight, I got up and decided to confront her. As I got closer, I noticed that the name on her name tag wasn't Harriet, but Jane.

"Harriet," I said. "It's me, Michelle." I smiled at her. With cold, blank eyes she stared back at me and in an almost robotic voice said, "I think you are mistaken. My name is not Harriet, it's Jane. We have never met before." She carried on serving the drinks she had on her trolley.

What could I say? I looked into her eyes and she knew and I knew that it wasn't true, but I wasn't about to embarrass her on the plane, so I sat back down and told my husband what had happened. We were both perplexed.

The journey continued without any further incidents except for her deliberately ignoring me. We hadn't even reached the baggage hall when I received a text from her.

I read her text to my husband: *"Sorry it was a bit awkward earlier, I've changed my name and my new colleagues don't know me as Harriet, so I panicked when I saw U. Hope we can speak soon. Harriet XXX"*

I replied that I understood. On the one hand, I could totally see why she wanted to make a clean start, but underneath there was something troubling me. The more I thought about it, the more it didn't add up. The following week in the office I spoke to my friend Dr Hilary and asked him what he made of it all.

He listened to the whole tale. How I had met her in the first place, how we had become friends, how she had climbed on the bridge and was thinking about taking her own life, how the child had died in a tragic accident, the mother had committed suicide and now how she had completely blanked me on a plane back from Egypt.

I was actually just asking for his advice on how to deal with her next time we spoke, but his reply took me by surprise.

"Can I ask you one question?" he said. "Do you believe her? It all sounds a bit farfetched to me."

What did he mean? Did I believe her? Of course, I believed her. How could it not be true? I had seen pictures of the child, the lock of hair and how distraught she was when all the events had happened. I had spent hours with her on the phone talking about all her experiences.

But then I reflected on it afterwards and I too started to doubt parts of her story. I tried to contact Harriet, but she had obviously changed her phone and I had no forwarding number. I tried emailing her, but got no response back.

I decided I needed to track down her mum. Not only to find out more, but also to check that Harriet was okay. I managed to find her through vague bits of information that Harriet had given me over the past year: the town she was from, her surname and what school she had attended.

When I spoke to her mum on the phone and explained who I was, she said she had never heard of me. In all the time I had known Harriet, she had never mentioned me to her mother once. Not only was this surprising, the next bit was even more shocking.

As I started to tell her about my dealings with Harriet, she stopped me. She sounded apologetic.

"Oh dear," she said. "I'm sorry you have had to deal with this. Jane always did have an active imagination. Harriet was her imaginary friend, from an early age. She often calls herself Harriet, but her name is really Jane.

"The fibs have become worse in recent years. What story has she told you this time?"

And so, I told Harriet, or should I say Jane's mum, my story. A story which I was to discover just wasn't true.

Yes, she had fallen pregnant in the sixth form, but she'd had the baby aborted. There was no Sophie with the dark hair and big brown eyes. There had been no moving to Spain, no swimming pool accident and no adoptive mother taking her own life. It was all a pack of lies.

I felt foolish that I had believed her. I was a journalist after all. Any story I covered for the show I would have checked the facts for, but this was one that I had got personally involved in. I had fallen for her web of deceit, but I also felt incredibly sad for her.

Harriet, or Jane, in simple words, was a fantasist. Bored with her life, she had made up a fake one. When her life had finally got interesting with a job travelling the world as cabin crew, she had realised she could live her life for real, rather than in a tragic world of make believe.

From that day on, I was always wary about mixing my job with my personal life. I tried to keep some form of detachment between the guests I put on the show and my own life. There have been the odd exceptions, but most of the time I have kept to that rule.

I have met all sorts of amazing people in my job, some with great stories and most of them true, but you have to be on the lookout for the 'Harriets' of this world, who just wanted some attention using fake stories to get noticed.

I never heard from Harriet again. I don't know whether she went on to spin other tragic tall tales with other people like me or whether she finally settled on being plain Jane.

I hoped that she had settled for the latter. She was smart, beautiful and could tell one hell of a good story, perhaps she went on to be an actress or saleswoman–she would have been good at both.

13

STRAWBERRY FILTERS AND CHAPATIS

The angry mob had surrounded our van and were banging their sticks on the bonnet and the roof and shouting loudly in Punjabi.

"Please can you say something to calm them down?" I asked our lovely Indian guide and fixer, Minty. "Explain to them, there's been a terrible mistake."

Not knowing a word of Punjabi, or any other Indian language for that matter, we were reliant on Minty to help us placate the crowd.

"Leave it to me," she said, and wound down the window to speak to them.

I could do little else; I could only pray that her words would calm them. I really had not expected a visit to meet the local bishop in his Anglican church to turn out like this.

As the one and only Producer on this Indian film shoot, I was responsible for everyone's safety, including my camera crew

Steve and Ian, my presenter Clare Nasir and our Indian driver and guide. We had come to Amritsar in Northern India to trace and film Clare Nasir's family tree.

Following in the footsteps of the BBC programme *Who Do You Think You Are?*, *GMTV* had commissioned me to make some films with our presenters tracing their own ancestral roots. I had already made films with *GMTV* presenters Ben Shephard, Lorraine Kelly, Kate Garraway and John Stapleton.

Ben's story had taken me to the mining district of Ironbridge in Shropshire, John's involved a trip to Manchester and a pub in Dublin, Lorraine's also involved a trip to Northern Ireland and a meeting with her lovely granny in the Gorbals district of Glasgow. Kate's story took us to the City of London where we surprised her with the news, she was a direct descendant of a Lord Mayor of London.

Now it was Clare's turn.

Clare had a fascinating background. Her paternal family had left India after partition in 1949 to live in Tanzania, before moving to Milton Keynes in the UK in the 1970s. Clare had some amazing stories of her family's time living in the Punjab.

Her great-grandfather and ancestors were famous Sikhs in the area–Amritsar is the home of the Golden Temple where Sikhs from around the world came on a pilgrimage. However, when British missionaries came to the area in the late 1900s, Clare's great-grandfather had converted to Christianity, and in doing so had been ostracised by his family. Undeterred, he had gone on to marry a Christian woman and have three children, including Clare's grandad–who then went on to have a Christian family of his own.

When Partition happened in 1949, the area of the Punjab where they were was quite literally cut in two. Overnight, the border was created, cutting off thousands of families including Clare's grandfather and some of his children.

Some of her families were in Amritsar, India and some just thirty-two miles away in Lahore, now part of Pakistan. No one was allowed to cross the border, unless for extreme circumstances.

Clare's father had told her an amazing story of how her grandad dressed up in a Red Cross uniform and rode his motorbike across the border from Pakistan to India in the dead of night to see his son (Clare's uncle) after the boy had been involved in an accident. You cannot imagine now how dangerous this was, and how scared he was doing it. Nor could you have imagined what the border police would have done if they had stopped this 'fake' Red Cross first aider on a motorbike. Thankfully, he made it across to his son and back again safely.

We had come here to Amritsar and Delhi to film at some of the places where her family had lived and where these stories had happened, hopefully to find out more.

At the time, I was not only responsible for planning the film shoot, I also had to be Production Manager. A production manager organises all the logistics in television, including booking crews, equipment, and managing the budget and the travel.

When I found out we were going to Amritsar, the first thing I did was find a fixer. A fixer in television is someone who normally comes from that region and can help you set up filming locations and permits, interpret from the local language where necessary and also advise and sort accommodation, travel and transport. Without one, I knew I would not have stood a chance of getting anything arranged in India.

Minty was a great fixer. A highly educated Indian woman from Delhi, she also had friends in high places who could sort out filming permits at breakneck speed, no mean feat in a country as bureaucratic as India. She also offered to find us places to stay.

"What type of accommodation do you want to stay in?" she asked, during one of our many research phone calls. "There's lots of 4-star chain hotels, or would you like something more authentic?"

I thought for a moment. If I was going to India for the first time, I wanted to stay somewhere that reflected the local culture. "Let's go authentic," I replied.

She came back with a perfect choice: Mrs Bhandari's Guesthouse had been run by her for twenty years, had good reviews in 'The Rough Guide to India' and was close to the Golden Temple where we were going to film. I instructed her to go ahead with the booking.

Steve, Ian, Clare and I arrived in the early evening, after a long flight from London. Minty and her driver were there to meet us.

By the time we got to the guesthouse it was dusk and so the plan was to head for bed, before an early start in the morning.

The place really was authentic. The rooms we were given were in converted cowsheds that had been painted in bright colours and fitted with a ceiling fan and a simple shower. The cowsheds also housed Mrs B's cows, who could be heard all night long, just on the other side of the thin walls.

Now Steve, our cameraman, obviously by the nature of his job likes taking a picture or two. He also had this habit of taking a photo of every room he had ever stayed in while working away.

He said it was because when his wife asked him what the room was like, rather than describing it, he would just send her the picture. Over the years, I know he had a great collection of pictures of fantastic rooms he had stayed in. Sadly, tonight's room would not be one of them.

After a night in a hot and sweaty room, with cows mooing beside us, we met for breakfast.

None of us had slept very well as milking had commenced at 3am, when the mooing had become even louder.

"I think we'll find somewhere less authentic to stay tonight. Shall we?" I suggested and they all nodded in agreement.

Ever since our stay at Mrs Bhandari's Guest House, I have always been a bit wary about staying in "authentic" accommodation.

The next day we went to the Golden Temple. We covered our heads and removed our shoes before entering the temple area. What we found was quite extraordinary. From the outside entrance, the streets were crowded with little souvenir shops offering miniature, gold-coloured plastic versions of the temple, an array of colourful headscarves and plastic bottles of water.

Noisy motorbikes and skinny cows jostled for position on the litter-strewn street. The motorbike riders were holding on to the handlebars with one hand, while trying to balance numerous family members and random bits of furniture on the back with the other.

However, when you walked through the foot baths into the grounds of the temple it was quite the opposite: clean, orderly and incredibly peaceful. Toothpaste-white marble pathways surrounded a large area of dark, crystal-clear water, which acted as a moat around a giant, gold, gleaming temple. Its large dome reflected the morning sun, dazzling my eyes so much that I had to squint through my sunglasses to look at it. It was breathtakingly beautiful. Hundreds of Sikh worshippers were queueing up to go into the temple and hundreds more were bathing in the calm waters around it.

Apart from being one of the holiest places in the world for people from the Sikh religion, the place was also home to one of the world's largest chapati machines, churning out millions of the flatbreads every day. In the Temple, it was customary to give everyone free food, so the kitchens here were enormous. All around us were huge metal vats bubbling away with red and green dhal and a giant machine making the chapatis to feed all the pilgrims.

Before starting our filming, we went for a recce to see what we could film and how. With a temperature of thirty-two degrees and a humidity level of over ninety per cent, there was no point lugging around heavy camera and sound equipment to places we didn't need to, so we left the gear in the safety of a van and went off for a tour around the temple and its grounds.

As we were walking around, a middle-aged Indian man with dark brown eyes, and a long, flowing grey beard which came to a point in the middle, tapped me on the shoulder.

"Excuse me," he said, in perfect English. "I'm doing a survey about what people think about the Golden Temple. Can I ask you some questions?"

"Sure," I replied. Of course, I was going to help him out. We were there at the invitation of the temple and it seemed only right and proper to do so.

"What is your name and where have you come from today?" he asked.

"Well today I've just come from down the road," I said, pointing in the direction of Mrs B's place. "But yesterday we flew in from London."

The man adjusted his white turban, took a pencil out of his bag, opened up his notebook and wrote down my name and what I had just said.

"What do you think about the Golden Temple?" he asked.

"'The Temple is one of the most beautiful things I have seen in the world and I am honoured and privileged to be here," I replied. Once again, he wrote down word for word what I had just said. He then asked me a couple of other questions, thanked me and disappeared into a crowd of people.

We carried on with our recce. Ten minutes later, he was back beside me. "Excuse me," he said in his perfect English. "I'm doing a survey about what people think about the Golden Temple. Can I ask you some questions?"

"You've already asked me," I answered politely. "You interviewed me over there, just ten minutes ago." I pointed to the water's edge. I suggested he ask some of my colleagues to fill in the questionnaire. He looked Clare and my crew up and down, but did not seem interested. He put his pen and notebook away and disappeared into the crowds as quickly as he had arrived.

Ten minutes later, he was back again, asking me the exact same question.

I found this very odd. What was so special about me and why did he want to keep asking me questions rather than anyone else? Perhaps he had been told to, as I was in charge of the film crew. I am all for being helpful, but I did have a job to do, so I declined. By now, I was getting a bit bored of this. "Why is he just asking me the questions and why does he keep coming back to me?" I asked the crew.

"Look around," said Steve. "You're the only fair-skinned blonde woman in the whole place, you do kind of stick out like a sore thumb." The thought had not dawned on me, but he was right, I did look very different to everyone around me.

"I think he's got a crush on you," Ian the soundman said, and we all laughed.

After our recce we started filming, and were there for about three hours. During that time, the man with the white beard and notebook appeared at regular intervals to ask me to answer his questionnaire. I finally said I would answer some more questions, but this time different ones.

He opened his notebook to write down some more of my answers. I managed to take a look inside his book, while writing something down for him, only to discover that my responses were the only words he had written in there. If he really was part of the Golden Temple survey team, I thought, this was not going to be a very comprehensive questionnaire!

After finishing filming in the Temple, we went on to the Wada Border Crossing between India and Pakistan. It was near here that Clare's grandfather's motorbike ride took place. The plan was to record Clare doing a piece to camera telling the fantastic story.

I was expecting the location to be a normal border crossing with cars and lorries queueing up to cross. What I had not expected was a stadium of seats on one side of the border gate and a stadium of seats on the other. The place, we discovered, was a popular tourist attraction. At dusk, the Indian soldiers dressed in starched khaki uniforms and the Pakistani soldiers dressed in black, with helmets and huge plumes on their heads, performed a goose-stepping routine, like something from *Monty Python*.

On the Indian side of the border, the stadium seats were full of hundreds of women in brightly-coloured saris cheering and chanting "Rajasthan, Rajasthan" at their Pakistani counterparts. On the Pakistan side, men in white robes and women in black burkas shouted back, "Pakistan, Pakistan", as the soldiers continued to posture and hiss at each other.

This scene reminded me more of a Premier league football match with two noisy ends of rival fans, rather than a formal border ceremony.

This spectacle apparently happened nightly, and while entertaining to watch, it was hardly the kind of background noise level for poor Clare to say her words. Shouting her words out over the chanting crowds, we finally got the take we needed and we were finished for the day.

That night we retired to a different hotel–free from cows and cowsheds–in preparation for the next day's filming.

This time our fixer had arranged for us to meet the local bishop at Amritsar's Anglican church.

This structure had been around when Clare's family lived there and was most likely the location where her family had worshipped all those years ago.

We arrived on time, but there was no sign of anyone. The building itself was huge, and looked like it had been plucked straight out of a typical English village scene, rather than by the side of a busy street in India. It was obviously a symbol of the country's colonial past and was surrounded by immaculately tended grounds, quite a contrast to the cramped shacks and shops just outside.

Half an hour went past and there was still no sign of our hosts. On film shoots, you do not tend to have a lot of spare time just to hang around. Thinking on my feet, I suggested that Clare film a piece to camera with the church in the background. If there was going to be no interview with the Bishop of Amritsar, at least we would have pictures of her standing in the church-yard explaining that this was where her family could have once worshipped.

We were just about to start recording when a huge 4x4 SUV with blacked-out windows rolled into the churchyard. The car seemed more suited to a rock star or drug baron than a bishop, so we assumed this was someone else paying a visit.

However, it quickly became apparent that this was indeed the bishop, the clue being in the number plate. In thick black letters, the SUV sported the car registration 'BISH 1'. We all looked at each other and laughed. Now there is nothing wrong with personalised number plates, but it seemed funny that a man of the cloth would be driving around in a vehicle with BISH 1 written on it. Surely it was pretty obvious who he was? The clothes were a definite giveaway.

From the front passenger seat, a thickset man emerged. He looked like a bodyguard, dressed in a tight black suit. He wore dark sunglasses and looked around furtively. He opened the back door and out stepped the bishop.

I have several recollections of him. He was incredibly tall. He wore purple robes with a giant gold chain and a golden cross in the middle of it. He had huge gold rings across his knuckles, and a gold tooth that glinted in the sun when he smiled. Indeed, all of these things could have been perfectly normal were it not for the top-of-the-range Nike trainers he wore underneath.

Judging by his appearance and the car, being the Bishop of Amritsar obviously had some benefits and some status attached to it.

We all walked over to meet him. Unfortunately, while incredibly friendly, he did not speak a word of English, so we spoke through Minty who acted as our interpreter. It quickly became clear that not only did he not know anything about Clare's family, he seemed to know nothing about the history of his church either.

I pulled Clare and the crew aside. "Let's do a strawberry filter," I said.

They all knew exactly what I meant.

There was no way this man was going to end up in our final film, but we needed to be polite, and so we were going to make out we were filming him, when actually we weren't filming at all.

The term strawberry filter was the term we used so the crew knew that we did not really want to interview someone. We would ask the minimum questions required for politeness and then end the interview.

The strawberry filter interview being over, and having not gleaned any information from the bishop, we asked if we could look inside the church. We were hoping this would give us some clues to Clare's family's past, or at least some nice footage of the interior of the church.

"Can we go inside?" I asked the bishop through his interpreter. The bishop shook his head. I thought at first, he was refusing on religious grounds, but the reason was much simpler. Not one of them seemed to have the key or knew how to get hold of one.

This seemed very odd to me. Surely the Bishop of Amritsar, who was in charge of this church, or one of his staff, must have a key. It would be like the King not being able to get into Buckingham Palace. Even if you didn't carry one yourself, surely you could summon up someone to find one for you?

But we didn't have time to question it. We were on a tight schedule, so we thanked him, said our goodbyes and decided to simply continue with the filming we had planned in the churchyard, before they had arrived.

We assumed the gold-toothed, Nike-wearing bishop and his bodyguard had things to do. Being the Bishop of Amritsar, I was sure he must be incredibly busy, but apparently not. He and his driver seemed in no hurry to go anywhere. They just hung around outside the car, chatting and smoking.

We had just started filming with Clare when another SUV roared into the drive. On spotting the other car, the gold-toothed Bishop and his driver jumped into BISH 1 and made a swift exit. An angry mob jumped out of the second car and chased after them as they sped out of the churchyard into the oncoming traffic.

We all looked at one another in bewilderment sensing something was not right.

"I think we need to get out of here?" said Steve. We quickly gathered up our equipment and headed back to the car. One of the new arrivals started shouting at us in Punjabi. I asked our fixer Minty to translate for us.

"He's asking, 'Who are you and why are you trespassing on our land?'" explained Minty.

Minty tried explaining the situation as the rest of us piled into our van. After a few minutes of conversation, she too made a hasty retreat.

"Let's get out of here," she said. The driver started the engine and we drove towards the exit.

But the mob had surrounded our vehicle, banging their sticks on the bonnet and the roof, shouting loudly in Punjabi. It was getting scary. I asked Minty to politely but firmly explain the situation, and ask that they let us leave.

"Please can you say something to calm them down?" I pleaded. "Explain to them there's been a terrible mistake."

The banging on the van was getting louder and they were starting to rock the van. I remember thinking of the headlines. "TV weather presenter killed in India by angry mob" or at least badly injured. This really was not looking good for my health and safety record.

"Leave it to me," she said, and wound down the window. The result was not what I expected.

Instead of calmly speaking to them, she started shouting at them and hitting them with her handbag. I had no idea what she was saying at the time, but this was definitely not my idea of gentle diplomacy.

Our fixer's handbag-bashing not surprisingly made the mob even angrier. I know we were on holy soil, but we needed a bit of holy intervention or we were in holy crap.

The intervention came in the shape of our driver, who decided to take matters into his own hands. He put his foot down and accelerated towards the gate. The angry crowd dispersed, but continued to run behind the van waving their sticks.

We made it out of the churchyard and into the busy streets. Fortunately for us, a mixture of cars, cows and motorbikes made it difficult for anyone to follow.

It was only later that the complete story emerged. Apparently, there were two Bishops of Amritsar. One who actually had the role and one who had decided he should have it instead. It turned out we had met the Fake Bishop of Amritsar, complete with gold tooth, Nike trainers and BISH 1 number plate.

We later found out that the church sat on a large, very valuable piece of land. Across India there were many disputes going on about who owned land like this, and who was in charge.

Being the Bishop of Amritsar was obviously a hugely prestigious gig with lots of financial benefits.

It seems the genuine Bishop of Amritsar had found out that a film crew was in his church interviewing his imposter, and neither he nor his team were happy about it. He had sent his mob there to chase us away.

We had interviewed the wrong bishop. Although, looking back, I'm not sure I would have wanted to interview the real one. Especially if he tended to hang around with men who liked bashing up cars and people with sticks.

In the final film though, just to be safe, we never mentioned the fake bishop–not that we were planning too anyway. I definitely didn't have time to explain the strawberry filter to the angry mob.

Now, strange as it may seem, whenever I meet any member of the clergy, I always check out their car number plate and range of footwear before fully believing them.

It certainly was a memorable trip and I know lots of people would love to have been in my shoes. Even if they weren't top of the range Nike trainers.

14

PLAYING WITH FIRE

The pathway of hot coals glowed a tangerine orange, spitting and crackling in front of us.

In the half-darkness behind them, I saw our four brave or just plain mad women, who were about to run across hot coals in bare feet LIVE on Breakfast Television.

"Will they have the courage to overcome their fears, and walk across this path of fire?" teased Kate Garraway into the camera, talking to the millions of viewers watching at home.

"Stay tuned and find out after the break."

The studio cut to an ad break.

We were all set for our dramatic live stunt.

What could possibly go wrong? As the main producer in charge of this feature, I was hoping that nothing, but you never quite know with live television, particularly when it involves something flammable.

When you are making television, you are always looking for a new spectacle or idea to grab viewers' attention. We never forgot that every morning they had the choice of whether to watch you or grab the remote control and switch over to the other side. In our case, to watch our rivals BBC Breakfast.

In recent months, the ratings war had got fiercer, as BBC Breakfast were catching up in terms of viewing figures. As producers, we were all being pushed harder than ever to come up with new ways to keep them watching, particularly over the ad breaks. Every viewing focus group you spoke to said how much they hated them, but ads were our bread and butter on a commercial station like ITV, and the fact was, they paid all our wages. While we might wish they weren't there, we couldn't survive or make a profit as a TV station without them.

The BBC didn't have any ads as they got all their money from the licence fee, so we were particularly vulnerable to losing viewers during commercials. So, before every break we would tease what was coming after it, just as Kate had done with the hot coals.

I was part of a team working on a week-long strand called Inch Loss Island, which involved repackaging the classic diet feature we always did in January. Almost everyone has been on a January diet at some time, and this would be our way of showing people how to lose weight in an entertaining way.

The TV show Big Brother was all the rage at the time, so this was our spin on it. The idea was simple: lock four overweight people on an island and watch how they got on as they were subjected to lots of exercise and a complete change in diet. With the help of nutritionist Amanda Ursell, fitness guru Nicki Waterman and life coach Pete Cohen, we would help them change habits of a lifetime and, in doing so, lose weight. In this case, lots of it.

The location was Burgh Island on the south coast of Devon, an island that was cut off by the sea for half of the day. There was one hotel and one tiny pub called the Pilchard Inn, and both of them were only accessible from the mainland when the tide was out.

The hotel was where Agatha Christie had reportedly written two of her books, 'And Then There Were None' and 'Evil Under the Sun'. Then, it was a swish 5-star hotel with beautiful Art Deco rooms. Now it was a tired hotel in need of refurbishment, with new owners hoping to restore it to its former glory. We managed to rent it at a cut-price rate because it was in the middle of the building work, and it was the first week in January (so off-peak).

There was no heating in the hotel, so we all spent the week in our thermals and coats. The weather also added to the drama; it was wet and windy, with howling gales that whipped around the island and the hotel.

To add to the suspense, we had searchlights installed like those in a prison yard, and we employed a security guard and his dog to keep watch on the island. To be honest though, it was so big that if one of our recruits wanted to slip off when the tide was out, nobody would have noticed. But it looked good for the cameras.

To put on a production like this required a large crew, too. There were at least thirty of us working on it. There was the on-screen talent, producers, researchers, camera, sound and lighting crew—and, of course, the Inch Loss recruits themselves.

Accommodation on the island was limited, so while half of us stayed in the hotel, the rest of the crew had to stay in local hotels and B&Bs on the mainland.

The tide times were a problem. You could only walk across the sand onto the island for six hours at a time, before the waves crashed back in again and cut it off for a further six hours. In summer, there was a sea tractor that shuttled guests backwards and forwards, but that winter it was broken.

Due to the unfavourable tide times, one night the fifteen or so crew members staying off the island, had to get up at 2.30am to walk across the sandy causeway in the dark, before the tide came in.

That morning, some of them almost didn't make it.

David the production manager came to see me. He took a long draw on his pipe, expelling a strong smell of liquorice into the air, before giving me the bad news.

"Some of the boys have overslept, and I'm not sure if they are going to make it onto the island in time," he said, downplaying the drama with a little laugh and a comical raising of his eyebrows. "You know Eddie and Steve and the boys, I'm sure they'll get here," he went on, as though he was telling me a light-hearted tale rather than the news that my broadcast was ruined.

I tried to look on the bright side, like he was, but I couldn't see it. If they didn't make it onto the island, I had no satellite engineer, no sound engineer and no live broadcast. While the truck was safely on the island, they were not.

I had watched Steve and Eddie power up our OB truck on many occasions, but I had no idea how to do it myself, nor did anyone else who was on the island.

Forget Inch Loss Island, this was Engineer-less Island. I had an island full of presenters and diet recruits, but no way to broadcast. I thought about maybe taking them all to the mainland and trying to do a broadcast from there, but quickly rejected that idea. What would be the point of Inch Loss Island if we'd all abandoned it just two days into the week?

There was nothing I could do but wait, and hope that they would make it, before the waters rose up too high.

I had enough health and safety issues to deal with that day, without a drowning crew to add to them.

David and I stood on the island, peering out into the dark, waiting to see any signs of life.

At about 3am we saw headlights come into view in the car park on the other side of the causeway. The vehicle parked up and the headlights were switched off.

We strained our eyes in the blackness looking for any signs of the crew heading in our direction.

David shone a torch onto the causeway. The water was rising; I could see the waves creeping towards each other on either side, like a pair of wet folded hands meeting in the lap of the sands in the middle.

There was no doubt that Steve, Eddie and the rest of the crew were going to get wet, but it was difficult to tell at this stage just how damp they would be.

I was worried, even if they weren't. Wading through knee-high freezing water is not fun at the best of times, but now they were doing it in the pitch dark.

We couldn't see anything. I went back to the hotel and asked someone to turn on the searchlights. While originally hired for TV effect, they were now going to come in handy trying to spot four soggy crew members in the dark.

The searchlight found them. We spotted the four men in anoraks, wading through the water which was now knee-deep.

They arrived on the island, tired, wet and grumpy, and immediately went to try and dry off and get a quick nap before our broadcast started at 6am.

Meanwhile, a crew of a different kind had managed to arrive on time. The specialist team was already out on the lawn of the hotel, creating the path of hot coals that our Inch Loss Islanders would walk over.

Pete Cohen, the life coach, had first suggested the idea. The premise was simple: if they could overcome their fears of walking over hot coals, then these women could overcome their fears of everything, including all the things in their lives that were stopping them from losing weight.

I was the producer responsible for looking after this segment of the show. With just minutes to go, we were all set.

Outside, I was a sea of tranquillity–these women were obviously very nervous and the last thing I wanted them to do was back out–but inside I was bricking it and I was terrified that someone would get hurt.

Many people I have worked with have told me how calm I am on a live broadcast, even when chaos is erupting around me. As the producer in charge of a shoot, I felt I had to be. You are like the captain of a ship; if anyone senses you are not in control, then you've got a mutiny on your hands.

I had learnt from experience that it all had to do with the planning. For every Plan A, you needed a B and C, to cover all eventualities from terrible weather to guests not turning up.

Production manager David and I had done everything we could to make the stunt safe, starting with the risk assessment. This was something we had to do before any broadcast took place, particularly one as complicated as this.

Answering the questions on this one was more difficult than normal:

Question: What is the risk?

Answer: Fire.

Question: What might happen with that risk?

Answer: One of my recruits might get badly burnt feet - or worse, fall over while running across the coals and burn something else as well.

We had hired an expert company to set up the coals, placing them at exactly the right depth so as to be thick enough to walk on, but not too thick as to hurt anyone's feet, and both we and they were confident that the risks were very minimal.

We also had Dr Hilary Jones, a bucket of cold water and the first aid kit standing by, in case of any minor burns or injuries.

Pete Cohen stood next to the four Inch Loss recruits, quietly talking to them, reinforcing his positive messages, encouraging them that they could do it.

We were in the ad break and Kate stood waiting for the studio to come back to us, softly rehearsing her lines under her breath.

The hot coals glowed like an amber runway in the cold, dark January morning.

I went over to Dr Hilary to check that he was on standby to act if needed.

"Are you happy?" I asked him, looking for some kind of reassurance that I wasn't completely mad for putting this stunt live on TV.

"Yes," he said, waving the plasters from his first aid kit at me and pointing at the bucket of water next to him.

I felt relieved.

"There's just one thing," he continued.

"What thing?" I said. I didn't like the sound of this.

"The fire crew have just asked me to tell you to check that none of the women are wearing any nail varnish on their toes, as that would make their feet very flammable."

"Nail varnish! Nail varnish! No one told me anything about nail varnish!" I screeched and grabbed David's torch. I went running over to the women, frantically shining the light at their feet.

What was I going to do? We had just a minute before we went on air. They were going to be barefoot on TV, so the chances of at least one, if not more of them having painted their toenails were pretty high. We definitely didn't have time for them to take it off, and even if we did have some nail polish remover handy on this remote Devon Island, I reckoned that it would be even more flammable than the varnish itself.

I was going to have to call the whole thing off. I picked up my mobile to make a frantic call to the office.

Hilary was behind me and stopped me. "Got you! Only joking!" he said. "I just made that up. It's all fine," he laughed.

While I always enjoyed having a joke with people, I was not in the mood for it then.

"Hilary, you almost gave me a heart attack," I said, punching his arm. "I thought doctors were supposed to prevent them, not cause them."

We quickly went back to our posts and seconds later, we were live on TV.

The fire path crackled in front of us, as the first woman stepped onto the hot coals. She walked with purpose across the burning pathway, with Pete and the other recruits cheering her on. The others followed. If I do say so myself, the broadcast was fantastic. The sight of four women walking across burning coals and then the exhilaration they felt having done it was truly motivating. They were all pumped and willing to try anything.

All the effort and stress of getting everyone there and setting up the stunt had been worth it.

The recruits all went off with Amanda, Nicki and Pete to have their Inch Loss-style healthy breakfast.

I stood with Hilary and Dave by the glowing coals. It was just starting to get light. A watery winter sun peeked over the horizon in the east, revealing the flooded causeway down below.

We would be cut off from the mainland for a further hour before the water receded again, and some of the crew could get off.

"That was quite a morning." said David, taking another puff from his liquorice scented pipe.

"You could say that. I don't know whose heart rate was higher, the women waiting to cross those hot coals, or mine, worrying about drowning crew and guests with painted toenails going up in smoke."

We all laughed.

"I got you though," said Hilary. "I know you are a good producer and you try to think of everything, but there's always something new that can catch you out."

It was true. Every day on the job I was learning new things; that's what made it so interesting.

I have no idea where I first heard this phrase, but it has been my motto ever since: the day you stop learning is the day you stop living. Although I have to admit, I would have preferred to have learnt some of these 'lessons' with a little less stress involved.

15

TRAINS, DIET PILLS AND BLACK MAMBAS

The clicking noises finally stopped. The San people's elders now sat silently in a semi-circle around me.

"What are they saying?" I asked my interpreter and driver Shaun as we sat in a small mud hut in the remote northern corner of Namibia.

Shaun was translating my questions into Afrikaans. The Afrikaans speaker in the group was then translating it into their local language which involved flicking his tongue around his mouth to make a gentle clicking noise. The Bushmen then chatted amongst themselves in clicking tones discussing what I had asked, before the same man translated it back into Afrikaans, and Shaun, then translated it back into English so I could understand what on earth was going on.

The room was hot and sticky and the flies buzzed around our eyes and noses. While I spent all my time flicking them away from my face, the San elders in front of me seemed unaware of them. It was a tense moment; I needed an answer to my question and their reply could make or break my trip.

I had come to Namibia and South Africa on a research trip funded by the Commonwealth Broadcasting Association. I had won a bursary from them to seek out and research stories that could potentially make it onto television. The aim of the bursary was to encourage journalists to find positive stories about developing countries in the Commonwealth, rather than the usual negative or depressing stories about famine or corruption that often filled the papers.

I now had a taste for foreign travel, so when I had seen the bursary advertised in the Guardian newspaper, I applied never thinking I would ever get it. My idea was to look at how people and plants from the developing world were helping shape medicine in developed countries like the UK, across Europe and the USA.

One such story I was researching was about the hoodia plant, used for centuries by the San Bushmen to suppress their appetite when they went out hunting for days on end. The plant was now being used in medical trials carried out by a major pharmaceutical company to develop a pill to aid weight loss. Diet pills were and still are big business, so if this pill worked it could revolutionise the way the growing problem of obesity was tackled.

Having been given the bursary of £10,000, one month later I found myself travelling out to Namibia to meet with them to ask if I could film their story.

There were other opportunities to cover positive stories on health in that region while I was there. Among them was filming with the Phelophepa health train. The remit of the train was simple: it travelled around rural South Africa, offering affordable eye and dental treatment to some of the poorest, predominantly black communities in the country.

Every week, the train would set off from one place along the barely-used South African railway track and then park up for a week in the next rural location, where long queues of people would await. This train only came every two years, so demand was very high. After a week of pulling out teeth and performing other eye and dental treatments, the staff and medical volunteers on board would pack everything back into the train and set off to the next location.

While we had a week to catch the staff working at a village, we had just one day (normally a Saturday) to film the train actually trundling along the tracks.

In order to film this event, I needed a camera operator. I had never been to South Africa before, so I called on our experienced production manager, Raj, to find me one. After years working for Reuters, Raj had a contacts book the size of a small encyclopaedia and could find you crews almost anywhere in the world.

He recommended a young black South African cameraman called Frank who had worked with us before on other news shoots.

Having picked me up from Johannesburg early in the morning, Frank and I made the three- and half-hour drive to Bloemfontein, and arrived about an hour before the train was departing.

The station was a buzz of activity, with lots of young doctors in white coats and train staff busily packing away all the equipment and chairs and putting them safely on board for transit to the next station.

We found the train driver, Moses, and confirmed the route the train would be taking. While we would be filming the train departing from the station, we also needed to get some pictures of it, in transit. Moses told Frank about a good spot on a bridge about an hour down the line that we could film from.

Unlike Britain, where there was a strict timetable, South Africa's railway service was non-existent apart from a tourist train called the Blue Train. The Phelophepa health train was the only one running along the tracks that day. Indeed, in most cases, the last time the tracks had been used was two years ago, the last time the health train was there. This meant that repair teams often had to go ahead of the train to make sure the track was free from broken rails, animals on the line and any debris.

Frank had agreed with the train driver that after filming it leaving the station, we would then race ahead in our car, to catch it at the suggested location, on a suitable railway bridge miles down the line.

"Are you sure we will get there in time?" I asked Frank and Moses. "I've never tried racing against a train in the UK, but if I did, I am sure it would get there long before I did!"

The boys both laughed.

"There are eighteen carriages on this train full of equipment, this old lady doesn't go anywhere in a hurry," said Moses. "We like to take it slowly just in case there's any stray animals on the line. If I see them coming, I can sound my horn and hopefully they get out of the way in time."

I hoped that they did. I didn't like the idea of filming splattered cows or sheep on the train windscreen.

Frank chipped in. "I think there's a bit more traffic to worry about in London than here in the Free State."

"Here's my mobile number," said Moses. "Feel free to call me anytime if you need to get hold of me." He went off to prepare for the train's departure.

While I was grateful that Moses was being so helpful, I was also a little worried about him giving out his mobile number. Wasn't he going to be busy driving an 18-carriage train? Was it safe for him to be in charge of this big engine while having a chat with us on the phone?

At midday the train slowly pulled away from the station. We set off too, racing through the countryside of the Free State. Along flat empty roads, through rolling grasslands and burnt-orange soil, the black mountains as a teasing backdrop in the distance.

We found the filming vantage point on the railway bridge easily. Hundreds of onlookers were already gathered, waiting for the train. Grandparents with their grandchildren, dads with their children. It was not every day that a train went through their town and they were not going to miss it.

Jostling with crowds to find a suitable spot to film, Frank started setting up his camera. I meanwhile started chatting to one grandpa and his young grandson about what was about to happen. The six-year-old had never seen a real train before, so this was a big occasion.

Across the flat open plains, I could see the steam from the train coming in the distance. As it got closer, the children around me started to squeal with excitement.

My cameraman Frank, meanwhile, seemed to be fiddling with his camera, trying to sort out a back-focus problem. As the train drew closer, I asked Frank if he was ready. "Yes, sure" he replied, but the nervousness in his voice unsettled me.

"It's coming now!" I shouted at him as the noise of the cheering crowd got louder and the train appeared into view, chugging along the tracks below us, blowing its whistle to greet the onlookers on the bridge. Frank, while filming, didn't seem to be happy.

The train–all eighteen carriages of it–was only travelling at 20mph so it took a while for it to pass underneath us. Halfway through, I asked Frank if we had got the shots we needed.

"How can I explain this? I wasn't ready. I missed it."

I could not quite believe what I was hearing. "You missed it?" I shouted at him. "You're joking, aren't you?"

"Sorry," he said again sheepishly. "Do you think you can phone up Moses and ask him to stop the train, reverse down the line and come through again?"

"I beg your pardon?" I asked in disbelief. "You're asking me to phone up the train driver and ask him to stop an 18-carriage train full of people and medical equipment and ask him to reverse back down the tracks just because you missed the shot?"

"Yes," he replied. "We've got his number."

So, with trepidation I phoned Moses and made my request.

I could hear the sound of the engine burbling in the background as we spoke.

"I'm really sorry," I shouted, hoping he could hear me above the noise. "But we had a technical problem with the camera." I told a small fib on that one. I was too embarrassed to explain what had really happened.

"Is there any chance you can back up the train and come through again?" As I said the words I winced, not believing in a million years that he would actually take my request seriously.

"No problem at all," he said, as I heard the screeching of the brakes kicking in on the train. Within ten seconds, the whole thing had ground to a halt.

The crowd around me looked on in amazement. Why had the train stopped? They muttered amongst themselves, trying to work out what had happened.

After two minutes, the train started reversing back down the tracks. The children on the bridge all squealed again with excitement. "Look Grandpa, the train is going backwards!" the six-year-old boy yelled.

The train continued coming back down the line, for a full mile before grinding to a halt.

My phone rang again. It was Moses.

"Let me know when you are ready and we'll come through under the bridge again," he shouted down the phone.

"Okay," I said. "Thanks so much, when I am ready to go I'll shout Action!"

I still couldn't quite believe that, on my cue, a twenty tonne, 18-carriage railway train was going to start moving again.

Holding the driver on the line, I shouted across to Frank. "Please tell me you are ready this time?"

"Yes, I'm ready," he replied.

"Are you sure about that?" I wanted confirmation. I did not want to do this again.

"Yes, I am definitely ready."

"Okay, standby Moses, let's go for it...5, 4, 3, 2, 1 and ACTION!" I shouted down the phone.

We all watched as the locomotive lurched into life, moving once again down the track toward us.

The waiting crowds cheered loudly. Not only would they get to see a train coming through their township once, but twice in two years.

As the train came chugging along the track underneath us, Frank filmed it perfectly this time. The final video we shot was stunning, capturing the gleaming white and red carriages coming into view against the backdrop of the golden fields and red-soiled southern African landscape.

After the train had gone completely through again, Frank and I started to pack up and get ready for our drive to the next filming point as the train arrived at its next destination.

Beside me, the grandfather and grandson watched in amazement. "Wow," said the six-year-old boy. "That woman is a superhero; she has power over the train."

I smiled to myself, I guess for just a moment in time, I did.

Back in Namibia, where I was hoping to film the hoodia plant story I felt less in control of the situation. Shaun had driven me in his SUV for two hours along a dusty red track. There were no towns, no petrol stations and no sign of anyone much. Just mile upon mile of dirt road. Shaun had brought enough water and food to keep us going for a few days, just in case we broke down. He also had a satellite phone, as the mobile phone network between towns was non-existent.

Also, on the back seat of the car was a pile of blankets in case we got cold at night. We stopped to have a refreshment and toilet break. Shaun produced two cans of ice-cold Coke from the icebox on the back seat. I was so thirsty; I drank one straight down.

"There are more drinks in there if you want them," he said, gesturing to the box. "Help yourself. I'm going for a pee." He disappeared into the nearby bushes.

I climbed into the back, making it easier for me to open the cool box. As I sat down on the blankets, I felt a hard object underneath them. I pulled one back to reveal a Magnum 358 gun on the back seat.

I was not sure how I felt about this. I was in a car with a man I had only met a few hours before, who had a gun hidden from me. I saw the headlines, "British TV Producer found shot dead in African Bush."

Although I quickly realised that by the time anyone found me, there probably wouldn't have been much left. My imagination started to go into overdrive, imagining some passing hyena tearing my flesh to bits.

On the one hand he could use the gun against me, but on the other it was probably for our own protection and, more importantly, if he didn't look after me, he wouldn't get paid. Also, Shaun had come highly recommended through friends of friends, so I was hoping I would never see the gun again.

I quickly put the blanket back as I'd found it, grabbed some water from the icebox, and made a mental note not to upset him at any point during our adventure.

For the next few hours, we continued along the dusty dirt track. He never spoke about the gun, and I never asked. That was, until we hit a black mamba snake that crossed our path. The snake reared up and hit the windscreen with a thud and landed in the road in front of us.

Shaun brought the car to a halt and stepped out to inspect it.

"Would you like to see her?" he asked, poking the twitching mamba with his stick.

"Is it poisonous and is it alive?" I asked.

"Yes, and yes," he confirmed.

"I think I'll just stay in the car," I said. It might be my first and only time seeing a black mamba, but as far I was concerned it was close enough.

"It's really beautiful," he said, taking the gun out from the back seat of the car.

I was going to have to take his word for it. Before I had time to change my mind, a loud bang rang out.

"It's dead now," he said, picking up the black snake which now had very little head left on it.

I didn't know whether to be happy or sad. On the one hand, the snake was dead and wouldn't be in any pain or poisoning either of us. On the other hand, it seemed a shame that, had we not run it over, and then shot it, it would still be alive and still able to slither around in the hot African sun.

Shaun got back in the car and continued driving. We had arrived at our destination just as the sun was setting, casting long shadows over the red soil. The area where the Bushmen lived was way off the tourist track. The only visitors were people prospecting for precious metals and minerals, or people like me who had come to meet them.

There was just one lodge to stay in in the town. It had a main building with a thatched roof that housed the reception desk and a dining area. The rooms were in separate concrete huts with corrugated iron roofs that were spread around the compound with glass and wire mesh on the windows. The lodge was surrounded by a huge barbed wire fence.

"Is it dangerous here?" I asked.

"It's not to protect you from the San people, it's to ward off the elephants. Otherwise, they would just stampede over everything and drink all the water in the tank," Shaun said pointing at a large water drum elevated on a simple wooden frame beside the main reception area.

I had always had this impression that elephants were cuddly creatures, but now I could see the simple reality of living beside them was less easy and downright dangerous at times.

I was shown to my concrete hut where I would be spending the night.

"Freshen up and we'll grab some dinner," Shaun suggested.

It was 6pm, and I didn't normally eat that early, but apparently dinner was served at 6pm or not at all. So, I followed him to the dining shack.

There was no choice on the menu. The chef served up skinny legs of chicken with maize. While very lean, the chicken meat was delicious, and obviously freshly sourced. I was really hungry by this point so gobbled it all up. It was accompanied by a cold bottle of beer, which was welcome in the dry heat. Outside it was not quite pitch dark. I could hear the click of crickets, the quiet buzz of mosquitos and other night noises.

"I'm off to bed," Shaun said. "We have an early start."

Now after years of working on Breakfast TV I wasn't averse to an early night, but it was still not even 7pm, and I wasn't remotely tired. I hung around for about ten minutes after Shaun had left, but got the impression the chef and lodge manager wanted to shut up for the night so I decided to head off too.

"Good night, thanks for dinner," I said. heading for the door.

"You'll be needing the torch and this," the manager said, handing me a hat with special netting over it. "The hat is to protect you from the mozzies, they are pretty vicious around here. The torch is to protect you from the black mambas. It's pitch-black out there and hard to see them, but step on one and you'll quickly know about it," he added, laughing. "Wave the torch around and stamp your feet and you'll scare them off."

The journey from the dining hut to my prefab hut was no more than ten metres, but it felt like a mile as I stamped my feet and waved around my torch, looking like I was performing some form of Namibian tribal dance. With every crack of twig and rustle of leaves, I was convinced there was a snake there. There was no sign of the mambas, but it was mozzie motorway around my face as they crashed into the netting.

I got into my room and shut the door. Switching on the light, a terrible clattering and banging started. I realised that, while not inside the prefab, the giant flies and mozzies were attracted to the light and were head-banging the corrugated iron and grilled windows, desperately trying to get in.

The noise got louder and louder as more mozzies were attracted to the single bulb that hung from my bedroom ceiling. There was nothing for it, I had to switch off the light. The noise was unbearable.

I climbed under my mosquito net and read my book by torchlight. While there were now fewer giant insects trying to headbutt their way into my room, there were still plenty of strange noises to distract me. At 9pm I finally switched off the light and tried to sleep with the sound of the animals around me. But with giant-sized mosquitoes, elephants and snakes supposedly in the vicinity, I was not sure how much sleep I would get that night.

The following morning, the sunlight woke me at 5am, as it streamed through the grilled window. I got up and went for breakfast. After a meal of bush tea, boiled eggs and sliced white bread, we set off in the car to meet the San elders. Shaun had set up the meeting through a contact of his. I had no idea what to expect. All I knew was that they had agreed to meet me–a rare honour in itself–and that Shaun would be helping with the translation.

I walked into the hut where the four tiny, San elders sat talking amongst themselves. I had expected them to be dressed in traditional loincloth clothing, but instead they all wore English football tops and shorts. One had a red Liverpool top on, the other sported a blue Chelsea shirt. I laughed to myself. Here I was already stereotyping these people. Why couldn't they watch a bit of football and support an English team and have the shirt to prove it? It just seemed weird to see it seven thousand miles away from home.

What I also hadn't expected was the language they were speaking. The oldest of them was talking using gentle clicking noises. He was obviously telling a joke or something funny as they were all falling about with laughter.

I smiled and held out my hand. One of them smiled revealing some black crooked teeth and gestured for me to sit down. I had prepared what I had wanted to say, but did not realise that it had to go through not one, but two rounds of interpretation.

I started by explaining who I was and why I had come there. I explained about the hoodia plant and my grant and how I wanted to film and interview them about the amazing knowledge they had and how they had used it. Shaun translated what I said into Afrikaans and George, the youngest of the group translated it into the gentle clicking language.

Every question asked and every response was taking several minutes. As the interpretation went backwards and forwards, I had no idea how accurate the translations were, but just had to trust both George and Shaun that they were telling them the right thing.

What I discovered was fascinating. The hoodia plant was something they used to stop them feeling hungry when they were out hunting for days at a time. They carried the root of the plant in their bags and would just chew on it every now and then. It meant they could survive several days without proper food. The South African Army had apparently come across it when working with the San peoples, and had then passed it onto the drug company who was now investigating it.

The Bushmen were not happy, however, as they felt that their intellectual property had been stolen with little compensation. The clicking got louder and angrier as they discussed how they felt they had been deceived into giving up the secrets of this indigenous plant. Lawyers were now involved and the drug company had tried to make amends, offering the community new medical facilities and transport to get around, but the damage had already been done.

I tried to reassure them that I was nothing to do with the drug company, but as far as they were concerned, I was just another white person coming to steal something from them. I tried another tactic. I asked them if I could make a financial contribution to something they cared about. The elders' ears seemed to prick up at this point. While they were elderly, a chance to help the younger people was widely appreciated–many of them now had no jobs and no prospect of employment and just spent their days drinking and gambling with what little money they had.

It was crunch time. I had been there for over two hours as the interpretation went backwards and forwards. I needed to ask them if they would be happy to be interviewed and filmed so that they could tell their side of the story. Once again, Shaun translated my request into Afrikaans and George translated that into the gentle clicking language. The four elders started talking amongst themselves, at times gesticulating in my direction, at others arguing and waving their hands around madly. I had no idea what they were saying.

After what seemed like ages, but was probably only five minutes, I asked my guide what had been said.

George paused for effect. Shaun then repeated it. "The San elders, they say 'No'."

I was gutted and also a little confused.

They had been speaking for a good five minutes, so it was definitely much more than 'No' they were saying. They could have been talking about the weather or even the English football results for all I knew, but when I pressed them, no one would tell me what they had actually said. They could have also been being very rude about me, but I had no idea, and to this day haven't a clue what their conversation was all about.

All I know is that I never got to film with the San peoples with their lilting, clicking language. I was very disappointed, but I learnt a valuable lesson that day. In the words of the Frozen song, you sometimes just have to 'Let It Go'.

I would have loved to have brought their discovery to a wider audience, but it never happened. The drug never happened either. After medical trials, the drug company decided not to pursue production. I never found out why, but no doubt the Bushmen are still using it when they go out hunting. The hoodia plant will remain their little secret.

Just because I wanted to film it and show it to a British audience, it didn't mean they did. I learnt a valuable lesson that day, not everyone wants to be on telly.

16

BOMBS AND BRAVADO

For any TV Producer covering a breaking news story, it can be thrilling, frustrating, sometimes terrifying, all in equal measure. When a major event like a terrorist attack happens, the newsroom ramps up a gear and everyone goes into overdrive trying to cover the story in the best way possible.

As *GMTV* was only actually on air from 6am to 9.30am, it was often the most important time for breaking news, as people wanted to catch up with what had been happening, while they were asleep.

If it happened in your airtime, you covered the story as best you could. If it didn't happen while you were broadcasting, then you still wanted to cover it, but had to consider that every other news bulletin would have featured it the night before you did, so you needed to think ahead about what the fresh news lines would be, the following morning.

The 7/7 London terrorist attacks in 2005 did happen in our airtime. The first reports we heard about the bombs going off were at Aldgate, Edgware Road and Russell Square at 8.47am, during the Lorraine segment of the show. Immediately, all the planned programme items were swept aside to cover the story.

Correspondents Richard Gaisford and Jonathan Swain were immediately sent to the scene to report on what was going on via phone link.

Everyone hit the phones trying to get hold of the Metropolitan Police, the London Fire Brigade and the London Ambulance Service to get an accurate account of what had happened. We also needed eyewitnesses. We all scoured the other networks–BBC and Sky–on both television and radio to see who they had found. We would then scribble down their names and try to get hold of a contact number for them. As rival stations we couldn't just phone them up and ask, and even if we did, they were unlikely to have given out their numbers.

A good eyewitness account was worth ten poor ones. In other words, if you had someone who had been near to the scene and could talk well about what they had seen, they were priceless. Often these were few and far between; people were either too shy or shaken to do an interview, or just clammed up when they got in front of the cameras. As a result, you would often see the same person popping up on rival channels. The trick was to get to them first.

By 9.25am *GMTV* was off air and we then had to think about how we would cover the story the next day. Getting some good eyewitness statements with different stories to the ones we had already heard or seen would be the key.

I was working in our features department at the time, but immediately went over to the news desk to offer my services.

This was before the time of video on mobile phones, so our news editor Pete told me to grab a small video camera and get up to the location of the bus bomb in Tavistock Square to film some footage and interview anyone who might have seen what had happened.

As a journalist you are used to blocking out the personal side of the story and concentrating on the job at hand, but even so, it was hard not to be a little nervous in this case. A terrorist attack happening right in the heart of London was worrying. There could have been people on those tube trains that I knew: colleagues, relatives and friends. Who knew if there would be more bombs and where?

I left our offices on the South Bank and tried to hail a cab. I managed to flag one down and we started heading north towards the site of the atrocity. We did not get very far. We were hoping to be able to get over Waterloo Bridge, but there were huge traffic jams. We then heard on the radio that the police had closed the bridges to all vehicles. It was pointless staying in the cab, so I paid the driver and started walking instead.

I knew the Underground would not be working either, but I hoped to be able to jump on a bus for at least part of the journey, as it was almost a two-mile walk. I was not dressed for a hike across town in my summery dress, but at least I had trainers on. I had not expected to be going out filming that day, but despite wearing high heels to work, years of experience had taught me to keep a pair of comfortable shoes under my desk.

In spite of my more appropriate footwear, by the time I had walked up to the scene of the bomb, I was hot and sweaty and my trainers were starting to rub on my toes–I had forgotten to bring socks to wear inside them.

The normally bustling London streets were eerily quiet. I was used to seeing them chequered with bright red London buses and black taxis weaving in and out of the traffic, but there were none.

The cafés and bars around the British Museum, normally full of tourists drinking tea and reading maps, were empty.

Anyone I did see on foot was beating a hasty retreat from the scene. walking away from the scene, rather than towards it. The only ones heading towards it were other journalists like myself.

By the time I arrived in Tavistock Square, the police had cordoned off the bus with a white large screen, so people could not take photos and onlookers could not witness the gory scene behind it.

Police helicopters whirred overhead like giant mechanical bumblebees, trying to survey the roads for signs of other possible attacks.

I set up my camera and filmed the scene. Initially I stood right next to the white screen, trying to make out the sounds and voices I could hear coming from the other side. I heard one paramedic trying to calm down someone in shock.

"Where's my bag? Where's my bag?" the distressed woman cried out.

"Don't worry about your bag," said the paramedic, "we need to get you to hospital."

She then tried to get the woman to move her leg. She let out a piercing scream. Her bag could wait.

I winced to hear her in pain, but as I was on the other side of the screen, I couldn't see her or the state she was in.

Soon more Metropolitan Police officers arrived with ropes to make a cordon and slowly and surely inched it away from the bus, until I was standing on the south side of the square.

Unable to see much from there, I decided to go in search of eyewitnesses. I stopped people on the street, but they were all hacks like me looking for someone to talk with.

It became a bit of a game, circling the streets trying to find someone who had seen or heard anything. I kept bumping into the same reporters from the Evening Standard and PA News. Every time we met, we asked each other if we'd had any luck and would swap stories.

"Anyone interesting to talk to?" I said to the reporter from the Standard.

"I have a bus driver who was on the same street as the other bus and heard the explosion, then heard over his radio about the attack. What about you?"

It was like a human game of Top Trumps.

"Well, I've found a lawyer who was working in her office in the square and heard the explosion, but didn't see it," I offered back.

Neither was the greatest case study, but at this point they were all we had, so we swapped details and carried on.

Normally a journalist would not give out his or her contacts, but there were so few of us on the ground and time was crucial, so we shared resources. The truth of it was that the Evening Standard and *GMTV* were not rivals. They were a London newspaper; we were a national TV programme. There was no problem if we used the same witnesses–it was a different audience.

I changed tack and tried knocking on office doors and going into local hotel receptions.

Half an hour later, I bumped into a snooty producer I recognised from our rival BBC Breakfast show, who was also wandering the streets doing exactly the same thing.

When I had met her previously at the Chelsea Flower Show, she was producing the BBC weather presenter Carol Kirkwood. We had almost come to blows, because we both wanted to broadcast in the same spot–an elevated garden created by designer Diarmuid Gavin - at the same time. As the BBC had rights for the whole show, and we were only allowed in for the first morning, I had to back down and let her go ahead, while we stood by. I remember her smug look and vowed that if I ever encountered her again, I would not lift a finger to help her.

"Terrible tragedy," she said. "How are you getting on finding eyewitnesses?"

"Great," I lied.

By this time, I had found just one good eyewitness who had been working on the scaffold of a building site just metres from where the bus bomb went off, but I wasn't going to admit that to *her*.

"We have some great people lined up, people who saw everything," she boasted, flicking through her pad and surveying her notes.

I suspected she was fibbing too, but didn't want to admit it in front of her ITV rival.

"Anyone you fancy sharing with us?" she asked cockily.

"Sure," I said, trying to purvey a fake cordiality between us. There was no way on earth I was giving her my best eyewitness, I was just going to trade her a lesser one.

I swapped my hotel chef—who had heard the bomb, but not seen anything—for her dog walker, who was streets away when it happened.

We both thanked each other for the helpful tip—NOT—and carried on with our mission.

I tried calling in to the office, but the lines were busy. I finally got through and gave them an update. "I've filmed the scene as best I can, but there's no one here apart from journalists," I said to our deputy editor Malcolm.

"Stay put," he advised. "There might be a press conference at the local hospital about casualties that you can cover."

So that's what I did. I made my way to University College Hospital, which had taken in some of the casualties. It was just around the corner from where the bomb attack had happened. There would be a news conference in an hour, so I grabbed a coffee and went to sit outside on a bench in the sunshine. Soon I was joined by some other journalists all waiting around for the same press briefing, and we started chatting.

One reporter was from Toronto in Canada, representing the national newspaper, another was from Tel Aviv, the third was a young guy from Darwin, Australia. It turned out he had only arrived in the country days before and had managed to get himself a week's work with a London news agency.

We were swapping information about what we did and did not know. It was then that the Canadian guy started shaking uncontrollably.

"Are you okay?" I asked.

He shook his head.

"Sit down," I said. "I'll get you some tea."

I ran off to the local coffee shop and came back with tea in a paper cup. By now, he had stopped shaking, but his face was still ashen.

"Where are you from?" he asked me.

I told him I was from Surrey, but had worked and studied in London all my adult life.

"I don't know how you can work and live here all the time," he said. "All these bombs going off everywhere. I just couldn't stomach it." He shook his head from side to side.

I tried to explain the situation.

"Bombs don't happen every day, you know and when they do, London is such a big place that the chances of getting involved in one are pretty slim."

He didn't seem convinced. He still had no colour in his face, and he was picking at the skin around his fingernails nervously.

"When I was growing up, we used to have IRA bombs," I went on. In fact, it wasn't long since the Northern Ireland Peace Treaty had been signed, so my journalism training had involved learning how to react to a call from the IRA.

"They weren't pleasant, but at least they gave you a telephone warning and they were pretty infrequent in London, so you just learnt to live with them."

He didn't seem comforted by my stories.

Eamonn Holmes–who had grown up in Belfast–told stories of daily near misses from snipers and bombs, so in comparison, I thought my experiences had been a doddle.

The journalist from Tel Aviv then piped up. "Phar! This is nothing," he said, dismissively. "In Israel, we have suicide bombers all the time. Every day in my job, I deal with things like this. This place is quiet by comparison."

He gave a sweeping gesture as though we were in a gentle daisy field, rather than just around the corner from a London terrorist attack.

I tried to explain to him that I was glad I did not have to cover daily bombings. While getting involved in the odd story was exciting, doing it on a regular basis must take its toll. At this, he nodded.

The young Australian then joined in.

"This place is fantastic," he grinned. "Where I come from in Darwin, I'm used to covering stories about country fairs and crocodiles. Already this week we've had the G8 summit in Scotland. Yesterday London found out they'd won their bid to host the Olympics, and now all these bombings. Who could ask for a better place to be?"

For a news-hungry young reporter, you had to agree that this was indeed an exciting place to work, but I could also see where the Canadian journalist was coming from.

I tried to explain to him that not every news week was as jam-packed as this one, and not to expect this level of excitement all the time.

It was time for the press conference.

My little crew of reporters–the shaking guy from Canada, the seasoned journalist from Israel and the over-excited young reporter from Australia–all entered the room and found some-where to sit. I went to the back of the room to set up my camera. Standing there, I spotted some of the other journalists I had met earlier, among them the reporter from the Evening Standard and the snobby BBC producer.

There was a general hush in the room: people talked in low whispers, conscious of the gravity of the situation. They had their notebooks and voice tape recorders out ready to record the words of the hospital press officer. I set up my little camera along with a row of others at the back.

By this time, I was feeling slightly inadequate. They all had proper large Digi Beta broadcast cameras, I just had my little camcorder. The BBC producer came back to speak to one of the cameramen; she glanced over at me and smirked. I felt myself get hot and flushed with embarrassment, but tried not to show it in front of her.

I looked around for someone from ITN–the news arm of ITV–who I could buddy up to, but they were nowhere to be seen. I phoned up our news desk to ask if they were sending anyone. Malcolm answered the phone again.

"Are we or ITN sending anyone to film this hospital press conference?" I asked him.

"Yes," he said. "You."

"No, I meant a proper cameraperson," I said, trying to explain myself better.

''You'll be fine," said Malcolm. "They're probably not going to say much anyway." He hung up.

The BBC producer continued to quietly brief her cameraman, while I fiddled with my camera next to them. I felt embarrassed, but what could I do? It was like when you turned up to school on your bicycle to find that the prettiest girl in school had a proper shiny Raleigh bike and you just had one with stabilisers.

There was nothing I could do but tough it out and look like I knew what I was doing.

I had never filmed anything before that might actually go out on air. Taking a few general shots of the scene of the bombings was one thing, actually filming someone important or even a victim of the attacks was quite another. I was petrified that I would miss the shot.

I had received some camera training, but it was a while ago. I went through my list of checks in my head. First of all, making sure the camera was level; a wonky interview would not go down well. Check.

Do a white balance–there was a white tablecloth on the table where the spokespeople would be sitting, so I focused on that. Unlike your eyes which adjust automatically, you have to tell the camera what light setting you are in, whether it's an inside artificial light or an outside natural one. by focusing on something white, the camera is able to adjust its settings. Check.

I stuck my tiny headphones in and tried to listen to the sound; I could definitely hear something but whether the camera would pick up what was happening all the way at the front was another matter, as I had no separate microphone. I would have to just hope we could hear them, even if the sound was a bit dodgy. Short of adjusting the focus when the people sat down, I was ready to go.

I didn't have to worry. When the press conference happened, it was over within five minutes as they didn't really have much to tell us. The bomb attacks had only happened a few hours earlier, so while they could confirm that the hospital had taken in a number of the injured, they wouldn't reveal any of their names, due to patient confidentiality and informing their relatives first.

There had been nothing really newsworthy to film, and I felt a wave of relief that my dodgy camerawork wouldn't be needed on air. I phoned into the office and told them the news about the victims. By now I had been hanging around the area by the bus bomb for four hours.

"You might as well come back," said Malcolm. "You can chase some more people by phone from here."

I felt a little dejected. I hadn't really found any eyewitnesses who were good enough. I felt like a bit of a failure.

Before I left, I decided to nip to the loo. It would be a long walk back to the office. As I sat in the cubicle, I could hear a woman crying in the one next to me. No doubt another young reporter was upset by the terrorists, I thought to myself. I was going to leave her to it- I had done enough comforting for one day–but then I changed my mind and decided to speak to her.

"Are you okay in there?"

"I'm fine," sniffed the woman next to me.

"Covering stories like this can be pretty scary," I said to her. "This is my first time on a story like this. Is it yours, too?" There was silence. "What paper or network do you work for?"

"I don't work for any paper," she snuffled.

I had definitely got that one wrong. I tried to think why else she would be in the toilet sobbing.

"Do you work here?" I asked, thinking perhaps she was a doctor or a nurse and was dealing with some of the injured. Now this could be more interesting.

"No, my sister was involved in the bomb attack. They've brought her in here, but I can't see her yet. No one will tell me what's going on." I heard her pull some toilet roll from the dispenser to blow her nose.

Bingo! There I had been, trawling around the streets for hours on end for eyewitnesses, but now I had come across something even better, a relative of one of the victims. This really was like getting the top trump. What's more, it had all happened in the glamorous location of a hospital toilet.

I obviously wanted to be sensitive to her plight, but I also needed to get all her contact details and persuade her to come on the show before anyone else could get to her, especially the snooty BBC producer.

We sat and talked inside our toilet cubicles for another five minutes, before I decided to ask her to come out.

"Would you like to grab a coffee?" I suggested. "If you are going to have to wait, you might as well wait with someone."

She agreed and we both came out of the cubicles.

"Can I carry a bag for you?" she asked. I wasn't going to turn down that offer - by now I was getting fed up with carrying the two heavy bags holding the camera and tripod.

As we left the hospital together, I bumped into the BBC producer.

"Any luck with any more eyewitnesses?" she enquired.

"No," I said–and I wasn't lying.

"Never mind, I am sure something will turn up." She gave a false smile and headed back into the hospital to find her crew.

I smiled to myself too. I knew something she didn't and that I had actually found something much better. She might have a cameraman and a fancy camera, but I had a much bigger prize.

I spent the rest of the afternoon with the young woman. After a few fraught hours with no information, in the end her sister was one of the lucky ones. She just had some minor shrapnel injuries. Having received the positive news, the sister happily agreed to come on the show the following morning.

I phoned the office and told them the news, feeling pleased with myself at finding such a good guest for the show.

Pete the news editor answered. "Great job," he said. "Take her number and we'll see if we can squeeze her in."

By now, the other reporters and producers in the field had found many more eyewitnesses and family members of victims, some of them much more seriously hurt than the sister of my guest.

She never did make it onto the show the following day. Her story was trumped by a family with a worse story to tell. Having spent all that time with her, I then had to phone her and let her down about coming on the show. She seemed to be fine about it, but I felt slightly embarrassed. So often in our job, you chased people to come on the show, then had to drop them for something or someone 'better'.

Fortunately, terrorist attacks did not become the norm in London (I am pleased to report to my Canadian journalist friend), but during my career I was going to cover several more of them. Some very nasty ones, where–unlike the IRA bombs–there was no warning.

Thankfully, they never became part of my normal everyday life, but for many other reporters, like the one from Israel, they were a constant reality. I do not envy them that job.

Give me the choice of producing stories on bombings, or crocodiles, I would take the country fairs and crocs any day–but there is something intoxicating about covering a breaking news story, particularly in the heart of London.

I had to agree with the young Aussie reporter: working as a producer in the UK definitely was fantastic.

17

LIGHTS, CAMERA, NIPPLES

S tanding there, wearing nothing on top other than an old bra and my light blue anorak, was not how I had pictured myself dressed for a swanky reception in a royal residence, but here I was and there was very little I could do about it.

"Pleased to meet you," I said, extending my sweaty palm to a member of the household at Kensington Palace. The staff member looked at me oddly, but was polite enough not to say anything.

We had just completed a broadcast at the former home of Princess Diana and I think it was no exaggeration to say I was underdressed.

In my defence, I had not started the morning that way.

Working in this job allowed me to broadcast in some of the most amazing locations, including several royal palaces, but normally it was very early in the morning, before anyone was there.

I have often watched the sunrise over different parts of Britain and heard dawn choruses of birds welcome us to a new day. In the summer, there is something quite magical about being up at this time. You feel like you are getting a sneak preview of nature before anyone else. In the winter, it's quite the opposite. There's nothing fun about standing on a cold, windy street corner, with your fingers going numb and your face chapped and red from the prevailing wind. Spring and autumn could give you either and were more difficult to judge, weather wise.

One spring morning, the Historic Royal Palaces had invited *GMTV* to get a sneak preview of the summer exhibition inside Kensington Palace. We would be doing live broadcasts from there between 6am to 8.30am, ahead of the opening of the exhibition that day to the general public.

Getting into these places at such an early hour always involved persuading someone to wake up early to let us in.

In the case of Kensington Palace, we had been told to meet the security guard at the north gate at 4am. Despite being well into spring, the morning was cold at around only five degrees, and it was dark. We were to enter via the north gate. There were multiple gates into the park that surrounded the palace, so it had not been easy to find the right one. After consulting the sat nav and using good guesswork, I thought I had figured it out. It had no name on it, but using my girl guide orienteering skills I had deduced that this was the only gate on the north side of the park, so it had to be the right one.

A taxi had dropped me outside the gate at 3.50am. I stood in the darkness and waited for everyone else to arrive. Once the camera crew and satellite truck had turned up, I went over to the gate and pressed the buzzer. There was no reply. I buzzed again. The intercom crackled, but then went dead. I could see a security camera pointing down to where I stood, so I started waving furiously at it.

I started to doubt my own orienteering skills. What if we had the wrong gate? I could have been waking up Prince Harry or William, who both still lived there at the time. I hated to think what the consequences would have been of waking up one of their Royal Highnesses.

I went over to the crew car, and tapped on the window. The cameraman wound it down and a plume of hot air hit my face. The car heating was on full pelt as they were trying to keep warm inside.

"I'll give them a few more minutes and then I'll try again," I said. The cameraman nodded and wound his window back up again. Leaving me standing out in the cold. I paced backwards and forwards, trying to keep my circulation going.

Five minutes went by and there was still no sign of anyone. It was now ten past four and no one had arrived to meet us, so I decided to contact the number on our call sheet. It was the number of the Royal Palaces' press officer, who had said I could call her in an emergency.

Was this an emergency? I had to think about that one. Well not a medical emergency maybe, but definitely a broadcasting one. If we didn't get in soon, we wouldn't be ready to go live at 6am.

Calling someone at that time in the morning is always painful. On breakfast TV we had plenty of experience of it. You may have been up at the crack of dawn, but most of the world was fast asleep in bed. The last thing you wanted to do was to have the wrong number and wake up a complete stranger. Similarly, even if it was the right person, I would be probably waking someone up who was in a deep sleep.

I decided to leave it for ten more minutes. By now I could feel my toes starting to numb. I only had on a light blue anorak, and a cotton top underneath. I had misjudged the May weather, choosing my summer coat over my winter puffer jacket, thinking we would have been inside by now.

At 4.20 I made the decision to call the press officer. After about ten rings she picked up.

"Hello," she said in the familiar, groggy voice I was used to hearing when waking someone up unexpectedly.

"I'm really sorry to bother you, but we're outside the north gate and no one has turned up to let us in?"

"But they should be there," she said adamantly. I was not in the mood for arguing with a press officer at that time in the morning, but soon convinced her that there most definitely was *not* anybody here to meet us.

"I'll contact someone," she said, and hung up.

Five minutes later, we saw a torch coming towards us and a security guard unlocked the gate and let us in.

"So sorry to disturb you, thanks so much for letting us in," I said, but to be honest I was not worried about disturbing him. It was his job to let us in and he hadn't. "I tried the buzzer, but no one answered," I explained.

"Oh, that hasn't worked for ages," he said unfussed. "We keep meaning to fix it."

While the crew car and satellite truck drove through the gates, I walked with him to keep him company. There were shades of light in the east and the dawn chorus had started around us. Chirping blackbirds were whistling their morning greetings to one another. I wondered if these blackbirds knew they were whistling inside the grounds of a royal residence?

We walked in silence towards Kensington Palace where the satellite truck had now parked up. Whenever he flashed his torch in my direction, I could see my breath in front of my face like layers of cold smoke blown in the dark air.

The crew had started unloading their kit ready to go into the house. It was now twenty to five. Time was ticking and we needed to set up quickly. Things have changed a lot now. New technology like "Live U" makes it quick and easy to broadcast from all sorts of places with little effort–as long as there is a good 4G signal. But back then, we needed a satellite truck to make a live broadcast and we had to feed any cables we needed directly from the truck to the back of the cameras. This involved long cable runs.

Having done a recce of the location a week before, we had worked out we needed to feed the cables up through the second-floor window and through a bathroom closet, before coming out into the grand King's staircase and hallway, next to where we would be broadcasting.

The problem with stately homes and lots of other old big buildings, especially early in the morning, was that the temperature inside was freezing. They had not put the heating on for us, and with the window open to feed the cables in, the chilly air was whipping down the staircase and making it feel even colder.

We were now half an hour behind schedule, so the crew and the satellite engineer–a lovely guy called Frank–were rushing to rig the cables and cameras and set up in time for the six o'clock news. It was going to be tight for us to make it.

Due to the high-vaulted ceilings, the deep colours of the paintings on the walls and the fact that it was still dark outside, we also needed to use some big TV lights to flood the area and make it look light enough for the broadcast. The lighting crew set to work putting up huge panel lights that cast warm glows across the staircase.

Meanwhile, our reporter (whose name I am changing for reasons that will become apparent) had turned up. For the purposes of this story, let's call her Karen.

While I had seen the location before, she had not, and she wanted to make sure she could walk and talk down the grand staircase, recounting all the facts I had sent her in the brief and script.

Fifteen minutes before we were due on air, the camera crew still weren't ready to rehearse anything.

They were still on the phone to the technical director, Doug, who was in the main TV gallery back at the studios, trying to establish the connections.

"I really need to rehearse this," Karen said. "We're on air shortly and I need to make sure I have all the lines right in my head."

I looked at the crew, who were all still fiddling around with cables and wires.

"Why don't you rehearse it with me?" I suggested. "Make out I am the camera. But keep your coat on because it's freezing in here."

Karen nodded and we rehearsed where she would walk and what she would say, two or three times until she was happy.

We had four broadcasts across the programme that morning. The first was to be in the news bulletin at around ten past six.

Fortunately, the lighting team had done a great job of brightening up the venue, and the viewers at home would have thought it was a warm spring day, rather than a cold, dark, dreary one.

Finally, just after six o'clock, the crew were ready to go. Just minutes before the broadcast, Karen took her coat off. She had a lovely, shimmery, blue blouse on with a smart black pencil skirt and patent black high heels. She looked incredibly glamorous. Her designer-label top was just the right tone for the setting. She stood by, waiting for the cue from the studio to start her first broadcast.

There were a lot of cables–and a lot of antiques–lying around, so my job involved not just producing Karen, but also 'cable bashing', i.e., stopping the camera crew from tripping up on the leads, as well as keeping the cables from the cameras from damaging the priceless artefacts around us.

The Palace was full of them: ancient giant porcelain urns covered in delicate pictures of birds and animals lined the corridors, while ornate frescos on the walls of the King's Staircase depicted the lively 18th century court of King George III.

In spite of my company having a hefty public liability insurance, I didn't want to be the first one to damage the artworks or explain to our hosts why one of their lovely 18th century pictures, now had a dirty great 21st century scratch or dent in it.

I grabbed the cables behind the crew and got ready to follow them as they tracked Karen up the staircase.

Despite the rush to set up, the first broadcast went very smoothly. Karen delivered her lines perfectly. As I was busy behind the cameraman, I couldn't actually see her, but I could see the staircase, which looked stunning. The huge TV lights and lamps had illuminated the shiny marble ceiling ten feet above us, in sharp contrast to the black wrought iron bannisters below.

Minutes later though, we were to discover that this was not the only thing that had been illuminated.

Karen was very sensitive to what people thought about her, so as soon as the broadcast was over, she was on the phone to the producer on the news desk to get their feedback.

I was in earshot as she made the call. "Thanks, yes, I thought it went really well," she said, as the producer on the other end of the phone spoke to her. "Yes, the place looks stunning, doesn't it?"

Then I watched the colour drain from her face.

"'No! You're not serious," she gasped. "'I'm so embarrassed," she spluttered. She finished her call and rushed towards the nearby toilet.

I decided not to follow her, as often presenters or reporters need a bit of time and space to get their head around things, so I waited for her to return.

Meanwhile, I was trying to find a member of staff to turn the heating on. My fingers and toes were numb from the cold. We were all toasting our hands in front of the hot TV lamps to try and thaw them and warm up the tips of our fingers. The sound man started doing star jumps to keep his circulation going.

I found a security guard who said he would go off and ask. Heating stately homes was expensive and he wasn't sure if we were important enough to warrant it.

We had another broadcast at ten to seven which we needed to rehearse, so after ten minutes I went in search of Karen. I found her still in the toilet.

"Is everything okay?" I asked. I did not know her that well, but my job as producer was to support her and make the broadcast as good as it could be.

"Why didn't you tell me?" she wailed.

"Tell you what?" At this point, I had no idea what she was talking about.

"The director in the gallery said that my blouse was see-through. They said he could see everything underneath, including my erect nipples."

Fortunately, I was in a separate toilet cubicle. I stuffed my anorak sleeve in my mouth so she couldn't hear me burst out laughing.

"I'm supposed to be a serious journalist, but instead I'm the laughing stock of the newsroom," Karen sobbed from inside her cubicle.

I tried to compose myself. "To be honest with you," I said, "I really didn't notice. I wasn't concentrating on your bosoms, but rather trying to stop cables damaging priceless antiques and getting *GMTV* a large repair bill."

I tried to reassure her. "Let's go down to the satellite truck and watch the broadcast back. I'm sure it's not that bad."

She seemed to like this idea and unlocked the toilet door and followed me to the truck.

Squeezed inside the tiny satellite truck minutes later, Frank the satellite engineer, Karen and myself stood and watched a replay of what had just gone out on air.

It all started well. We watched as Karen walked elegantly up the stairs, introducing the item with the fact that this was the former home of Princess Diana and a new exhibition was opening to the public that morning.

There was no sign of any bra, or any nipples for that matter, just a reporter in a very swish designer top walking up the grand staircase. I really couldn't see what all the fuss was about.

Then it happened. About a minute into the broadcast, just as she was explaining how Queen Victoria herself would have walked up these historic steps a century before, Karen turned the corner and revealed everything.

I let out a stifled gasp. Frank just blushed and turned away.

Our very expensive TV lamps, hired to illuminate the magnificent staircase, had made her top completely translucent and revealed my correspondent's bra and her pert breasts and nipples beneath. It probably wouldn't have been so much of an issue if we'd managed to get the heating on in time.

I was trying to think of something positive to say to Karen, but was struggling to think of anything. Karen, however, wasn't sticking around to listen. She slid open the side door and ran from the truck, sobbing.

I went after her. I found her sitting back inside the toilet cubicle, using some royal toilet paper to wipe the tears from her face.

"'What am I going to do?" she cried. "I love this designer top, but it's useless on TV. I look like a porn star."

To tell the truth, at that moment I agreed with her. She did indeed look like a porn star, albeit a very high class one, but I decided this was not the right thing to say at that moment, so I kept quiet. From my point of view, we still had three more broadcasts to get through and I needed a reporter. I had to think of a way of getting her out of this toilet and back to the staircase.

"Do you have a spare blouse with you?" I asked, as I knew that sometimes female reporters weren't sure what to wear in the mornings and came prepared with a couple of options.

"No, I don't have a spare top with me," she snapped back. "The shops are shut and there's no way I can get home and back again before the next hit. What are we going to do?"

What she really meant was, what was I going to do? As the producer, it was often up to me to come up with a solution - and quickly. Without a new top, Karen wasn't going anywhere near a TV camera.

As I stood there, rubbing my hands together and blowing into my fingers to get my circulation going, I tried to assess the situation. I could have jumped in a cab and tried to find an early morning market stall, or have grabbed another top from our TV studios just a mile away - but with the London traffic, I wouldn't have made it back for at least an hour, by which time two more broadcasts would have gone by.

I looked around me for inspiration and suddenly had a brainwave. "I know! Why don't we swap tops?" I suggested. "I have a smart, non-see-through cotton top on, why not put that on, and I can wear your top beneath my anorak?"

More importantly, I was not the one on screen so it would not matter if I wore the sheer blouse. I might be even more cold, but it was worth the sacrifice to save the situation.

"That's a great idea. Let's do it," she said and started to take her top off. I did the same and handed her mine.

She looked at my plain cotton top and back at her designer blouse.

"I've got a better idea. How about I put your top underneath mine, and that will stop it from being see-through?" She was obviously pleased with her suggestion.

"But what am I going to wear?".

"Well, it doesn't matter about you," she replied. "You're not on camera. Also, my top is really expensive and I'd love to show it off a bit more and yours is just, well, *ordinary.*"

"Charming!" I thought. My top may not have been designer, but it was perfectly nice. I had just offered her a way out of her current fix and her response was to insult me.

I tried to protest, but we had just ten minutes until her next broadcast and we either had her on air showing her nipples to the world, or me wearing just my bra underneath my anorak. Reluctantly, I did what she asked.

I had been cold before, but now I was freezing. At every opportunity I huddled around the TV lamps trying to keep warm, crossing my arms to make sure my chest didn't suffer the same fate as Karen's had in the cold palace.

For the rest of the morning Karen wore my top underneath hers, which stopped a repeat of the unfortunate nipples' incident. I spent the morning in my bra and cagoule. The plastic was scratchy against my white, cold skin and I could feel a red-hot, itchy rash developing where it rubbed.

Neither Karen nor I told anyone about our arrangement and my state of semi-undress. The crew and Palace staff were oblivious, but I did feel slightly naked and exposed, even though I wasn't showing anything.

The broadcasts went well, and when we came off air that morning, everyone in the studio was very happy.

"Thanks for the loan of your blouse," Karen said. "You're a lifesaver." She smiled and promptly walked off to chat on her phone to the studio about her performance.

I thanked all the crew, including the lighting team, who then started to de-rig before heading home.

By this time the Palace press officer and other members of the Royal Palace team had arrived and came up to thank me.

"That was great," they said. "Fantastic publicity for the exhibition and even better for ticket sales. We've sold over 500 this morning off the back of your broadcasts. Thanks so much for coming." The press officer shook my hand vigorously.

"We would really like you to come to the private opening of the exhibition. It's happening in about ten minutes; would you like to join us?" she smiled. "There'll be a short reception with refreshments afterwards."

"Of course, I'd love to," I said, completely forgetting at that moment how I was dressed.

As soon as she walked away, I remembered my predicament. I needed my blouse back as soon as possible. I searched frantically for Karen in the grand corridors, in the gardens, in the satellite truck, but I could not find her anywhere. She had disappeared–along with my top.

I was thinking about making my excuses and just leaving, but just as I made for the exit, the press officer reappeared with one of the members of the royal household who had been invited. I had no choice but to stay and greet them. There was no escape. He held out his hand to me.

"Pleased to meet you," I said, extending my sweaty palm to shake his hand. The smartly-dressed gentleman looked at me oddly, but was polite enough not to say anything.

Not only was I standing there with nothing on top but a bra–a very old one at that–and anorak, but now someone had helpfully put on the heating. I was boiling. I could feel the sweat sliding down from my armpits, like fat from a hot, greasy chip pan, inside my plastic anorak. I also was in serious need of some deodorant.

I caught a glimpse of myself in one of the gilded, antique mirrors on the wall. I could see my face had turned beetroot with the heat, but there was nothing I could do about it. I couldn't unzip my anorak, or take it off, for fear of revealing my lack of top. I would have done anything now for a cold blast of early morning air to cool me down, but instead I had to stand drinking tea and eating pastries while severely overheating.

Ten minutes later, Karen reappeared, still wearing my top underneath her designer see-through number.

"Any chance I could have my top back?" I whispered in her ear. "I'm standing here in my anorak and feeling a right fool."

"Sure," she said. "I'm just having a tour of the galleries with the press officer. I'll give it to you after that."

I was livid. I had spent the morning first freezing my butt off and now roasting like a cooked turkey, all to help her out, and she wouldn't help me out of my own embarrassing hole.

I grabbed her arm to stop her from leaving. I was just about to escort her to the nearby toilets when the press officer stopped us.

"I must say that is a beautiful top you have on," she said to Karen. "Where did you get it?"

I then had to stand there while Karen gave her a detailed account of where she got it and what designer it was from.

"I thought so," said the press officer. "You can tell a good quality blouse. It looked great on the television this morning, very fitting." She smiled and Karen nodded in agreement.

Meanwhile I stood there, quietly fuming. *It only looked great on the telly because your poor producer had to make her own clothing sacrifice.*

My face had now turned from a light shade of beetroot to bright scarlet.

I pulled Karen to one side.

"I need my top back and I need it now," I hissed.

"Sure," she said breezily and we went back to the nearby toilets where she returned it.

Putting her own coat back on, she headed for the exit to hail a cab home.

I could now take my sweaty anorak off and just wear my own blouse. The problem was that my skin was now red and itchy underneath it. It also reeked of her expensive perfume, but at least it was better than the smell of body odour that now clung to me. I decided not to return to the reception and quietly slipped out of the palace and left.

Walking through the gardens, I stopped and reflected on my morning. If only the viewers had known what had gone on behind the scenes. My ordinary top and I had saved the day and helped avoid an unfortunate 'nipplegate' incident live on Breakfast TV.

As a TV Producer you definitely have to be prepared to give it your all. Even, sometimes, the shirt off your own back.

18

TANTRUMS AT NUMBER 10

I t was 7.30 in the morning and I was standing outside 10 Downing Street, not only one of the most famous streets in Britain, but also one of the coldest.

As any television crew or photographer will tell you, the narrow street gets very little sunlight due to the angle of buildings around it, even in the height of summer. The only thing that does get in, is a biting wind that whistles through the iron gates. To stand there for hours on end, first thing in the morning, can be mind-numbingly cold at any time of year. Luckily, thanks to previous chilly experiences, I had come prepared.

The Prime Minister Gordon Brown had invited our presenter Fiona Phillips to bring a young family from the Midlands to meet and ask him questions live on the show from inside Number 10. This was a big deal. *GMTV* had never been live inside the building before, so as I was now one of our more experienced outside broadcast producers, I was asked to produce it.

I had stood outside on the street watching the comings and goings of everyone from politicians to pizza delivery drivers doing live broadcasts before, but this was the first time I would be going in.

I was a little nervous. I kept telling myself it was just like producing any other interview, but the difference was, this was a very important big house and it had a very famous resident. It's not every day you get to go inside, so I didn't want to mess it up.

It was the height of the financial crash in 2008 and families, many of them our viewers, were struggling. Caroline, my fellow producer, had found a young family, a teacher and her husband and their 18th month daughter Jessie who were happy to take part in the show. After all, how often do you get the chance to put your questions to a Prime Minister face to face?

The front of 10 Downing Street might look small, but inside it's a maze of rooms, most of them working offices, connected to Number 11 – which is where Mr Brown and his family actually lived in a flat, because it was bigger than the one in Number 10.

The plan was as follows: at 7.30am the family would ring the bell of the famous black front door and be let in and taken to meet the Prime Minister, his wife Sarah and their two children in the private quarters, before returning in plenty of time for the sit-down interview on *GMTV* at 8.10am.

For this show, Fiona Phillips was in Downing Street, while the rest of the presenting team stayed put in the studio.

After a brief introduction from telly towers, Andrew Castle handed over to Fiona.

The cameraman started on a close-up of the black door and pulled out to reveal Fiona and the family standing there. Fiona started her tease.

"Good morning, live from Number 10. In just half an hour, this family will walk through the famous black door and meet the Prime Minister. In a TV exclusive, they will have a chance to ask him their burning questions on how he can help them through the current financial crisis. All live on *GMTV*. Join us later," and threw back to Andrew in the studio.

Our next broadcast was in twenty minutes, so we had to just stand around as there are no handy benches or chairs to sit on. We had a more pressing problem, though. The little girl needed the toilet.

As any parent knows, trying to find a loo when your child has a burning desire to go is incredibly stressful, even more so when you are locked inside Downing Street. Before 1989 anyone could just walk into it, but during the IRA bombings, a gate was put across the entrance. Thereafter everyone had to go through airport style security.

For the record, there are no public toilets in the street, nor can you just pop into Number 10 or 11 to use the facilities. Instead, any toilet breaks involve going back through security, and heading down Whitehall to the nearest coffee shop with a public convenience. Along with their political know-how, the correspondents, TV crews and photographers who cover Downing Street all learn to develop extra strong bladders, holding it in until they can get to the safety of their offices in Millbank.

We had twenty minutes until the next broadcast so my colleague Caroline–who was looking after the family–quickly walked them down Whitehall.

While they were gone I re-briefed Fiona on what would happen next.

"You introduce the family; explain why they are here and then you invite them to go and ring the doorbell"

"Okay, great."

"The police officer behind the door will open it and they will all go inside."

"What do I do then?" asked Fiona.

"Once our broadcast is over, they will let the rest of us in and we can grab some pictures of the Prime Minister meeting them inside."

"Okay, understood," she said and went back to reading her notes.

Shortly afterwards, our family returned from their excursion and Fiona started chatting to them to keep them from feeling nervous while we were waiting around. Fiona always had a great way of putting guests at ease.

Then Big Ben chimed nearby on the half hour, and it was all systems go as Fiona heard the cue from the *GMTV* gallery to start talking.

"In just forty minutes' time this family will be grilling Gordon Brown live on *GMTV*, but first they need to get inside Number 10," she said to the camera.

"Are you ready to meet the Prime Minister?" She turned to the family who all nodded in excitement.

"Okay, off you go." Fiona said, gesturing for them to go forward.

The family approached the door and rang the doorbell, but nothing happened. They looked back to us in bewilderment. They rang it again, still nothing, none of us knew what to do.

There was an awkward pause. Should I run in and bang on the door for them, I wondered, or should I send Fiona in to intervene?

As I was later to discover, the doorbell didn't work! You can understand why. There were always so many people coming in and out of the door, you could imagine the doorbell would be going all the time, which would have definitely got on your nerves.

To my relief, seconds later the door opened. The policeman must have finally spotted them on the security camera and let them in.

But, to our utter shock, they were greeted not by a friendly Met police officer, but by the Prime Minister himself! Gordon Brown smiled at the family and invited them in.

We all looked at each other in disbelief. What on earth was he doing there, hovering behind the door? Didn't he have world leaders to speak to, or important government documents to sign rather than playing the role of doorman live on Breakfast Television?

Having welcomed the family inside, Mr Brown shut the door, leaving the rest of us outside.

"Well, that was a turn up for the books," I said to Fiona and my crew. "I really wasn't expecting the PM to open his own front door."

"But what do *we* do now?" they said. They had a point. I was going to have to act quickly to get us into Number 10 or all our plans would be ruined. I beckoned Fiona and the crew to grab their equipment and follow me.

We ran to the door and waved to the security camera. This time a policeman opened it.

Inside, the main reception area was empty.

"Where's the family who just came in with the Prime Minister?" I asked, looking along the corridors to see if I could spot them.

"He's taken them upstairs to meet Mrs Brown and the boys," the copper replied.

Now this was not how I had planned it. "We were supposed to be filming him here greeting the *GMTV* family," I said exasperated.

"Nothing to do with me," said the officer.

"Can we follow him?"

"Nope. They are private quarters, no cameras allowed."

I protested a bit more, but knew in my heart it was pointless arguing. I had to admit, I was pretty annoyed with the PM. We had it all planned out beautifully and he had ruined it by opening the front door and running off with my family. In other circumstances, with other less important guests, I would have demanded they go and fetch him.

However, in this case I thought better of it. After all, he was the leader of the country and could do what he jolly well wanted.

Resigning myself to the fact that we would have to adapt our plans, I took time to look around the hallway. It was much larger than I had imagined. It had a black and white marble floor, set out like a checkerboard. I wondered if anyone had ever tried to play giant games of chess on it. Perhaps past prime ministers like Winston Churchill or Harold Wilson had snuck down in the night when it was quiet and had a quick game with one of the police officers on security duty?

I took in more of my surroundings. Beautiful red velvet drapes hung at the windows, framing lace net curtains. No one I knew had net curtains at their windows anymore, but obviously prime ministers didn't want any Tom, Dick or Harry from the press peering in.

In the middle of the black and white floor, a giant red carpet led the way to a long sweeping corridor that went on as far as the eye could see. Everyone had told me how deceptively small Number 10 looked from the outside, but how large it was inside. Made up of more than one-hundred rooms, I could see why some people called it the Westminster Tardis.

On one side of the hall stood a wooden shelf with tiny compartments in it.

"Please leave your mobile phones here and someone will come and collect you," said the policeman on the door.

At which point my phone rang. It was probably the office. "I'm just going to take this call, and then I'll hand it in," I promised.

It was the studio producer looking after my item on the show that morning.

"When are you sending me the eight o'clock tease pictures of Gordon meeting the family?" she asked.

"A slight problem there," I said. "We, err, didn't film it."

"What do you mean you didn't film it?" She sounded annoyed.

"Well, it's a bit of a long story," I started, and went on to explain the recent shenanigans.

"Well, that's no use to me," said the producer. "What am I going to put in the eight o'clock menu now?"

I thought she was being a little selfish. Forget what she was going to do. What was *I* going to do? *I* was the one who had lost a Prime Minister, a young couple and a toddler inside Number 10!

"Don't worry, I have a plan," I said, trying to sound convincing. I actually had no plan at all, but I was going to have to come up with one - and fast. We would be on air again in less than twenty minutes. "Give me a couple of minutes and I'll call you back."

The crew were waiting for me so they could go upstairs and get set up for the interview. While we had one camera crew already up there, the boys who had been filming outside with me would also rig up their camera, so that we could have separate shots of the Prime Minister (on one camera) and Fiona and the family (on the other). The director in the gallery would then be able to cut between the two during the live interview.

"You go on ahead," I said to the crew. "I'm just going to stay here for a minute and make another call."

I called the office again and spoke to the same producer as before. "Can you have a look at the playback tape of the programme? Did we record the bit where the Prime Minister opened the door?"

She quickly looked. "The good news is we recorded it. The bad news is that you can see someone opening the door, but you can't really make out who it is. It just looks like someone in the shadows."

I couldn't believe it. Probably the one time in history when a Prime Minister opened his own front door, and we didn't get it on tape.

I had to think of another plan. "Turn around that footage anyway, and then I'll get the family sitting in the room with Fiona, with an empty chair where Mr Brown will sit," I said, thinking on my feet.

"She'll say something along the lines of, 'Join us in just ten minutes' time when this empty chair will be filled by the Prime Minister himself, answering questions from this family about how he is going to deal with their financial worries. All Live on *GMTV*.'"

It wasn't perfect, but it would do. Also, I knew I could rely on Fiona to jazz it up a bit and put it in her own words.

"Okay, got it," she said. "I'll go and cut the footage now and change the script."

Having spoken to the office, I dumped my mobile in one of the hallway's wooden compartments and waited for the Downing Street official to return to escort me to our interview room.

She appeared and we made our way up the stairs.

It was only then that it dawned on me that I had seen this staircase before. It was the famous Grand Staircase you always saw in the newspapers and the one Hugh Grant dances up and down in the film 'Love Actually' (well, a mock-up of it anyway).

As I climbed the thickly-carpeted stairs I saw portraits of all the past prime ministers. Among them Harold Wilson, Ted Heath, Jim Callaghan, Margaret Thatcher, John Major, Tony Blair. All those who had led the country during my lifetime.

It was then that it struck me how lucky I was to be doing this job. Here I was inside the home of the Leader of the United Kingdom, and I was about to meet my first Prime Minister, Gordon Brown—whose portrait would be the next one to be placed on these walls.

I was walking up the same stairs as hundreds of world leaders before me. Everyone from Nelson Mandela to Bill Clinton. I wondered whether they had paused to admire the portraits, or whether they were more like me–in a rush and having to give them a fleeting glance as I dashed to get to the room we would be broadcasting from.

I arrived with just ten minutes to spare. The two crews were set to go. Fiona was all miked up and sitting in her seat, ready for the eight o'clock tease. The problem was that there was no sign of the family.

"Any chance we can get the family to come and sit in for our broadcast?" I asked the woman who had just escorted me upstairs.

"Let me find out," she said and disappeared into one of the many corridors around us. Without my mobile phone, I couldn't call the family to find out where they were, and they couldn't call me either.

It was just a few minutes until we were going live now, and Fiona was getting twitchy.

"Where are they?" she asked. "Can't you go and find them?"

I shook my head. For a start I wasn't allowed to go anywhere without an escort, and she had gone off to find the family. Even if I was allowed to wander off by myself, with one-hundred rooms to choose from, the chances of me finding them were pretty slim.

I told Fiona she might need to adapt her opening tease. She immediately started scribbling some new notes of what she might say.

Two minutes before we were due on air, I spotted the family at the end of the corridor walking towards us.

"Run!" I shouted. "We've got less than a minute to get you in here and put your microphones on."

They obeyed, but what I hadn't noticed was that the Prime Minister was behind them, and hearing my command, he started jogging along the carpet, too.

I really didn't feel like I could tell him to stop.

It was one of the most memorable moments of my television career, having the Prime Minister at my command. Seeing him trotting obediently towards me really was a picture.

The family arrived and we quickly put microphones on them. We had made it with just seconds to spare.

Having sat them down and told them which camera to look at, I then turned around to see Gordon Brown sitting down in his chair, too.

Now this was awkward. We actually didn't want him for another ten minutes. We wanted an empty chair, so we could tease the fact that he was on his way. Him sitting there, kind of blew the suspense of it all.

I did not have the heart to tell him to budge. After all, he was the leader of the country and he had already obeyed one instruction from me—I didn't feel I could give him another. Plus, I was so used to politicians being late for everything, it was refreshing to have one turn up early.

Fiona was taken by surprise, too. She had launched into her menu tease as planned and was just about to talk about the empty chair when she spotted him sitting there.

"Hello Prime Minister, thanks for joining us early!" she ad-libbed.

Mr Brown didn't have a microphone on at that moment, so he just nodded and smiled, but no one noticed anything amiss.

The eight o'clock menu teases out of the way; we then miked him up ready for the interview at ten past eight.

My fellow producer Caroline and I stood behind the cameras, ready to direct them or answer any last-minute questions that might arise as we prepared to go live.

Everything was calm. With IFB earpieces in place, we could hear exactly what was happening in the *GMTV* gallery, just across the river from us. We received our one-minute reminder from the director.

Until this point, 18-month-old Jessie had been happily sitting on her mother's knee, but now she was bored and tried to wriggle free. Aware that the interview was due to start any moment, her mum clung on to her tightly. Jessie was having none of it, and started to squeal like a trapped piglet. Prime Minister or not, she did not want to sit still a second longer.

The broadcast began. We were now live on air. Fiona introduced the PM and the family, but the little girl would not sit still and started to wriggle and squirm and wail even louder. As her mother held her tighter on her lap, she increased the decibels, letting out a shriek that could pierce any nearby eardrum. No one could hear a word that was being said.

I tried distracting her from behind the camera, pulling silly faces, giving her some keys to play with, but nothing worked. She squirmed off her mum's lap and made a beeline for the door. Caroline and I went after her, worried that she might use my keys, which she still had in her hand, to drag along the ornate–and no doubt very expensive–flock wallpaper in the corridor outside. Fiona was left doing the interview without us.

As soon as she was out of the room, the little girl stopped crying and started doing roly-polys on the thick-carpeted floor. We played peek-a-boo with her hiding behind an 18th century walnut sideboard. This was far more interesting to her than sitting on her mum's lap next to the Prime Minister. Having calmed her down, we tried to take her back inside, but every time we led her to the door, she started wailing again.

On the plus side, entertaining the little girl meant that the *GMTV* audience could at least hear her mum and dad talking to the most powerful man in Britain.

The interview over, Gordon Brown thanked everyone and disappeared down one of the many corridors inside No 10. Everyone including Fiona and my bosses in the studio were very happy with the broadcast.

I have to therefore admit that, for the first piece of television I ever produced from Downing Street, I was not actually there. Fiona did a fine job to be fair, but it wasn't exactly how I imagined the morning going. As so often happens, my job involved not just controlling the big things in front of the camera, but managing the small things (and people) behind it.

19

THINGS THAT GO BUMP IN EAST ANGLIA

T revor's face was as pale as the bedsheets we were standing next to. I imagined my face was pretty similar.

We were standing alone together in a tiny attic room in the oldest pub in Ipswich.

"Did that really just happen?" I said, looking across at him in the dimly-lit room.

"I'm not sure," he said, "but I'm not sticking around any longer to find out." We both made for the door and left the room as fast as our legs could carry us.

When we had told the viewers, we were on the hunt for ghosts, we never expected to actually find one.

I was working with Richard Arnold, our entertainment presenter, on a week-long feature strand called 'The Ghosts of Christmas Past'. This involved us doing live broadcasts from locations with tales of ghouls who were particularly active around Christmas.

Of course, ghosts themselves paid no attention whatsoever to what time of the year it was, so for this feature we had to stretch the truth a little. Trying to find paranormal activity that just flared up over the yuletide period was not easy, but obviously cold, winter nights did lend themselves to a sighting.

My editor had come up with the idea, but it was my job to find suitable locations in time for us to film them during a week in early December.

Ghosts, I learnt, tended to hang out in some of Britain's oldest towns, so our trip had taken us to the dark walls of Chester and now to Ipswich, which I discovered from my research had its fair share of spooky sightings. So much so, that it even had a ghostly walking tour. Depending on who you spoke to, Ipswich was the oldest, or second oldest town in the UK–the folk of Colchester also claimed the top spot. Ipswich, dating back to the 7th century, and with some buildings still standing from mediaeval times, had no shortage of locations for spooky characters to haunt.

The pub we had picked claimed to be one of the most haunted in Britain, having not one, but four spooks. The one we were particularly interested in was a monk, who could apparently be seen at Christmas time, drinking a flagon of ale by the pub fire.

We had employed the services of the celebrity spirit medium Derek Acorah–star of the Most Haunted series–to help us find out more about the ghosts we had found.

We had told Derek nothing about the pub's haunted occupants, but were planning just to go around the building seeing what Derek could discover.

Before he and Richard arrived, my cameraman Trevor and I went to do a recce of the locations and rooms where we would be filming. Firstly, to see how big they were—not all rooms are meant for a camera crew. Secondly, old, mediaeval buildings can be very dark—in this case a plus, to help create a spooky atmosphere—but too dark and we wouldn't be able to see anything at all.

The pub landlord first showed us the snug next to the fireplace where the jolly monk had been spotted. At this point it was 4pm, and there was no sign of the spirited fella.

"When was the last time the customers saw him?" I asked.

"Well, one of my regulars swore he saw him last week. It was just before closing time, and he was convinced there was an old guy in a brown cloak sitting there having a quiet draft of ale. Next to the Christmas tree."

"And what happened then?" I was intrigued to know about this encounter.

"It was last orders and he offered to buy him a drink, but by the time he had got to the bar, the man in the brown cloak had disappeared."

"Perhaps it had something to do with his eyesight, and the amount of alcohol he had consumed?" I joked with the landlord.

You can gather I was quite sceptical about all things paranormal, but the pub manager was adamant that he had seen him too.

"Do people ever get spooked by him?" I asked.

"Thankfully he's a happy ghost who is content to just mind his own business. A lot of the drinkers here just think he's another customer having a quiet drink in the corner."

I have to say, I have seen a few odd people sitting in pub corners over the years, so perhaps I had sat next to a ghost and not realised it, too.

"He's no problem though, it's the other ones we have who are mischievous," the landlord continued, and with that, he led us down to the cellar.

Standing beside all the barrels, he told us about another, more annoying ghoul.

"This one keeps turning the beer taps off. You can be halfway through a busy night and suddenly the pumps stop working," he explained. "You open the trap door to go down to the cellar and find that they have been turned off. There's no way anyone can get in or out of the cellar without me seeing, so it has *got* to be a ghost."

"I wouldn't care," he said, "but it's always at our busiest time, and can happen three or four times a night."

I could indeed see how this would be very annoying, but I really didn't believe it had anything to do with ghosts; surely it was some technical problem, or one of the staff pulling his leg.

He went on. "The other problem we have is with a room at the very top of the pub, in the staff lodgings. There's a small bedroom in the corner of the building which staff refuse to sleep in, because they say it's haunted. I wouldn't mind, but I am losing staff because of it," he added ruefully.

"The ghostly goings-on have made some staff move bedrooms in the middle of the night, or in other cases quit their jobs completely."

Wiping his hands on his beer-stained apron, he pointed us towards the steep stairs at the back of the pub. "We'll go and take a look at the room if you like."

Trevor and I followed the landlord up three flights of stairs and along the landing until we came to a door right at the back of the house, which opened onto a small corner room with two single neatly-made beds and a chest of drawers. It had a tiny window the size of an A4 piece of paper in the corner.

Trevor and I both looked at each other.

"I'm not sure I'd like to sleep in this room," he said, "but it's probably because there's hardly any light in here and no heating."

I nodded in agreement. It was freezing cold—not surprising as it was December and the room had two outside walls which did not help. Either way, it did feel a bit creepy.

"How about I go and get some lights and we'll set them up to make it look even spookier?" Trevor suggested, and headed back down the three flights of stairs to the pub below.

"I need to change a barrel," the landlord said. "Call me if you need me." He followed Trevor down the stairs.

I looked around and shuddered. I felt glad I was only visiting this tiny, dark room for just a few minutes, unlike the poor members of the bar staff who'd actually had to sleep there all night. I closed the door and headed back downstairs to help Trevor carry some of the equipment. Fifteen minutes later, we returned to the room with the camera and lights and opened the door.

Inside, one of the beds was still made as we had left it, but the other now had dishevelled sheets as though someone had been sleeping in it. I tried to rewind to the scene just a quarter of an hour before. I might have been mistaken, but I was sure both the beds had been made when we had been in there.

"Trevor, I may be imagining things, but weren't both of those beds made when we were in here before?"

Trevor looked at me. "I really don't remember," he said, before adding, "perhaps that naughty ghost has been up to something?"

"Or perhaps I just dreamt it?" I tried to laugh it off. I had no intention of believing these ghostly tales.

While Trevor set to work lighting the room, I made the untidy bed and smoothed down the covers, then we both went back downstairs to meet Richard Arnold and Derek Acorah, who had just arrived.

For the next hour or so, we followed Richard and Derek around the pub rooms as Derek talked about the spirits he could feel and who they might be. He was spot-on with all of them, including the jolly monk sipping ale beside the fire, but then my cynical mind said that he could have looked up the information on the website, just like I had, and so I was still unconvinced.

The final room we were due to film in was the cold corner room at the top of the house. This story had not featured on any website, so I was keen to see what Derek would feel in this small, dark attic.

When I opened the door, the two beds were as I had left them, made up and ready to sleep in. The four of us squeezed into the tiny room and started filming. "I sense a good spirit, here in the room," said Derek. "It's the spirit of a little girl who had smallpox and died in here."

Richard looked shocked. "Don't worry," said Derek. "She's perfectly happy, she just likes appearing every now and again and playing games in the room and laughing."

Richard looked a bit happier at this piece of information. Derek continued: "She likes doing things like playing with the curtains or lying in the bed and ruffling up the bedsheets."

At that moment, the room seemed to get ten degrees colder. I looked at Trevor and he looked at me. Neither of us had mentioned the bed sheet incident from earlier to anyone else, especially not to Richard or Derek.

We remained silent and continued with the filming until we were finished. Derek and Richard left the room and went back down the stairs.

"Did that really happen?" I asked Trevor. "Did we really just have a young child ghost play a trick on us?"

"I'm not sure," he said, "but I'm not sticking around to find out."

He quickly packed up his lights and camera and left the room. I wasn't planning on staying around either. Even though at this point the beds were both untouched, I knew what I had seen earlier, it hadn't been a figment of my imagination.

I switched off the light, shut the door on the small corner room at the top of the house and followed him down the stairs.

We had finished our filming for the day, so Richard and Derek were now having a drink at the bar and I decided to join them, while Trevor packed his equipment into the car. It was then that I realised that I had left my notebook in the room upstairs. It contained all my notes and numbers, and I really needed it, so I reluctantly climbed the stairs back up to the top of the house.

I opened the door and switched on the light. Once again, one of the single beds was unmade and this time bore a small indentation in the shape of a child's body. I felt the hairs stand up on the back of my neck. I snatched the book, switched off the light and ran as fast as I could back down to the bar below.

As I sat and gulped down a very large glass of cider, I tried to make sense of what I had just seen. Surely it was just one of the staff playing tricks on me. But no one had passed me in the corridor on the way down or up, and all the staff were in the bar. Also, no one knew what Derek had said, apart from the people in the room, and they were all now downstairs. I had definitely been the last person to close the door and reopen it.

To this day, I have no idea if it was an elaborate joke or if I had actually witnessed the prank of a mischievous young child ghost. All I knew was that working in television you could expect all sorts of guests to turn up, not all of them invited.

20

THE BRIDE, THE HORSE AND THE ZIMMER FRAME

W e had planned for most things, but none of us had factored in how the bride would end up coming down the aisle.

However, with less than twenty-four hours to go until the wedding, we were all coming to terms with that reality.

For four years, we ran an interactive wedding competition where one lucky couple got the chance to have their dream wedding paid for by *GMTV*. The catch was that the viewers got to pick everything about the wedding. This was long before programmes like *Don't Tell the Bride* or *Four Weddings*, so it was still a novel idea (and much less brutal).

First the viewers got to vote on which one of three couples they wanted to see married live on TV, then they had to vote on the venue, then what dress the bride was going to wear, what outfit the groom wore, the flowers, the cake–and so the list went on, right down to the style of the wedding invites.

The couple were picked in early June, and every week during the summer, we followed them as they discovered what decisions the viewers had made for them, until the wedding itself took place on the last Friday of August.

The first year had been a huge success. The viewers had voted for Leicestershire-based couple Liz and Tim to get married on the Greek island of Rhodes. The weather was gorgeous and the wedding took place against the backdrop of a deep blue Aegean Sea and a pearl-white windmill.

Liz walked down the aisle in a stunning strapless designer dress and Tim wore an elegant white suit. We only had two minor hiccups on the day; the first was when the presenter Carla Romano got her heel caught in one of the tassels on her dress live on air, which almost sent her flying. She looked like a glamorous pirate with a peg leg, dragging it behind her as she walked and talked. The second was when the radio mike pack, which was strapped to Liz's leg so it couldn't be seen by the viewers, started sliding down just as she was about to walk down the aisle. Someone had to hastily put their head up her dress to adjust it. Apart from that, the wedding had gone like clockwork.

Not surprisingly, lots of people had tuned in for the big day and the following year we received hundreds more entries from engaged couples. Having gone through them all to make sure they fitted the criteria–in other words, that they were legally able to marry–we then went through the lengthy process of phoning them all up to find out more about them.

We asked them quite personal questions about how they met, why they wanted to get married on television and, more importantly, if they were happy to spend the next three months of their life on TV. You cannot believe the number of entrants who said 'no', they didn't want to be on television, in spite of the fact that this was quite plainly stated in the terms and conditions. For some reason, they expected us to give them a free £20,000 wedding with nothing in return.

We also had to ask them if they had criminal records and whether there were any reasons they could think of why it might be wiser *not* to get married live on TV.

From my professional experience, I knew that if you had any skeletons in your closet, putting yourself on national television was a sure way for them to pop out and say hello. While we didn't necessarily rule people out if they had a conviction–a mild misdemeanour was fine–obviously we tried not to put any mass murderers or sex offenders on the show. The purpose of asking about the skeletons was so that we and our press office could be aware of them, just in case the newspapers got wind of them. Vetting complete, we then put the shortlist to an internal judging panel who whittled it down to three couples.

Next, I sent my colleague Ali around the country to make profile films with all of them.

The couples were then due to appear on the show separately on the Monday, Tuesday and Wednesday in early June, before the viewers voted on Thursday and we surprised the winning couple at their home on the Friday.

All was going well. We interviewed the first two finalists in the studio. At the end of Tuesday's item, we 'teased' ahead to our final couple–let's call them Craig and Carrie–who would be joining us the next day. We showed some footage we had shot with them the week before.

It was then that the problems started.

A woman phoned our duty office. This was where all the calls from viewers who wanted to comment, ask questions or complain about the show were directed. Our duty officer, Annie, had taken a call from a woman who had apparently been sobbing down the phone.

"This woman is really upset," said Annie. "She told me that she was shocked to see Craig's picture pop up, as he had proposed marriage to *her* and then disappeared into thin air. That was a year ago and she hasn't seen him since, not until this morning when his face appeared on *GMTV*."

I felt my mouth go dry like sandpaper. How on earth had we missed this fact on our research chats–but then again, how on earth could we have known?

While my researchers and I had asked the question 'are you legally able to get married?', we hadn't thought about asking 'how many women are you planning to get married to?'

I gathered my thoughts for a moment. While we took claims like this very seriously, I also knew from experience, that there was also a chance this woman could be making things up. As much as people like seeing friends and family on TV, there are also lots of ex-friends and scorned lovers out there, who like nothing better than making false accusations to cause trouble.

The first step was to call the potential groom and ask him if the allegations were true.

I took a deep breath as this was going to be a tricky call.

"Hello Craig, how are you?" I said.

"Fine," he replied. "Looking forward to being on the show tomorrow."

"I've got something difficult to ask you," I started. "We've had a woman calling our duty office, claiming that you are supposed to be marrying her rather than Carrie."

I paused for a reaction, but there was none. I continued.

"Now before you say anything, I have to tell you that we have to investigate these things. As we stated before, the viewers and the national press may not react well to the fact that you are due to be marrying one woman live on TV, but you've promised another woman to marry her as well."

Once again, I paused for a reaction. There was silence at the end of the phone.

"Craig, are you still there?" I asked, thinking perhaps he had just hung up.

"Yeah, I'm still here," he said.

"Do you have anything to say?"

"Yeah, I know all about it." He sighed. "It's totally not a problem. I did go out with this woman on a few dates a while back, but she got the wrong end of the stick."

"Did you ask her to marry you?" I needed a straight answer from him, if we were ever going to get out of this mess.

"I might have said something once when I was drunk," he said.

"But I was only joking! These girls, you know what they are like, they get crazy ideas in their heads, particularly when they are dating someone as good-looking as me," he went on, giving a cocky laugh.

Now I really was not expecting that reaction. I thought he would be angry, apologetic or even embarrassed, but he actually seemed quite proud that another woman wanted to marry him. I had to admit he was handsome, but to shamelessly tell me how good a catch he was took me by surprise.

"Does Carrie know about this?"

"Yeah, she knows," he said. "She's cool with it, she knows about Tina, but as I said, Tina's just got the wrong end of the stick."

I felt my chest tighten like someone had clamped my heart. I gulped loud enough that he would have heard it over the phone. At no point had I given the woman's name. However, I knew for sure her name was *not* Tina. What was going on here?

"Actually, the woman who called isn't called Tina. She's called Chris." I was now in full-scale panic.

"Oh, of course she is. I just used to call her Tina, it was my pet name for her," he went on, without skipping a beat.

My mind was racing. Did I believe him? Trying to give him the benefit of the doubt, she could have been a Christina, I thought, so maybe I did not need to worry after all.

"Okay," I said. "So, you are happy for me to phone this woman back and tell her what you have just told me?"

"Sure," he replied. "It's a misunderstanding. We are just friends, that's all. She'll be cool with it. Sorry I've got to go now, I've got a work call to make," and he hung up.

I met up with my boss and our press and legal teams and told them what had happened. Our lawyers explained the situation. On the one hand, it did not look good that we had a woman claiming Craig was supposed to be engaged to her, but on the other hand, he had done nothing legally wrong. Either way, we had to do some damage limitation. If this woman wanted to go to the press about Craig, she was more than justified to do so.

After our meeting, my boss Karen decided to call the woman who had called in. She was expecting her to be angry; instead, she seemed to have calmed down. Yes, she had been furious when she saw him pop up on the TV, but now Craig had called her and they'd had a good chat, so she didn't want to take the matter any further.

Lord knows what spell Craig had cast on her, but she had completely backed down. I was relieved that we had averted a crisis, but I had a nagging feeling about all this, that wouldn't leave me. I just wanted to get the next day's interview out of the way.

The following morning, Craig and Carrie appeared on the show. The interview went as planned, and both were charming and great interviewees. Back in the duty office, things were not so rosy. Duty officer Annie came to find me in the green room.

"I don't like to tell you this," she said. "But we've now had calls from several other women around the country, all with similar stories, all telling me that Craig had proposed to them."

I felt physically sick. As if one scorned woman wasn't bad enough, there now seemed to be a whole posse of them. What type of man was Craig and how had he thought he could get away with this, in front of millions of people on Breakfast TV?

As they came out of the studio, I pulled Craig to one side and told him what had just happened.

Instead of looking worried, he just grinned. "I'm a bit of a stud, aren't I?" he bragged. "All these women want to marry me." He gave a big belly laugh.

It was one time in my career where I honestly felt like giving a guest a good slap, but I tried to stay calm.

I gave him one of my Paddington Bear 'hard stares' instead.

"Craig, this is serious. Does Carrie know about this?" I asked, trying to make it clear to him how much hot water he was in. I envisaged all the headlines the next day: '*GMTV* love rat was supposed to marry me!' or 'Interactive Wedding Sham'.

It was not the best start to our wedding competition and, if true, we might have had to scrap the wedding competition altogether. It could have scuppered the next three months' worth of content.

"Yeah, she knows about all of them, she's fine with it," he replied, without batting an eyelid.

"Okay," I said. "Stay in the green room and I'll get my boss to come and speak with you both."

I found Karen and we went into the green room to confront him. Craig calmly told us that in his job as a computer salesman he had to travel around the UK, where he met lots of women. He and his fiancée had an open relationship and she was fully aware of all these other women. He may have proposed marriage to one or two of them in the past, but Carrie was the woman he loved and she was the one he really wanted to marry.

All the time I was watching his fiancée for her reaction. If it had been me, I would have been shouting and screaming by now, but she sat there expressionless. There was no anger and no tears. After he had stopped speaking, we asked Carrie for her reaction.

"Did you know about these other women?" Karen asked.

"Yes, but it doesn't bother me," she said, turning to Craig. He gave her an approving look.

"Craig loves me and I love him. He may have proposed to a lot of women, but what matters is that he wants to marry *me*." She grasped his hands tightly and kissed him lightly on the cheek. She was obviously smitten with him and was keeping up the united front.

Karen and I left the room, not quite believing what we had just seen and heard. We consulted our legal and press teams again, but there was still nothing we could do.

This couple were not doing anything illegal, and as far as they were concerned these women were not 'skeletons in their closet', they were quite open about them. Other people might not think it was the normal way to behave in a relationship, but they were happy with it. They hadn't broken any rules, so they were still allowed to stay in the competition.

Then followed one of the most stressful thirty-six-hour work periods of my life. The viewers were voting the next day on who should win the wedding, but we wouldn't know until voting closed at twelve o'clock who had won. I was hoping and praying it wouldn't be Craig and Carrie.

Fortunately, they lost by quite a large margin and the press frenzy was avoided, apart from one small piece in their local newspaper.

Instead, the viewers voted for Suzie and James, a young couple from the North West of England, to be our chosen bride and groom.

I thought all my stress was over, but it was actually just beginning.

Having picked the couple, the viewers had to choose a venue. The choice was a little church in Cyprus, a wedding chapel in Las Vegas or a Scottish castle. The viewers voted for them to get married in Paphos, Cyprus, in a lovely little chapel adjacent to the St George Hotel, where they and a select number of guests would have the reception afterwards.

The happy couple, the top wedding planner Siobhan Craven-Robins, a film crew and myself then went out to Cyprus to organise all the different options for the wedding. We also filmed the couple seeing the venue for the first time.

During filming, Suzie told us how she had dreamed of having a horse-drawn carriage to take her to the church. To be fair, the trip from the hotel reception to the chapel was walkable, but having heard her request, the extremely helpful hotel manager, Costas, duly obliged.

Before we knew it, Darius the horse was standing outside the hotel reception, pulling a beautiful wooden white carriage behind him. He too was pure white, apart from a large black freckle on his nose. He flicked his ears back and forth, swatting the nearby flies. He was definitely a fine specimen.

But there was one small issue: Darius was a bit fussy. While he would happily trot over cobbles and concrete, as soon as he saw anything metal, he just screeched to a halt. During the short journey from the hotel entrance to church, he had to go over a metal grate. Every time we tried to film Darius trotting up to the church, he just stopped in front of it, refusing to cross. Try as we might, he would not budge.

I really didn't have time to deal with the odd preferences of a temperamental horse, I still had lots of filming to do, but Costas the hotel manager was more accommodating.

"I know! We have a red carpet we could cover the grate up with, so Darius doesn't see it."

I was sceptical of this idea, but it was worth a try. Ten minutes later, a member of staff returned with the red carpet and promptly laid it over the grate. On the next take, Darius happily trotted over it.

In all my years as a TV Producer, I had seen many red carpets laid down for celebrities, but never for a five foot white horse.

Initially, the couple were hugely excited about winning the prize and loved coming down to London and staying overnight and appearing on the show each Friday. But, as the weeks wore on – twelve weeks in total from being picked in early June to the wedding in late August – the train journeys took their toll and the bride in particular began to moan... a lot!

Why did they have to come down? Why couldn't they just have the wedding without all this hassle? As I patiently pointed out to them, they were getting a dream wedding costing at least £20,000, and they hardly had to pay for anything. Like it or not, they had signed a contract to take part in the show.

In addition, the bride was a bit of a hypochondriac. One week her head hurt, another week it was her stomach, or she was getting travel sickness, or she had hay fever. The truth was, she was fed up with heading down to London each week to appear on TV. But rather than tell us this herself, she would get her fiancé James to phone us up.

"Suzie isn't feeling very well," he'd tell me. "Can she not just do the interview from our home?"

While initially compassionate to her illnesses, we soon worked out that they always occurred on a Thursday morning, just hours before she was due to travel to London.

By the time the wedding week arrived, I think they were fed up with us, and we were certainly fed up with them.

We all had to fly out to the venue again a week before the big day, in order to do all the legal paperwork and sort out the finishing touches to the wedding.

Costas, the lovely hotel manager, had gone out of his way to make us all very welcome. There was a welcome dinner, the happy couple had a separate five-star villa on the resort, and when the twenty wedding guests arrived, he threw a pirate party to celebrate. We were all invited.

I was exhausted, however, and just ready for my bed. By this time, I had spent twelve weeks filming and producing live segments each week with this couple. I was incredibly tired.

Everyone thinks working in these lovely locations is easy, but from the time I got up to the time I went to bed, I was busy talking to my production team, working out the big day's choreography with our director Andrew, on the phone to the editorial team in London, writing scripts, or just dealing with last minute wedding problems. It had been a busy few days and that morning I had been up at 5am producing a live segment. I also had to get up at 5am the following morning to do another interview with Suzie and James. Pirate party or no pirate party, I was going to bed.

I had also just received the devastating news that day that my sister-in-law Christine had incurable cancer, so I really was not in the mood for a party. I left the wedding guests and the team to attend the do without me.

I climbed into bed at about 10pm and lay listening to the sounds of the bouzouki band, their tinkling melodies seeping out into the hot and sultry night, and the wedding party laughing and chatting as they danced to the music. In less than forty-eight hours they would get married live on *GMTV* with twenty of their closest friends and relatives to witness it, and millions more viewers on TV. While they were looking forward to it, I couldn't wait for it to be over. I fell into a deep sleep.

At midnight, I was woken up by the hotel phone.

It was my boss Karen, who had arrived that day to help with the main event.

"I don't want to alarm you," she said, "but Suzie has fallen over and we think she may have broken her ankle. We've taken her to hospital and they're looking at her now. Don't worry, we've got it all under control."

Immediately I thought of our hypochondriac bride, and assumed this was just her latest imaginary ailment.

"Thanks Karen, keep me posted." I put the phone down, turned over and went straight back to sleep.

Three hours later, I was woken up again, this time by a loud thumping on the door.

I got up to open it. It was Karen, standing there still dressed in her pirate outfit, looking shattered.

"Just to let you know, Suzie hasn't broken her ankle, but it is badly sprained, so she has had it bandaged up. She's now back at the villa," she told me.

Now I really felt guilty for staying in my bed.

"Thanks for going to the hospital with her, Karen. I really appreciate it. I was so tired, I just had to go to bed. I'll look after her in the morning. Please go and get some sleep."

Karen started walking away down the corridor, but then stopped and turned.

"Be prepared though, she might be on crutches."

I was really annoyed with Suzie. I had put up with her fake illnesses all summer, and now she was giving my boss the same grief. I shut the door and tried to get a couple more hours of sleep before I had to be up.

Two hours later, I walked down to the seafront where the crew were setting up. They could speak of nothing else.

"We were all having an amazing time; lots of food, lots of drink and lots of dancing, when suddenly we saw Suzie being stretchered off in an ambulance," Darren the cameraman exclaimed.

"We never saw her again. Do you know what happened after that?" asked Glenn the soundie.

I filled them in about Karen and the hospital.

"Karen says she's going to turn up on crutches this morning," I said, rolling my eyes. "Just another stunt from Suzie to get attention." I picked up the phone to call the office.

I was still on that call, when out of the corner of my eye I caught the expression on both of their faces. They both looked genuinely flabbergasted. Glenn's mouth sprung open in shock, wide enough that I could see his tonsils.

"I think you need to turn around, Michelle," he said.

I did. There coming towards me was Suzie, not on crutches, but being pushed by James in a wheelchair, her right foot bound up in a huge white bandage like an Egyptian mummy's leg.

I was dumbstruck. Perhaps she really had done something serious – or was this her being a drama queen again? I had no idea, but what I *did* know was that our presenter Carla Romano was going to be interviewing a bride-to-be in a wheelchair live on *GMTV*.

Carla asked her how she had done it. Suzie said that she had not been drinking, but had just been a bit overenthusiastic with her dancing and had fallen down a step.

While I was seething at her stupidity, when I spoke to my editor he was delighted. "This is brilliant!" he said. "Will she/won't she make it down the aisle? You can't make up this jeopardy," he added gleefully.

I, meanwhile, still had something at the back of my brain that did not believe her. After all the made-up illnesses she had apparently had in the last three months, I still expected her to make a miraculous recovery. Every bride I knew wanted to WALK down the aisle. My guess was she would play on it for a few more hours and then be fine.

By 4pm that afternoon, we got the news I really was not expecting. A doctor had come to her villa to inspect the injury. "The only way she can walk down the aisle," he told us, "is if she's on a Zimmer frame."

This was definitely not on the agenda. For the last three months, we had been arranging venues, dresses, cakes, wedding invitations, but not walking frames. Firstly, with less than a day to go to the wedding, where was I going to get one from? And secondly, how were we going to make it look glamorous and romantic against the beautiful setting of the Cypriot church?

Our lovely hotel manager Costas came to the rescue once again. An hour later, a Zimmer frame appeared. In the meantime, I was thinking about what we could do to jazz it up a bit.

"Do you have any spare flowers we could use?" I asked sheepishly to our top London florist Matthew. He looked at me in disbelief. Having flown all the way from London to Paphos, he was hoping that his bridal bouquets would be the centre of attention at our live television wedding. He had not factored in flowers for a metal walking frame.

After Matthew had recovered from the shock, he miraculously came up with some more flowers and florist wire.

"I brought a few spare blooms just in case," he said. "Don't worry, Michelle, I'll make it look lovely." And he did.

And so, this is how I found myself producing a bride on a Zimmer frame for the live *GMTV* Interactive Wedding.

The wedding would take place live at 9am UK Time–11am in Cyprus. Across the morning we would be making live inserts into the show. Carla Romano and Clare Nasir were our presenters building up to the big event.

The preparations started well. The hairdresser and make-up artist could still go to the villa and make up Suzie as previously planned. We could still start the morning with live shots of the bride getting ready while the groom and best man were interviewed outside the church.

The problems started when it came to moving the bride. Firstly, we had to get her into the horse and carriage. We had delicately suggested to Suzie that we might lose this element of the wedding, but she was still adamant she wanted to do it.

It took four people, over five minutes to get her into the carriage with her big dress, bandaged foot and frame. It took lots of pushing and shoving of the bride's bottom, before she was finally in.

Fortunately, we didn't show that bit live on national television, just Darius the horse trotting her round the whole fifty metres, over the strategically placed red carpet to the church steps. It then took us another five minutes to get her out again. The clock was ticking, and everything was running late.

Poor Carla and Clare had to do a lot of 'filling' from inside the chapel where the groom and congregation were waiting. I had given them enough notes to cover Suzie walking down the aisle. Notes on what she was wearing, what James was wearing, who had done the flowers etc, but they had now been on air for three minutes and there was still no sign of the bride.

Finally, Suzie appeared at the chapel front door, complete with a flower-covered Zimmer frame for her short walk–or hop–down the aisle.

We were all set. I retreated to the hotel room which had doubled up as a live gallery, with the director Andrew beside me.

The wedding itself had been planned down to the second. Andrew had worked out every camera shot and every word to match the script. The studio in London had allocated us ten minutes for the ceremony. But what we hadn't factored in was how long it would take a bride to walk down the 10-metre aisle with a sprained ankle.

We had planned for it to take thirty seconds. She managed to make it last two minutes and forty-three seconds, hopping on one foot down the aisle.

She was really milking the attention. After every shuffle on the walking frame, she would look up, look around, smile and pause for effect, before taking another tiny step-hop forward. I really wanted to go in and push her down the aisle, but there was nothing I could do. Believe me, two minutes forty-three seconds is an excruciatingly long time to watch someone hobbling down a very short aisle.

The next unforeseen problem was the vicar. Having gone through with him exactly what he planned to say, he then started ad libbing. This was to be his starring moment on television and he was making the most of it. Once again, we could do nothing but watch in horror as the service got longer and longer and longer.

In London, our editor was in the gallery and getting bored. Unbeknown to us, he decided to cut off the wordy vicar and instead cross to our reporter who was broadcasting live with a group of relatives who had not been able to go to the wedding. One of them was Suzie's chain-smoking sister. There was a reason she had not been invited, and it soon became obvious to the viewing nation why.

It was just nine o'clock in the morning and she was already very tipsy.

"Doesn't she look beautiful," she slurred into the microphone. "She's my bestest, bestest sister." She took a large drag from her cigarette before tottering off to refill her glass.

As the ceremony went on, the gallery in London kept cutting from the service in the little church in Paphos to the inebriated fag-ash sister, who now could hardly stand up.

"I love her sooo much, and that's even though she dissed me and didn't invite me to her own bloody wedding. What type of sister does that to her own flesh and blood?" she slurred. She started to cry.

The studio cut her off at this point. In Cyprus, meanwhile, we were still focused on the never-ending ceremony, totally unaware of what was going on back in the UK.

After twenty-five long minutes, the wedding was over, and we all collapsed in a heap of exhaustion and relief that we had made it that far. The married couple then went off to have their reception. I was exhausted and went back to bed.

Later that afternoon though, things turned sour. As a special treat, Costas had set up a big TV screen in the hotel, so that all the wedding and hotel guests could watch a replay of the wedding that he had recorded via satellite that morning. It was then that we all found out about the drunk, chain-smoking sister hogging so much of the broadcast.

Suzie the bride was apoplectic with rage. "I specifically didn't invite my sister as I knew she'd ruin the wedding," she wailed. "But thanks to *GMTV*, she did anyway."

Frankly, I was pretty angry too. I had to apologise to the couple and all the guests, even though it was nothing to do with me, but in this job, you represent your company whatever has happened. I had to bite my lip, while inside I was fuming. I had spent months working on this wedding, I was functioning on barely any sleep over the last seven days, and now I was being blamed for something which was not my fault.

Fortunately, Andrew the director had recorded a full 'Cyprus only' version of the wedding from Cyprus, showing none of the sister's antics in the UK. This pacified Suzie and James, who now had a 'proper' wedding video, tape minus the deviant sister and they went on to have a lovely evening with their guests

Still cross, however, I decided to phone my editor up and tell him how I felt. This was not a good idea. Firstly, because he was my boss and secondly, he had the power to fire me.

I really didn't want this wedding to be my last act as a Breakfast TV Producer, but I had principles too. I would take responsibility for the overrunning part (though how was I to know the bride was going to take so long to come down the aisle?) What I had a beef about was taking the flak for putting so much of the tipsy sister on the show.

I plucked up the courage and made the call to London and went for it. While surprised to hear from me, he listened to my complaints and didn't fire me. He was the editor and he could do what he wanted, but he acknowledged my hard work and flexibility in the challenging circumstances.

We all laughed about it afterwards, but it was incredibly stressful.

My boss Karen sadly died a few years later of cancer, but I will never forget her help with taking Suzie to the hospital, or the image of her standing at my door at 3am, dressed as a pirate, telling me I had to be prepared for a bride with a broken ankle on crutches.

I went on to produce many more TV weddings, but what with the 'love rat' contestant, hopping hypochondriac bride, temperamental horse and flower-covered Zimmer frame, this one will definitely stick in my mind.

As Suzie and James made their wedding vows, I made a vow of my own, never to work on such a crazy wedding again. Unfortunately, I didn't keep that promise.

21

HELPING MATHAPELO

I was off to Africa again. In my wildest dreams I had imagined myself like Meryl Streep in a scene from Out of Africa, whizzing through the golden plains in a shiny jeep to the soundtrack of a light orchestra filled with the romantic sound of violins and flutes. What definitely *hadn't* been in my dreams, wild or otherwise, was that we would be towing a portable toilet.

Instead of orchestral strings, the only sound I could hear was the portaloo on wheels, as it rattled and bounced on the tarmac behind us.

The car wasn't particularly shiny either. It wasn't even a jeep. Instead, my husband Ian and I were in a battered pickup truck owned and driven by Frank, my South African cameraman.

Health and safety, as I have already told you from my Inch loss island nail polish scare, was a big part of my job. Ultimately, on a shoot or live broadcast I was responsible for everyone there: the presenter, the crew, the members of the public who would be on air. If something went wrong, I would be the one hauled up in front of the Health and Safety police to answer for it.

This wasn't the only thing you had to guard against, but after playing with fire, I thought I could tackle anything when it came to health and safety.

What I hadn't bargained for was arranging for a clean, functioning toilet. A clean place to go to the bathroom and somewhere to wash your hands was apparently part of my job too.

Off the back of my successful trip making a report about the Phelophepa health train, and my less successful one trying to get the San tribe in Namibia to film with me, my editor Martin had asked me to use my contacts to find some young South Africans to film with.

It was ten years since Nelson Mandela had become President and Martin wanted us to make a series of films about how life had changed for the average black person in South Africa. One story I suggested we cover was how much life had changed for the average black South African child.

Sue Jameson, one of our most senior and highly respected correspondents, was being sent to South Africa to cover the ten year anniversary.

We needed some school children for Sue to film with. I called upon my fixer and cameraman Frank - who had been involved in my Phelophepa health train adventure - to help me.

Getting into a South African school wouldn't be easy. He suggested a school in the north of the country, where his friend was the headmaster. His friend agreed that Sue could go there and interview some of the children.

Sue met lots of black teenagers at the school who, thanks to Nelson Mandela's leadership, now had big aspirations. They wanted to be doctors and teachers, engineers and lawyers. In reality, the chances of them achieving their goals were very small. While they received a good free education until they were sixteen, going on to college or university cost money, money which most of them did not have.

While walking round the school, one 14-year-old girl slipped her arm through Sue's and walked with her. Her name was Mathapelo.

The teenager was smartly dressed in her school uniform. She wore a crisply starched yellow blouse, a green striped tie and a dark green pleated skirt, the colours of the South African flag. Her dark afro hair was divided into two small plaits pinned to her head. She had big brown eyes and a beautiful smile.

It always amazed me how all the children managed to look so smart in their school uniforms, considering there were no washing machines and no running water in their own homes, but they did. Far smarter than many of the children I had seen in UK schools.

Mathapelo told Sue she wanted to be a teacher. Every day she would come into school early to study and do her homework under the white strip lighting in the classroom, because there were no lights at home. She wanted to make a better life for herself and build a new South Africa.

She talked eloquently about world and South African history and how she wanted to be an example to young black women like herself. Sue was immediately taken with her courage and bubbly personality and so decided to film a story about her.

While the education she received was excellent, she had to walk six kilometres to school each day, and lived in a very basic, small, two room house built with homemade mud bricks. The house had no running water and no electricity. She slept next to her sisters on a simple mat on the floor.

She was not alone; all the children who attended the school came from similar backgrounds. Education, they had quickly learnt, was their only way out of poverty.

Sue returned from South Africa and set to work editing the report she had made about the young teenager.

When we screened the film a few weeks later, our switchboard lit up with viewers wanting to help her and the other children from the school to achieve their dreams. People wanted to give money and clothes. It was interesting to see the enthusiasm with which our viewers took to Mathapelo and the other children in this remote South African village.

Seeing the public response, my editor Martin asked me if we could do something to help the teenager and her family - and indeed the whole village. I was sent on a scouting mission to South Africa to find out.

Frank picked me up from the airport and we headed north towards Limpopo. We left the shiny, tall buildings of Johannesburg and headed out onto the highway, passing the township of Soweto - mile upon mile of small concrete buildings set out in uniform dusty streets - before the landscape and the buildings changed dramatically.

Now we were driving through lush green pastures, full of golden fields of wheat and corn. Every now and then jacaranda trees dotted the landscape with their beautiful violet leaves, like purple Quality Street wrappers stuck on a brown canvas. Here there were more makeshift buildings, either mud huts with little nets at the window and sturdy black women in colourful dresses sweeping their porches, or tin shacks made from corrugated iron and whatever else the owners could get their hands on, surrounded by a few chickens pecking away at the dirt.

By the time we reached Limpopo the scenery had turned into vast expanses of red soil, with large dramatic red boulders, where nothing grew apart from the occasional cactus. It looked like a landscape for the moon. This was the part of South Africa that time had forgotten. The new South Africa with all its promise had not reached these parts.

We entered the village off the main road. At this point it was still concrete and passable, but it ended abruptly at the Catholic church. I later found out that they had had the funds to extend it throughout the village, but the money had mysteriously disappeared. A battered sign still showed the details of the planned project, but the villagers had long since given up on it ever happening.

As we proceeded along what was now a bumpy track towards the school, we saw women washing clothes by the tiny stream that served the village, slapping them against the big boulders and laying them out to bake and dry in the sun.

Frank carried on driving us along the rough track until we reached the two brick-built buildings and red dusty playground of the school.

We met with the headmaster, a tall sombre-looking black man called Stompy.

I asked him what was most needed at the school.

"Our classrooms are overcrowded," he said, pointing at the children squeezed inside.

"We really need another one to deal with all the extra children that are now coming to school."

I looked through the metal-framed window into one of the two classrooms on the site. Inside, the children sat in their smart green and yellow uniforms, repeating back everything the teacher was telling them and writing on the blackboard. The room had twenty desks and chairs, but there were twice as many children in it, so there were two squeezed onto each seat.

"And what about computers?" I asked, looking around the bare rooms.

Stompy shook his head. "There are no computers here," he said, looking surprised that I had asked that question. "We have no textbooks either," he continued.

I looked at the sparse classroom, so different to the ones we have in the UK. The real difference here, though, was that all the children *wanted* to go to school and turned up every day, even though they only had one exercise book and one pencil each and no textbooks or computers at all.

It was September, springtime in South Africa, but it was already hot. I needed more water as my bottle was empty.

"And where can I get water from?" I said, looking around for a tap.

"You'll have to go back down the road about two miles," he said, pointing back the way we had come. "We have just one freshwater standpipe in the village. Women queue for hours to fill up their jerry cans with clean water."

Again, this surprised me. I knew water was an issue in Africa, but South Africa was supposed to be the shining beacon of the continent and the fact that they didn't have it shocked me.

Frank told me we could buy bottled water from the local shack, but said most locals didn't bother as they couldn't afford it, and so the children were drinking dirty water, leading to all sorts of illnesses.

What I also needed right now was the toilet. We had been on the road for three hours and I really needed to spend a penny.

"Where can I use the bathroom?" I asked. I wasn't expecting much (after all, I had used one in the hut of the Namibian tribesman, which was very basic to say the least) and I knew it wasn't going to be pleasant. As we were here at a school, I was hoping to see a little block of neatly spaced-out toilets for the children.

"It's over there," he said, pointing behind a straw fence. I had started to walk towards it when Frank stopped me. "It won't have any toilet paper," he said, "but I've got some in the car, I will get it for you," and he ran off to find it.

The toilet was just a hole in the ground with two slats. I carefully squatted over it trying not to fall down the pit that had been dug underneath it. The smell was terrible. Flies buzzed around the stinking hole. I made a mental note not to use it again.

"At least the internet is great here," I said, trying to sound positive and showing him the four bars and 3G signal I was getting on my BlackBerry phone. "It's a better signal than I get at home!"

"The problem," Frank explained, "is that most people here don't have access to a computer or a phone, so they can't benefit from it."

I hadn't thought about that. I had also noticed that there were very few cars. "How do people get around?" I asked, trying to get a sense of the lives they led.

"For longer distances they might take one of the minibuses that ply for trade on the street, but that costs money. Most of them just walk," he told me.

Just like Mathapelo did.

"But what if they live miles away?" I wanted to know. He shrugged. "They just get up earlier and start walking."

There were so many things this village needed, but where did we start? Armed with all this information, I returned to London to report back to my boss.

Whatever we decided to do could not be for their benefit alone, we also needed something that would be interesting for the cameras to film. Everything in breakfast television needs a 'hook' or reason for being on air. Every day we had hundreds of emails from PR companies, lots of news stories and plenty of feature items all pitching for those elusive slots on the show. I needed to provide a good reason for us to have not just one slot, but several slots a day across a whole week.

My editor Peter McHugh always used to say, "Why am I putting this on the TV this morning? Why would Mrs Smith from Scunthorpe be interested in watching this today?"

While I already knew that our viewers were interested in Mathapelo, we had to have a good reason for going back there to see her again.

We decided to do something like the show DIY SOS and set ourselves a challenge: to build a classroom, dig a water borehole and give them some form of transport all in one week. This gave us much needed jeopardy. Will we/won't we finish it on time?

Having pitched the story in the monthly planning meeting, it was approved.

Now all I needed to do was make it happen. Although we had some budget for the project, there was no way it would stretch to building a classroom or providing a water borehole.

My husband Ian (who, as you may remember, once helped me conjure up a red sleigh for Santa at short notice) worked in the construction industry. I asked if he could help me out again and his firm came up trumps, agreeing to help build the classroom.

They not only agreed to pay for all the materials and send Ian and a colleague out from the UK to help supervise the work, but they also wanted to employ local labour, giving much needed employment to the community.

Their one caveat was that the construction workers all wore hi vis jackets and hard hats, as these were the safety requirements of their employees in the UK. We agreed to their terms, but getting the workers to wear them, we thought, would be a tough one.

We regularly saw the African workers balancing on roofs or carrying bricks on their heads without even a pair of gloves between them.

The next item on the list was transport.

Lorraine O'Brien, my friend and leading businesswoman, came up with another great idea. "I can get you a meeting with the Post Office," she said. "I know they have lots of old postal bikes that they no longer need, perhaps they could donate them to the project."

And true to her word, she did. And they did. Fifty red postal bikes were shipped to South Africa ready to surprise the children. They also sent a bike mechanic to show them how to repair and maintain them.

The headmaster Stompy thought this was a great idea. Not only could the children use them, but their families could borrow them to get around, too. The bikes would be useful for the whole community, long after we had left.

We also decided to invite two girls who were the same age as Mathapelo and a deputy headteacher from a British school to come out to South Africa to take part in the project. The difference between her life and theirs was stark.

Having sorted out where we could source all the materials we needed in South Africa. My husband and I arrived in Joburg and were picked up by Frank at the airport.

We had a busy week ahead of us, so we needed to get cracking to get all of it finished in the allotted time frame.

We were going to the site straightaway, so Ian could start sorting things out.

Or so we thought. On the way, we stopped in an industrial estate. I thought we were stopping for a loo break; we were, but of a different kind.

Rather than going to the loo, we were picking one up to tow with us to the site in Limpopo.

"I couldn't bear the thought of you and all the crew using that hole in the ground, so I took the liberty of hiring a toilet," said Frank.

He had a point. Although I had experienced the local school's lavatories and survived, I didn't think the teacher, the two English school children and the rest of our crew would be able to stomach them.

So, there we were driving along the highway in northern South Africa towing a public convenience - and *everyone* knew it. Advertised on the side in bright green letters were the words 'No need to rush, when you can flush', alongside a picture of a man holding a giant toilet brush. You had to admire the entrepreneurial spirit of the company. If someone is going to hire and tow your toilet, you might as well get some free advertising out of it.

Ian had already met with the builders and arranged for the supplies to be delivered to the site of the new classroom. All they had to do now was build it.

He handed out the hi vis yellow jackets and hard hats to all the workers. "Good luck getting them to wear them," I said, not believing for a moment that any of them would put them on.

But I was wrong. The bricklayers, the carpenters, the labourers all absolutely loved them. So much so that they never took them off, the whole time we were there. All week long we saw them walking around the village in their new fluorescent yellow uniforms.

Sue Jameson, who had originally covered the story for *GMTV*, had now joined us, flying in with the crew and presenter Andrea McLean, to host the week-long live reports from the village.

On site we had set up a little tent with tea and coffee, bread and boiled eggs for breakfast. It not only kept us out of the sun, but also stopped the flies coming in.

The toilet, which was parked up on the side of the site was also getting good use. That was until after two days, when it broke.

"Michelle, the toilet doesn't seem to be working?" piped up the deputy headteacher from the British school.

I had many producer skills under my belt by this point, but fixing toilets wasn't one of them.

I was not sure what she expected me to do about it, so I just ignored her and carried on with the filming we were doing. Getting no response from me, she went in search of my husband.

Ian is a construction manager, not a toilet attendant, but she insisted he go and fix it.

He reluctantly did so, and managed to unblock it and get it working again for the rest of the week.

Meanwhile, the building work was going great guns, so much so that I had to tell Ian to *slow* the workers down.

To work as a week-long TV production, I needed that all-important jeopardy. Will we/won't we make it by the end of the week? The rate these builders were going, it would all be finished by Thursday and we would have no grand finale on Friday.

Getting water for the village was more of an issue. Originally, we had planned for the borehole to be drilled on Monday, so that on Tuesday we could turn on the tap live on TV.

We had paid for a special drilling company to come in and sink the well. The problem was that they had drilled the borehole to one hundred metres, but they had still not found water. This was surprising. We knew this was an area with little rain, but to not find water at that depth was worrying.

We broke the news to the viewers and the children on Tuesday that we had not found water yet, but we would keep trying.

Meanwhile, the two teenagers who had travelled from the UK with their deputy headteacher were getting to know their South African counterpart. They had been amazed by how little she had, but how positive she was about life. They decided that they wanted to help her family by sprucing up her house with some brightly-coloured paint and a few soft furnishings, like curtains at the window.

Andrea and Sue got stuck in, too, helping. Not only did we have to paint her house, but we also had to pump up all the tyres on the 50 bicycles, which had- as they had to be, been deflated, before they were shipped from the UK.

Every day after we came off air, the work carried on, while Martin and Nigel, our crew, set about filming either at the school or her home.

As we only had one camera, we just had to make sure we were at the right location at the right time, when things were happening.

On Wednesday, we had decided to park the satellite truck and do the live broadcast from Mathapelo's home, with Andrea.

The good news was that we had finally hit water in the borehole at about one-hundred-and-twenty metres on Tuesday afternoon. We would be able to switch it on in front of the children the following morning. The problem was that the well was several miles away back at the school.

We couldn't be in two places at once.

So, at first light, Sue, Mathapelo and the crew went over to the school to film the first water coming out of the pump. We would play in the footage 'As Live', a term we used when we had recorded something, but still wanted to make it look as live as possible.

During the actual live broadcast, Andrea would be (genuinely) live from the teenager's house, then hand over to Sue for the recorded bit with Mathapelo and the children watching the first water coming out of the well. We would then come back to Andrea afterwards to wrap up the broadcast. The middle section with Sue in it would just be played 'As Live' from the truck. To the viewers at home, it would all look like it was happening at the same time, and no one would be any the wiser.

Or so we thought. The broadcasts that morning went smoothly. Andrea showed us how things were getting on in the house, Andrea then linked to the recorded piece from earlier with Sue at the well, then she picked up again and we saw the two British schoolgirls and Mathapelo having fun painting her bedroom a pretty shade of yellow.

The broadcast finished and we all congratulated ourselves on a great morning of television.

The viewers adored it. We had lots of them contacting our duty office saying how much they loved Mathapelo. We all stood round the satellite truck to watch it back. It was only then that it dawned on me. Not only had she been with Sue turning on the pump, but you could plainly see her painting the walls of her house with the two other teenagers.

There was no way on earth she could have been in the two places at once, but there she was. Turning on the pump at the school and the next minute in her house with a big smile on her face, even though they were 6km apart.

I waited for someone in the office to spot our mistake, but no one did.

"Oh well," said Sue. "This African teenager may not have electricity or running water, but at least she can time travel!" We all burst out laughing.

On Thursday, it was time to give the children their bicycles. In the early morning when they were distracted in the classroom, we quietly stored the fifty bright red Post Office bikes with their baskets behind the back of the school building, ready to surprise them.

When the moment came, Andrea went into the classroom and told Mathepelo and the children to follow her outside.

"These bikes are for you," she announced as she revealed the surprise. The children just looked at her in bewilderment.

Andrea repeated what she had just said. There was still no reaction. She thought perhaps the children had not understood her. While many of them spoke English, they mostly used their native local language.

"Mathapelo, can you tell these children that these bikes are for them. Come and take them and ride them," Andrea said again, gesturing to her to translate what Andrea had said into her local tongue.

The teenager realised what she was saying, but rather than translating it, she just turned around with a beaming smile and shouted, "These bicycles are for us! Let's play with them! Hurrah!" and raised her hands in the air in wild excitement. All said in perfect English. All the children let out a loud cheer then, and slowly came forward to take the red bikes.

What followed was one of the hilarious, but most joyous, moments of my TV career. Many of the children had never seen a bicycle before, let alone learnt how to ride one. They were wobbling and crashing to the floor around us, falling off but then getting back on again, determined to try and master this strange contraption.

There was no orderly riding around in circles, they all just rode them in every direction like a giant spaghetti junction. There were screams of laughter everywhere, and by the time the studio came back to us for the final broadcast of the morning, it was hard to hear Andrea above the sounds of screeching brakes and children shouting.

The children were supposed to be back in the classroom by this time, but they were having far too much fun to do any learning. It was a wonderful broadcast, full of life and laughter - and Andrea trying to avoid being mown down by an oncoming cyclist.

It was a TV broadcast that I will never forget.

Meanwhile, back on the building site, things were a lot more stressful. Having told the builders to slow down, it now looked like we would struggle to finish in time.

This was not just made-up 'jeopardy' for the cameras; this was for real.

The South African builders were totally confused by now. First of all, they had been told to slow down. Now they were being told to speed up. I am sure they thought it was some kind of strange British building custom, but they couldn't quite fathom out what, or why.

On Thursday, Ian and the local builders worked late into the night, using torchlight to try and get things almost finished for the next day's grand reveal.

They knocked off around midnight, but we needed them back again at sunrise to put panes of glass in the windows, paint some of the walls, put all the new furniture in and give the place a good clean before the children entered.

We all got up extra early on Friday and were on site while it was still dark. Everyone was excited, but also very nervous. This wasn't like other shoots, where we could do it again, or postpone the finish; the classroom had to be ready for the children to sit in by the end of that morning's broadcasts.

The problem was that it was now 5.30am local time and the builders had still not turned up. The late night had obviously taken its toll on them.

We all started to worry. If they didn't show up, how were we going to get this building finished? We couldn't do it without them. I might be able to do a bit of painting and cleaning, but there was no way I could fit panes of glass to windows. We needed the specialist skills of this local crew.

Ten minutes passed and there was still no sign of them, until we spotted the first one, then another of them walking towards us, their hi vis jackets reflecting the sun's early morning rays like little fireflies in the early morning light. One by one they appeared from across the landscape until they had all arrived on site.

The problem we now faced was that everyone had turned up to do all the jobs all at once. What followed in the next few hours was a mixture of organised chaos and sheer good luck. The glazier had only just finished fitting the glass panes in the windows, when the cleaner came along trying to clean them.

Unfortunately, the putty around them hadn't had time to set, so as the cleaner tried to do her job, the glass just kept popping out. Eventually we decided that a few dirty windows were better than no windows at all.

The paint was also still wet when the children came into the classroom, but we managed to warn them and keep them far enough away that they didn't get marks on their lovely clean school uniforms.

But thanks to the magic of television, the viewers never knew a thing. When the grand reveal happened at twenty past eight, no one watching would be any the wiser about the wet paint or the slightly dusty windows.

We had completed all we had set out to do, and the South African headteacher and the children were extremely happy.

Everyone was happy, in fact - well, everyone except the deputy head from the British school. "Michelle, can you tell Ian the toilets aren't working again?" she whined, expecting poor Ian to fix it, but we were both too caught up in the last-minute preparations to do anything about it.

When it came to health and safety, as a producer I had done my job well on the toilet front, and Ian had done his job by getting the builders to wear their hi-vis jackets and hats.

But I had failed spectacularly on the bicycle front. There were a few minor injuries on the day we gave the children the bikes. While they loved having them, we hadn't thought that we needed to show them how to ride them. Despite a few grazed knees, there were no complaints from them, however, because they now had a much quicker way to get around the village and they were happy.

We didn't change the world that week, but we did make a little bit of difference. We also helped shine a light on a part of the world that most viewers never normally thought about. Mathapelo was just like their children, with hopes and worries of her own. Like their children, she wanted to create a better life for herself and her village. She just needed somewhere to sleep, something to eat and drink and someone to care about her. She was just trying to make the best of her life in challenging circumstances.

I kept in touch with her and some of the other children, and, thanks to viewers' generosity and fundraising, we managed to pay for some of them to go to college. Mathapelo didn't become a teacher, but is now a mother and has a local government job.

For years afterwards, there was a twin learning programme between the school in Africa and the one in the UK. Stompy the headteacher even came over to the UK school to learn more about education here.

I invited him to the *GMTV* studios, too, so he could see how they operated and to watch some of the films we had made in South Africa. I thought he would be impressed, but he seemed more interested in the canteen and the large cooked breakfast I was buying him.

The canteen overlooked the river Thames. It really was a great spot with a great view of the famous London waterway, but he seemed too engrossed in his egg and bacon to notice it. I tried to draw his attention to the view and the river boats outside.

"This is the river Thames," I said. "Just along there are the Houses of Parliament and the London Eye."

Stompy looked up.

"I suppose that dries up in the summer?" he said, pointing at the waters below, and went back to munching away at his sausages.

And it reminded me how different his life was to mine. Where he came from, that's what the rivers did. It made me realise that his priorities and worries were very different to mine. Having enough to eat and a river to get water from were everyday concerns I didn't even think about.

The teachers from the UK school also went out to visit and teach at their South African counterpart. The exchange programme lasted for several years.

Although Lord knows what the teachers did when they came to spend a penny, as we had returned the portable toilet.

22

UNDER PRESSURE

The only things I knew about Scotland before I joined Breakfast TV were that it had a Loch Ness Monster, bagpipes, lots of golf courses and was the birthplace of Billy Connolly and Lorraine Kelly.

What I discovered while I worked there is that it is also where JK Rowling wrote her Harry Potter books, it was home to the ancestors of Piers Morgan and it has the largest percentage of people with high blood pressure or hypertension in the whole of the UK. Whether the last two are related has yet to be scientifically proven. But when our Scottish viewers discovered that, through his DNA, Piers had Scottish roots, it definitely did nothing to help the problem.

My first trip to Scotland also had a medical theme and I was excited to be heading north of the border. By now I had worked on Lorraine Kelly's show for a while and had got to know her a bit better. I had also worked with her husband Steve–a very good cameraman who had joined me on many shoots, including the infamous one with the fake bishop in Amritsar.

I had found out lots about Lorraine. Not only was she a great presenter, but I learnt that there were two things that she absolutely loved: Star Trek and babies. Offer her the chance to meet Patrick Stewart or Leonard Nimoy and she would jump at the chance. And if any guest brought a baby into the green room, she was one of the first in there, asking if she could have a cuddle.

I knew that a live broadcast from the premature baby unit at the Edinburgh Royal Infirmary would be right up her street.

We were doing a broadcast there on Christmas Eve, to highlight the fact that while many people would be spending their Christmas at home with their families, there were others who would not. We would be filming premature babies and talking to the parents, and also the doctors and nurses who were working over Christmas to look after them.

As I've mentioned before, Breakfast TV doesn't stop. Viewers still expect to see you on air, even when they are all off work. *Especially* when most of the nation is off work, in fact. As a result, we all had to draw straws about who would cover the Christmas shifts.

To be honest, though, I often offered to work the shifts around Christmas, in particular Christmas Eve as it was always a fun show to be part of. I didn't have children, and my family were all local to me, so I preferred to allow my colleagues with kids, or those who had to travel to far-flung parts of the country, to take leave during the festive period.

Not only were we planning to interview the parents and staff at the Infirmary for this particular broadcast, we were also going to surprise them with presents. Thinking about it later, I should have just asked my Scottish cameraman Martin to buy them and wrap them up. Instead, I rushed around buying a ton of small cuddly toys from Argos, several packets of bath bombs from Boots and some wrapping paper from Paperchase and then stuffed them all into my hand luggage for the short flight from London City Airport to Edinburgh.

I was just about to leave the office with my small wheelie suitcase, when I had a call from Martin. He had gone to do a recce at the hospital and was reporting back.

"The hospital is really helpful," he said. "There are lots of parents and babies we can film with."

This was good news, I thought, as there was no way on earth, I was going to find another location this late on the day for Christmas Eve.

"The only problem," he continued, "is that the location, well, it's not very Christmassy!"

"What do you mean it's not very Christmassy?

Surely a children's ward in a hospital had to be the most festive place of all in order to cheer the kids up.

"They don't like having decorations in the main ward, as they need to keep it sterile for the babies," Martin explained.

"They are suggesting we film in the parents' room, which is plenty big enough, but it's pretty bare."

"Okay, I'll see what I can do," I said, looking around our office which was full of tinsel and Christmas decorations. I dismantled a few glittery bits and pieces and stuffed them in my bag, as lots of people were already on leave for the holidays I was sure they wouldn't miss it.

I then had another bright idea: as well as the presents I was giving them, if I could find some boxes, I could also decorate a few 'fake' ones with some of my wrapping paper to dress the room and make it look more festive.

Looking around our office for inspiration, I spotted exactly what I needed by the photocopier. There were loads of A4 size cardboard boxes full of packs of printer paper, ideal for creating small fake 'gifts'. My years as a Girl Guide and watching Blue Peter were coming in handy. I could turn my hand to making something out of anything.

I emptied seven or eight of the boxes and flat-packed them to make them easier to carry. I had no room left in my case, so I just tied some string around them, making them into a small cardboard parcel.

Now running a bit late, I jumped into a cab and went directly to the airport. Since I didn't need to check anything in, I headed straight for security.

I took off my winter coat and placed it in the first bin, so it could pass through the security scanner. I then unpacked my computer and my 100ml bottles into a plastic bag and put my suitcase into another. In the final one, I placed the nicely pack-aged cardboard boxes.

The security guard standing by the conveyor belt stared at them quizzically. "Got nowhere to sleep tonight?" he said, with a smirk on his face.

It hadn't occurred to me until that moment, but it must have looked pretty bizarre. My suitcase was full of cuddly toys, bath bombs and gift wrap. I would guess the security guys had seen all sorts of different things go through the scanners, but I think

I must have been the first person ever to have thought about taking flat-packed cardboard on a flight.

"Wrap up warm, it's going to be cold tonight," he added, keeping a deadpan face as he pushed the cardboard along the conveyor belt.

I gave a mini-laugh, but he didn't respond. I never did find out whether he was joking or not.

In the hospital, the cardboard boxes worked a treat. Covered in wrapping paper the following morning, you would never have known that there was nothing in them.

They made the perfect Christmas backdrop to interview our families and their babies and, when the broadcast was over, the team in London called me to thank me for a lovely heart-warming and Christmassy broadcast.

I worked on a lot of medical stories on Breakfast TV over the years and I'm proud to say that some of them were campaigns that also saved lives.

Our resident medic Dr Hilary Jones had become famous for doing the 'tumbler test' for meningitis; a dangerous and, in some cases, deadly disease if not caught early enough in children and teenagers. Dr Hilary showed parents a very simple test they could do to check if a rash was a symptom of meningitis or not. If you rolled a glass on the spotty area and it did not disappear, then there was every chance your child had the infection. It was a medical emergency and you needed to get your child to hospital very quickly. This simple test being shown on TV had saved hundreds of children's lives. Hilary was always getting letters from people thanking him.

Another time, we had not gone out expecting to save a life, but it had just happened anyway.

We were doing a week-long campaign to help the nation identify and deal with some serious conditions affecting women, like diabetes, heart problems and high blood pressure.

Trying to bring a regional spread to our broadcasts, I did some research to find out which nation had the highest percentage of people suffering from these conditions. Unfortunately, Scotland came out top in all of them. I really didn't think it was fair to do every single broadcast from Scotland, so I had to just pick one of them. I chose high blood pressure, or hypertension.

To illustrate this, we needed to diagnose someone who didn't know they had high blood pressure and then Hilary would explain what they could do to reduce it and manage it so it didn't have more dire consequences.

We decided to test a large group of dinner ladies in a school on the outskirts of Glasgow. Armed with a film crew, Dr Hilary, his medical bag and an old-fashioned blood pressure monitor, we arrived at the school just after they had finished serving lunch.

All the women were excited about meeting Dr Hilary. He was well known across the UK and we often had women stopping him in the street and wanting to have their photo taken with him. One thing I hadn't factored in was the effect it would have on their blood pressure.

There is a condition called White Coat Syndrome, where it's quite common for a patient's blood pressure or heart rate to go up when they see a doctor. The problem I discovered was even worse when they saw a TV doctor. Dr Hilary made all their levels increase so much that we had to wait to get them used to the idea of him being there. After thirty minutes in his company, they finally calmed down enough for us to start filming.

Most of the women had slightly inflated BP readings, but nothing too serious. Then Jean arrived. A short, very plump woman in her early thirties, you could tell she was going to have high blood pressure even before she sat down. Her face was beetroot red and she was sweating profusely.

Hilary sat her down and took her readings. He was using an old-fashioned monitor, the one where you pumped a rubber balloon until the cuff was tight around the arm and then slowly let it go. He had a stethoscope in his ears and was watching the levels on the monitor as he did it. Having worked with Hilary before, I knew there were two readings he was looking for: the systolic pressure, when the heart pushes blood out (which ideally needed to be below 140), and the diastolic pressure, when the heart rests between beats (which needed to be below 100).

Hilary pumped the cuff tight and looked at the reading. Both he and I could see it was high, but his expression remained the same. Years of being a doctor had taught him not to show any emotion or cause any panic in the patient. He decided to take the pressure again. He did it one more time just to be sure. Not only was it high, it was at an impending stroke level: 210 over 140.

Once again, he remained calm. "Okay, Jean," he said, pausing before delivering his diagnosis.

"I am afraid your blood pressure level is dangerously high. This really is very serious; you need to get an appointment with your doctor as soon as possible." He spoke in a calm but authoritative voice. The young woman nodded.

"I'll call them when I get home," she said.

Hilary wrote down the readings and reiterated his point. "They need to see you as soon as possible, not next week, not next month, but *as soon as possible*."

I now had a more delicate thing to ask her. "Would you mind if we came to your house and broadcast live tomorrow morning? You would be encouraging hundreds of women like you to go and get their blood pressure checked out, so they can find out early if they have a problem," I explained.

"That would be great," she said in her soft Glaswegian accent. "My son Rory will love it that I'm going to be on the telly."

"I'll need to come and do a recce later this afternoon," I said. "Just to see if there's somewhere we can park the truck and easily get the camera cables into your flat."

"That's fine," she replied. "I'll be in after four, so just pop round whenever." She scribbled down her address.

Later that afternoon, myself and our Scottish cameraman Martin turned up outside Jean's block of flats. We rang the doorbell, but no one answered. I tried calling her, but nobody picked up. Unable to enter the building, we managed to work out which flat she lived in and how we could feed cables from the satellite truck over the balcony.

We returned to our hotel, but I kept trying to call her over the next few hours. I was getting more and more worried. Firstly, because without confirmation that she would be there, I had no one and nowhere to do the live broadcast in the morning. Secondly, having seen her blood pressure, I was worried that she'd been rushed into hospital.

Finally, around 7.30pm, she answered the phone.

"Are you okay?" I asked. "Have you spoken to the doctor?"

"I'm fine," she said. "I was out at Weightwatchers and I forgot the time. I'm back now, though—Rory and I have just bought ourselves a takeaway if you want to pop round."

"What about the doctors?" I asked.

"Oh aye," she said. "I've arranged an appointment in the morning."

The following morning, the crew and I met outside her block of flats at five o'clock. Our broadcast wasn't until 7.40 but we thought it would be good to get things sorted early. Having powered up the satellite truck, we knocked on her door at 5.30. Jean let us in, still in her dressing gown. The flat was in darkness. She told us to come in and set up while she went for a wash and put some clothes on.

The flat was tiny. Filming in it would be a challenge, but there was just enough room to stick a light out on her balcony and shine it into the room.

While Martin and the crew set up, I decided to sit down on the sofa to make a call to the office. As I sat down, the sofa made a large squelching noise. I could also feel something wet coming through my jeans. I touched the damp sofa cushion and cautiously put my fingers to my nose. It was wee, and judging by the dog now trying to join me on the sofa, it wasvdefinitely dog wee. I quickly jumped up again and stood in the middle of the room.

I went into the kitchen to wash my hands under the tap. Last night's takeaway cartons were on the counter, the bin was over-flowing and the sink was full of unwashed cups. Hilary arrived and we all stood together in the middle of the flat, not daring to sit down, and not daring to drink anything.

"What time is your appointment with the doctor?" Hilary asked Jean.

"Oh, I haven't made it yet," she said, starting to make herself a peanut butter and jam sandwich.

"I thought you said you had made an appointment?" I quizzed her.

"Oh aye. I told you I was going to phone up for one this morning, or I might do it later," she said, taking a bite out of her sandwich.

I must have misheard her and got the wrong end of the stick, I thought.

In all the years I'd worked with him, it was the only time I'd ever seen Dr Hilary get angry.

"Jean, you have blood pressure that's through the roof. You need to see a doctor as soon as possible, or you are going to have a stroke," he said sternly. "Have I made myself clear?"

Jean looked shocked, but nodded. She now realised just how serious the condition was.

As soon as the broadcast was over, Hilary made Jean call the doctors there and then. The GP's receptionist tried to give her an appointment for the following week, but Hilary, who was listening in, grabbed the phone.

"This is Dr Hilary Jones and I don't think you understand. This woman's blood pressure is 210 over 140. She needs to see a doctor and she needs to see one first thing this morning. Do you understand?" he said forcefully. I could see him trying to control his anger.

The receptionist–who was probably now suffering from TV Doctor White Coat Syndrome herself–immediately found Jean an appointment.

That day Jean was sent straight to hospital. After receiving treatment and medication, she is now managing her high blood pressure. She sent a lovely note to Dr Hilary thanking him for saving her life.

I had discovered a lot more about Scotland than when I started the job, but best of all, I knew that there was one less person with hypertension.

23

SUNSHINE AND STRESS IN LEITH

My next trip to Scotland was to Edinburgh again, this time to film with The Proclaimers. I jumped at the chance of producing them. I loved their song 'I'm Gonna Be' and had spent many school discos marching around to the lyrics "and I have walked five-hundred miles."

I was more than happy to fly three-hundred miles to meet them in person and spend some time with them. They had a new album out and a UK tour on the way. It was a bright spring day, and the idea was to film live with them at the docks in the Edinburgh port district of Leith where they now lived.

Scottish cameraman Martin and I were there early at 5.30am to set up and the satellite truck turned up shortly afterwards. We didn't have a regular satellite truck in Scotland, so this one had been hired in. The engineer introduced himself and started setting up, opening the dish on top and pointing it in a southerly direction, looking for the satellite to lock onto. The dish hummed and buzzed like a giant bee as it opened up to the sky like a sunflower searching for the sun.

Meanwhile, I was on the phone to our office, getting last-minute notes about the twin brothers Craig and Charlie Reid. The interview was scheduled to take place at 7.20am and they were due to arrive at around 6.30 in plenty of time for a seven o'clock menu tease.

By 6.30, though, we still weren't ready to broadcast. "We've got a problem," said Martin. "Either the engineer doesn't know what he's doing, or the dish is broken. I think we need a Plan B."

That was all very well, but where was I going to find a Plan B standing in the empty streets of Leith at that time in the morning? There definitely weren't any spare satellite trucks hanging around waiting to be used.

The only person around was a man in a little street sweeper snaking backwards and forwards across the pavement, trying to wash and brush off the beer and dirt left by late-night revellers. Fortunately, Martin had an idea.

"I think you need to take them to the STV studio, and do the interview from there," he suggested. "I'll phone London and let them know about the change of plan."

At this point, The Proclaimers brothers Charlie and Craig arrived in an Edinburgh taxi. I stopped them before they got out and Charlie wound down the window.

"I'm really sorry," I said, having introduced myself. "We seem to have a technical problem with the truck and we need to go to the STV studios. Would you mind if I jumped in with you and we all went there together?" I realised it was a bit of a cheek asking them this when I had only just met them, but it made sense.

"No problem," said Craig, "Hop in."

I climbed into the back of the cab with them and their two guitars and we turned around and headed back into town.

I have to admit, I was a little starstruck. By then I had already met quite a few well-known faces, but these guys were different. I felt they had been part of my teenage years and I had grown up with them. I found myself looking out of the window rather than talking to them, trying desperately to compose myself.

After several minutes of silence, I managed to start briefing them about what was going to happen that morning. Who was interviewing them, and the type of questions they would be asked.

They were both absolutely lovely. You never quite know with famous faces until you meet them, but the brothers were really chilled and laid back.

The streets of Edinburgh were empty, so we arrived at the STV studios in just fifteen minutes. To my surprise, the front doors were locked. I pressed the buzzer so we could be let in. No one answered. I pressed the button again and this time a distant voice replied.

"Hello. I'm from *GMTV*, I have The Proclaimers with me and we need to come in to use your studio for a down-the-line interview," I said, using TV jargon for a chat between people at two different studio locations. I expected the person at the other end to buzz us straight up.

"Of course, you have," said the security guard sarcastically through the intercom.

"Our studio in London should have phoned you and told you we were coming," I said, trying to get the man to understand my urgency, but he was having none of it. The door remained firmly shut.

"Honestly, I *do* have them with me," I said, turning around and gesturing to the boys to come forward. "Why don't you come down and let us in?" It was now 6.45 and they were due to do a live tease in just fifteen minutes.

"Can you imagine how many people I get pulling my leg, telling me they have Lorraine Kelly, Billy Connolly or The Proclaimers with them?" he said mockingly. "What on earth would The Proclaimers be doing standing on a doorstep with you at this time in the morning?"

I was furious and also really embarrassed. What could I do to prove to this man that I really did have The Proclaimers with me? There was no video security for us to wave at, and definitely no mobile phones with cameras at the time.

There was just one thing for it. I asked Craig if he wouldn't mind going up to the intercom and speaking to this rude and very unhelpful security man.

"We can do one better than that," said Craig.

Unzipping the guitars from their cases, they both began playing and singing into the STV intercom: "When I wake up, well I know I'm gonna be, I'm gonna be the man who wakes up next to you."

It was wonderful. There I was on a street corner in Edinburgh being treated to an impromptu performance by The Proclaimers. The security guard, who I really didn't think deserved it, was hearing it too.

Having finished the first verse, I told them to stop and spoke to the security man again.

"Well, why didn't you say?" he exclaimed. "I'd recognise those guys anywhere."

I waited for him to finally release the door.

"Are you going to let us in now?" I was surprised he hadn't already.

"No, hen, I meant to tell you–there's no engineers here at the moment. They don't start until 8am. Come back then."

Now I could feel my blood pressure rising. What did he mean there was no one there? Surely, he could have told us that before we wasted ten minutes and an impromptu performance by The Proclaimers on him? Now I really felt really stupid. I had dragged Craig and Charlie to a TV studio for no reason.

I phoned Martin to explain the problem.

"Ah yes, I thought that might be the case," he said. "Since the regional cutbacks, they only bring staff in early on request.".

I wished he had told me that before I had jumped into the taxi, but I guess it had been worth a try.

"Good news, though. The engineer has said he's fixed the truck. Get back here as soon as you can, and you should just make it in time for the broadcast."

This was even more awkward. I now had to explain to Craig and Charlie that we needed to get back in a taxi and return to Leith where it had all started.

"No bother," said Charlie pleasantly. If only other celebrities were so easy to work with, I thought to myself, as we hailed a passing cab and jumped in again.

This time, it was their turn to do the talking. They knew much more about Edinburgh than I did, so they gave me a guided tour. They pointed out some of the architecture on the magnificent, tall, grey granite buildings. They told me about the elegant green squares and finally they pointed out venues they had played during their career.

I remember thinking then what a bizarre, but brilliant experience this was. It's not every day you get to meet The Proclaimers, but here I was getting a personal guided tour from them as well.

The traffic was taking longer than expected. I was still hopeful that we would make our 7.20 slot, but it was going to be tight. Having exhausted everything to do with the sights of Edinburgh, the boys then started to tell me about their tours of Australia and New Zealand.

Every winter they headed Down Under to perform at festivals and special concerts which were often set in vineyards. They made a great living out of it, spending the winters in sunny Australia and the rest of the year back in Scotland.

We arrived back at the satellite truck with just five minutes to spare. We jumped out of the cab, and headed over to the camera so we could put microphones and earpieces on them.

"You are not going to believe it," said Martin. "The engineer has just told me the truck isn't working again."

By now, I had definitely joined the ranks of the Scottish population who had high blood pressure.

"What do you mean, it's not working again?" I ran over to the engineer, who started giving me the full story of how the transponders were working, and then they weren't, but I wasn't really listening.

I phoned London to tell them the bad news. The producers in the studio looked at the running order to see if there was another available slot, but the show was packed and there was no room for them anywhere–not that we actually had a working satellite truck or a studio to go into anyway. In the end, they managed to squeeze in a telephone interview with Craig and Charlie from a busy Leith Street. It was far from ideal–pictures are everything on TV–but it was better than nothing.

The interview was over, I apologised again to the guys. "Don't worry," Charlie said. "These things happen."

They were so nice to me, I really could have hugged them, but felt that was probably stretching my producer responsibilities just a touch. They got back into a taxi and left.

As a broadcast it had been a disaster, but I actually had a lovely time that morning, in spite of all the stress. Not only did I get to meet The Proclaimers and hang out with them in the back of a taxi twice, but I also got to hear them perform, live and unplugged, on a busy street outside STV.

There was nothing I could have done about the truck, these things just happen, but from that day onwards I always tried to have a Plan B. It could have been making sure we had an engineer booked to come in early at a local studio, or in later years, having a phone with a good video camera that we could use instead. It could have been having a wet weather plan for soggy outside broadcasts, or making sure there was a standby guest just in case your first choice didn't turn up.

But sometimes, despite all your Plan B's and C's, you just didn't make it on air at all. It was just the nature of live television and that's what I loved about it. The jeopardy was part of the fun of it. I loved waking up and producing live broadcasts every morning, not knowing exactly how they would go, thinking on my feet and often having to change things at the last moment.

Even if, at times, it did give me high blood pressure.

24

HOW TO PRODUCE A BABY

"Unless you produce a baby before 7am today, you're not coming on air," the angry programme editor screamed down the phone at me. It was five o'clock in the morning and she was in our noisy and very busy breakfast show newsroom in London. I stood outside a surprisingly quiet labour ward in a Scottish maternity hospital.

By now I was Deputy Head of our Features Department and I had plenty of experience producing live television. It was no exaggeration to say that I was one of the most experienced live producers at the station. I had produced so many different types of outside broadcasts, with everyone from Prime Ministers to petulant popstars and from half-naked football fans to South African workmen. I could turn my hand to most things when it came to live broadcasts, but as good and experienced as I was, there was one thing even I could not produce to schedule and that was a new born baby.

Let me recap a bit. It was 2010 and we were about to launch a new breakfast show to take over from *GMTV*, called *Daybreak*.

GMTV used to be a separate TV company owned by shareholders Disney, Scottish Media Group and ITV, but ITV had bought out the other partners and officially taken full control the year before.

Since *GMTV* had been losing the ratings war to BBC Breakfast over the last two or three years, they decided to relaunch the show.

Not only that, but the new editors wanted to totally reinvent it. They had spent months deliberating over the new format. As someone who had been there for twelve years at this point, I knew the show needed a refresh, but was shocked at the extent of their plans.

Breakfast TV is a strange beast. You need to understand that people are watching you when they are most vulnerable, they are often still in their pyjamas, eating their breakfast, trying to wake up and get out of the house.

I had learnt by now that people are creatures of habit at that time of the day, from what time they get up to what time they shower. Changing anything in that routine can really affect the equilibrium–including what they are watching on TV.

I remember viewers phoning in, years before, in their droves complaining that we had changed the sofa on the set and they didn't like it. To them, it was as if we had changed the sofa in their own front room. On another occasion, they phoned to complain that Ben Shephard wasn't wearing a tie; some were personally offended.

"How dare this young man present the news without a tie on," one viewer complained. "Does he not know how serious the news is?" said another.

People have a personal relationship with Breakfast TV. Watching us was like putting on your favourite pair of slippers. If we were going to change things, it had to be done gradually.

Yes, the show needed a refresh, but we all knew people had to be eased in, like the Abbey Bank, which first switched its colours to red, before a year later changing the name to Santander.

Our new ITV bosses had other ideas, however: there was to be a new set in a new studio, a new name and new presenters–Christine Bleakley and Adrian Chiles–who had been poached from *The One Show*. There were also lots of new staff who arrived.

The 'old timers', as we were now called, had to make way for a new guard, but wanting to fit in, we all enthusiastically put forward ideas of new features and things we might be able to do for the first day of the new show.

Everything was pinned on that first Monday in September when viewers would be tuning in to see *Daybreak* for the first time. About two weeks before the launch, I was asked to set up and produce a live segment featuring a 'Daybreak baby'.

By this time, I'd produced weddings, live marriage proposals and even state funerals, so really the only thing left was to cover the birth of a baby. Ideally, the baby needed to have been born after midnight on the morning of 6th September, our first day on air. The plan was for us to be *live* at a hospital that morning with the new *Daybreak* baby and the proud parents.

I had achieved lots of firsts in my career, but this one was going to be a real challenge. If I pulled this one off, it really would prove to my new bosses that I could produce anything.

The problem was that babies, as you know, do not just pop out on cue. Short of a planned caesarean, babies come when they want to, and no amount of money, influence or planning, even from an experienced TV Producer like myself, would change that.

Also, asking hospitals to let a television crew into their maternity wards was not an easy job. Hospitals, quite rightly, are nervous of letting any TV cameras in. The whole issue of patient consent and confidentiality is the first obstacle, and in addition, many hospitals are quite nervous that you might film other things that might show them in a bad light.

To give myself a fighting chance of success, I looked for friendly hospitals we had worked with before, with large maternity units where plenty of babies were born each day, so that, by the law of averages, we would see a *Daybreak* baby.

By now, I had worked for many years with Dr Hilary Jones. We had become friends as well as colleagues. So, my first call was to a hospital in Hampshire where Dr Hilary had a connection. His premature twins had been born at the Basingstoke and North Hampshire Hospital many years before, and over the years, I had built up a good relationship with the place. After explaining that I needed to have access to their labour and maternity ward, and after lots of negotiation, they agreed to let us in. Everything was set. The film crew, Dr Hilary and I were to be there on the Monday morning, 6th September.

The Wednesday before the launch of the new show, we all gathered in the editor's office to talk about the content for the following Monday. The editor surveyed the stories we had set up.

"We are a national TV station so we need to make sure we are in England, Scotland, Wales and Northern Ireland," he said, scanning the planning list.

I looked down the list. England, Wales and Northern Ireland were all covered, but we were still lacking something in Scotland.

The editor had spotted it, too. "What can we do from Scotland?" he said, questioning the assembled group. The news editor piped up.

"How about we put the weather presenter up there?" he suggested.

We all agreed. This was an easy fix for the problem, and there were some stunning locations across Scotland that Lucy Verasamy could report from.

"Slight problem with that," said the editor. "Lucy is new, so I would prefer that she's in the studio. I'd like her to be here so she can meet Adrian and Christine."

I tentatively shared another thought.

"The problem with Scotland is that it will still be dark at 6am," I said, trying not to sound too negative.

The deputy editor scanned the list and piped up. "Well, we can't change the location of these stories," he said, pointing to the top news features on the list. "Why don't we change the location of the *Daybreak* baby?"

I couldn't believe what I was hearing.

"Find us a Scottish baby," he said looking at me and pleased with himself that he had found a solution.

"That's not as easy as you think," I explained. "It took me a long time to persuade the first hospital to let us in."

"I'm sure you can use your magic to find us another one," he said.

Maybe I could use my producer magician skills to find us another location, but I would also have to use them to grovel to the hospital in Basingstoke to explain why we weren't going there after all.

Despite my protests, the editor and deputy editor were adamant. "We want to be *live* from a Scottish hospital on Monday morning."

By now, I was used to my items being set up and then scrapped, then sometimes rebooked again. The running order of a Breakfast TV show is always in a state of flux, from the planning stages right through to when you were actually on air. You had to just go with the flow, but in this case, I felt pretty miffed.

What could I do, though? They were my new bosses and I didn't want to come across as a 'moaning Minnie', so after trying and failing one more time to save my Basingstoke location, I gave in. I was going to have to let them down and find another hospital in Scotland. I had four days to do it. Two, if you took out the weekend.

I called our Scottish camera operator Martin for some advice. In the last twelve years we had done many stories together, so if anyone had a good Scottish hospital contact, it would be him. Fortunately, he did. He recommended a very nice maternity unit in Kirkcaldy in Fife that he had filmed at before. After calling them, they very kindly agreed to host us.

The day before the show's launch on Monday, I flew up to Edinburgh and then drove to the hospital, ready to spend the next eighteen hours waiting for babies to be born.

The idea was that, as the mothers-to-be arrived, we would ask their permission to interview and film them before and after giving birth. We would then get them or their partner– depending on how distracted they were with the contractions– to sign a consent form.

Some babies take longer to come out than others, of course, so I thought if I got there at midday, there was a chance that some women might come in and be in labour for over twelve hours - and so not give birth until after midnight. In short, giving us a Daybreak baby.

A maternity nurse in a starched blue uniform greeted me at reception.

"You canna believe how busy we were yesterday," she said, wiping her brow. "There were wee babies being born all over the place. I'm hoping for a quieter shift today," she confided, showing me around the hospital.

"I don't want to be rude," I said, "but I'm hoping for the opposite."

She let out a hearty laugh, but I was serious. I needed a baby, only one baby, to be born after midnight.

"Bring your stuff to the staff room," she said, "and I'll make you a brew while we're waiting."

I spent the afternoon drinking tea and eating biscuits with not a single newborn baby in sight. The maternity nurse had got her wish. A couple of heavily pregnant women came in, but were sent home again, as the nurses had decided they were not yet ready to give birth. Other than that, it was extremely quiet.

Having asked the nurses every question I could think of about the different types of births we might encounter, from birthing pools to epidurals, I had run out of childbirth-related things to talk about. Instead, I began to question the sister in charge–who was due to retire shortly–about how things had changed over her thirty-odd years working in this maternity hospital.

She told us many stories, but the most interesting one was about a ghost that was said to haunt an old ward.

"When I first started, there was a very stern matron who was a stickler for running the ward just so," she said.

"Lots of the nurses were terrified of her, as she was very strict on how everything should be, from the cleanliness of the ward, to the neatness of our hair and uniforms. She was a spinster and gave her life to this ward, and sadly died not soon after she retired. I hope that doesn't happen to me."

Looking at her kind face, I was sure she wouldn't, but even if she did, my experiences of ghosts made me think she would be a friendly one.

"We all used to moan about her behind her back, but looking back now, I realise how much she cared about all the nurses and the women giving birth here. She was like a mother hen looking after us all, and we were her family. I learnt a lot from her."

She sighed, tucking into another custard cream biscuit from the tin.

"The problem is, I think she loved this place so much that she hasn't really left. Lots of new nurses on the night shift have said they have seen her walking along the corridors of the old part of the hospital where the maternity unit used to be."

"Have you seen her?" I asked. After my encounter with the little girl ghost in Ipswich, I was now more tolerant of spooky goings-on.

"Yes, I've seen her two or three times," she said, "but unlike the new recruits, I find it quite comforting. It's like she's still looking out for us all."

She got up. "I'm going to go and check on the wards." She left me in the staff room on my own to reflect on what she had just said.

As interesting as this all was, it was not helping me with my quest to produce a *Daybreak* baby.

At six o'clock that evening, Martin and Dr Hilary arrived at the hospital. I called our office in London to give them an update.

"I'm not worrying," I said. "There's still a long time to go until the item is due on air," I reassured them. Thirteen hours is a long time in both television news and Breakfast TV. In the past, I had seen complete running orders change in that time.

I was getting slightly anxious, though, so I went outside the main entrance to get some fresh air. It was already dark and a light drizzle had started to fall, creating a slight mist across the half-empty hospital car park.

Several minutes later, a car driven at high speed came screeching in through the entrance. A man jumped out and ran in search of a wheelchair, returning a minute later to find that his pregnant girlfriend had climbed out of the car just as her waters broke, leaving a large puddle next to the passenger door. I ran to help her, and between us both, we got her into the wheelchair and through the doors to the maternity ward. As her boyfriend pushed her down the corridor, I hurriedly tried to explain who I was and why I was there.

"Would you be happy to take part?"

"Aye," said the father-to-be, "just give us a wee moment to get her into bed."

I felt terrible for asking, but relieved that they had agreed to allow us to film. Twenty minutes later, having had all the check-ups from the midwife, Hilary, myself and my cameraman Martin were allowed in to film them.

"Make it quick though," said the midwife. "The baby could be coming out any minute."

This was of no help to me, as it was only seven o'clock in the evening, and I needed her to hold on for a further five hours to make it a *Daybreak* baby. At this point, however, it was the closest we had got to a birth, so I decided to film it anyway.

Martin quickly set up the camera and I briefed Dr Hilary, then he started the interview next to the puffing and panting expectant mum. It transpired that this was her fourth child. She and her partner thought they were expecting another girl, but didn't know for certain, and had already named her Jessica.

"What if it's not a girl?" I asked.

"It has to be," said the father. "I've already had the name tattooed on my chest." He whipped up his tee-shirt to reveal the name inked next to those of his three other children, whose names also began with a J. "I'm Jimmy," he smiled.

I was both shocked and impressed by their conviction. I was not keen on tattoos, but even if I had been, I knew I would probably get something done, change my mind and then regret it. I found it difficult enough to decide what I was going to wear each day, usually changing my mind three or four times, let alone trying to decide what tattoo I was going to get for the rest of my life.

This guy had not only decided the sex of his baby, but named her and got the body art to prove it. They would make great guests on TV the following morning, I thought to myself, if only 'Jessica' could hang on for another five hours before making her appearance.

Fortunately, he did not need to change the tattoo. Baby Jessica arrived into the world. Unfortunately for us, it was just thirty-five minutes later.

Half an hour after that, once the baby had been cleaned up and the mum was comfortable, we went in to congratulate them and film the new arrival. It was incredible to think that just an hour earlier I had been interviewing them with Jessica inside her and now here she was, a little girl with a crinkly red face, tiny hands and a mop of black hair.

Mum and Dad were crying tears of joy. I was crying too, but for a different reason. Secretly I was cursing that she had popped out so quickly and would not count as my *Daybreak* baby.

Jessica and her parents left as quickly as they had arrived. As there were no complications, they all went home just two hours later. The maternity unit fell quiet again and Martin and I just sat and waited, and waited.

At 9.30pm, we were just raiding the vending machine for coffees when the midwife told us another woman had come in. "This one could take a little longer to come out," she confided.

I heard her before I saw her. The pregnant woman was lying on a trolley, waiting to be allocated a labour ward. Her husband stood beside her trying to help. She growled and screamed as her contractions came and went. Her face contorted every time a wave of labour pains came over her.

She gripped her husband's hand tightly, so much so that his hand was white. I saw him wince, but he was too nervous to say anything, obviously aware that any complaints would be met by a torrent of abuse from his wife, who was no doubt feeling a hundred times worse. Martin and I hovered around the corridor waiting for an appropriate time to intervene.

Sometimes you feel like the luckiest person on earth to be able to witness these moments, but you also feel like you are intruding. Here they were, waiting for the birth of their precious child, and we were asking them if we could stick a camera in their faces to record the moment for TV.

I picked my moment cautiously. Not surprisingly, the woman had more important things to worry about than talking to a TV crew, so she said she was happy for her husband to answer on her behalf.

This was their second baby, he explained, but this pregnancy had been more complicated than the first. He wasn't sure how long it was going to be, but we were welcome to film once it had arrived, if everything was okay with the baby.

I phoned my office to tell them the good news. As long as the baby came out after midnight – in less than two and a half hours' time – and before 7am the following morning, we would have our *Daybreak* baby.

Thinking we had time on our hands, Dr Hilary went to his hotel and Martin and I went in search of some dinner. On a Sunday night in Kirkcaldy, there was not much open, but we found a petrol station which sold sandwiches. We grabbed the food and headed back to the hospital to eat.

We were met by a beaming new father. "She's had the baby!" he cried, with tears of joy running down his face. "He's beautiful, he's a little boy.'"

While I was happy for them, secretly I was deflated. Their baby had been born before midnight and my editorial team would not be happy.

I managed to give a false smile and congratulated him and asked if we could film with them. Thirty minutes later, Martin and I set up the cameras and started rolling. The couple beamed from ear to ear and I tried to hide my disappointment. I looked up at the clock, quietly ticking away and taunting me. It was 11pm, just sixty minutes short of the magical midnight hour.

I remember looking at their smiling faces and feeling terrible for the thoughts going through my head. If they could have just held on for one more hour, I would have had the baby I needed and all the stress of the last eleven hours would be over. I felt cruel for thinking it, but it was true.

I still had no idea whether any other babies would pop into the world at that hospital that night, so as a Plan B I asked the new dad if he would come back the following morning for a bedside interview with his wife and their new arrival.

The parents were 'good talkers' in TV terms. In other words, they were chatty on screen and I knew they wouldn't clam up in front of the cameras. More importantly, Hamish the baby was unbelievably cute, even to a non-maternal woman like me. He had tiny blue eyes that gazed back at you and a fluffy small carpet of red hair. I knew the viewers would love him.

We still had over eight hours to go before we went on air, so there was still a chance of another birth, but at least I had this one up my sleeve.

Time goes very slowly when you are waiting around in hospitals. Even more so when you are constantly checking the door for screaming or puffing and panting pregnant women to appear. At midnight there were still no new arrivals. My bottom had now gone numb from sitting on the blue plastic waiting room chairs for hours on end, and I had run out of new snacks to eat. There's only so many packets of cheese and onion crisps and cans of Coke a girl can take.

The TV in the waiting area–which had been on all day–had now been switched off. At 1am, the corridors were eerily quiet.

The senior overnight nurse suggested Martin and I follow her to a disused maternity ward.

"I know you have to be up early," she said. "Try and grab a few hours' sleep." She led us towards an old, empty wing in the hospital.

"We have some spare beds in here you can lie on," she said, gesturing to four beds. There were no pillows or sheets, but at least we would be horizontal, and sleeping on a mattress rather than a plastic chair.

"I'll call you straight away if any expectant mums appear," she promised and disappeared into the darkness.

I lay down on the bed fully clothed and tried to sleep. Martin was in the bed next to me.

Even with the lights off it was still not completely dark. The street lights outside cast weird orange shadows across the ward and lit up the droplets of rain on the window panes like tiny diamonds glinting in the dark.

Needless to say, I didn't get any sleep. Not only was I anxious about getting a *Daybreak* baby, but I kept thinking that this was the ward where the haunted matron supposedly hung out. I was spooked by every noise and shadow in the darkness. It gave me the creeps.

I remember lying there and thinking about all the amazing locations I had been to with my job, from the beautiful plains of South Africa and the historic paddle steamer in New Zealand to the beauty of the Golden Temple in India. A spooky hospital ward at the dead of night was definitely the less glamorous side of the job.

I wondered if the ghost of the matron was really there and what she would have made of two fully-clothed, non-pregnant people lying in her ward in the dark.

I lay there, wide awake, for two hours before finally deciding that I might as well just get up. Martin had had little or no sleep either and he followed me back to the corridor and the plastic chairs.

It was now 3am and there was still no sign of a baby. There had been no new arrivals while we had been away. Meanwhile, in the newsroom in London, I knew a team of people working overnight would be expecting me to give them an update.

I really didn't want to call them and tell them the bad news. I kept walking backwards and forwards to the hospital entrance, peering into the dark Kirkcaldy night, hoping that I would spot a car's headlights coming into view in the dark, empty car park.

I left it as long as possible, but finally plucked up the courage to call the office at about 4.30am.

I felt like a soldier phoning their commanding officer to admit defeat in battle. There was just an hour and half to the launch of the new show and I knew people would be panicking in the office. I also knew that our senior team would be briefing new presenters Adrian and Christine shortly, and they needed to know what was coming up in the show.

I tried to put a positive spin on it. As anyone who knows me will tell you, the milk bottle of my life is always half-full, but on this occasion, I was struggling to find a way to celebrate the fact that this one had no more than a few smelly dregs in it.

The overnight producer looking after my item picked up the phone.

"There's bad news and good news," I said. "We may not have a *Daybreak* baby yet, but we do have a baby who is celebrating his first daybreak!" I tried to sound chirpy. "And what's more, the parents have agreed to be here live on the show with the new baby Hamish at 7.40."

"That's great," said the producer, sounding distracted by something else going on at the end of the phone. I could hear lots of noise from the busy newsroom in the background. Everyone wanted the new show to go well so all the bosses were in, ordering people around. She said she would pass the information on.

Half an hour later, I got the call from the overnight programme editor.

"Unless you produce a baby before 7am today, you're not coming on air," she screamed.

I was shocked, but not surprised. Tensions were running high in the office and everyone was very stressed. I tried to reason with her.

"The hospital has been so kind to us, letting us in in the first place. I've got Hamish's dad coming back in at 6.30am to prepare for the broadcast. He has told all his friends and family that he and his new born son are going to be on TV. Surely, we can just interview them for two minutes?"

"I don't care," said the programme editor. "Unless you produce a newborn baby, you're not coming on." She hung up.

Over the last twelve years, I had got used to people shouting at me, but I felt this was uncalled for.

I had produced all sorts over the years and had even learnt a few magic tricks along the way, but even with all the skills and experiences I had gathered, I couldn't magic up a newborn baby from nothing, in the middle of Scotland in the dark.

I tried to work out what the hell I was going to do next. How was I going to let this family down gently and tell them they weren't coming on the air? I was going to have to come up with a stellar excuse, or perhaps we would just do a 'strawberry filter' and leg it out of the hospital before anyone noticed we weren't actually broadcasting anything.

In the meantime, Martin had been asked to get a shot of the sunrise over Kirkcaldy for the weather segment at the start of the show at 6am.

The idea was that all the live teams out on the road that morning would show a live shot of the sunrise, to show that *Daybreak* was broadcasting live and nationwide. They had clearly forgotten that, as we had told them, the sunrise in this part of the world in September wouldn't be until 6.20 and it was also pretty typical Scottish weather for the time of year. It had stopped raining, but there were still thick clouds in the sky.

But Martin did what he was told and went outside to film the cloudy sky above Kirkcaldy. I went outside to join him, get some fresh air and gather my thoughts.

Martin was not surprised to hear what the editor had said about our *Daybreak* baby. As an outside-broadcast cameraman, he was used to standing on cold street corners waiting to go on air, then being dropped at the last minute because things were over-running, or because something more important had come up. But even he was annoyed that they would not let this lovely family on the air for just two minutes.

By now I had all but given up on producing another baby–that was until I spotted the headlights of a Ford Fiesta coming into the car park. I dared not hope it was an expectant mum, but it was. Her husband carefully walked beside her as she puffed and panted her way into the reception area, with me gingerly walking behind her, waiting to ask her permission to film once the baby arrived.

All the time I was thinking that, if this baby was going to make it on air, it was going to have to come out quickly. This was, I discovered, their third child–tick–she was in the late stages of labour–tick–and finally, and most importantly, she'd agreed to be filmed once the baby was born. Brilliant!

All I could hope for now was a super-fast labour and delivery. I called in to the *Daybreak* newsroom and gave them the good news.

"Tell her to push," the producer in the office replied.

Charming, I thought. I was sure the mother wouldn't appreciate that piece of advice, and decided it was better not to pass it on.

And so, it was, without any production skills from me, that at 6.48am a *Daybreak* baby was born. Naturally, the mother was pretty exhausted and not looking her best, so she didn't want to be live on Breakfast TV, but she and her husband did agree to a pre-recorded interview with Dr Hilary twenty minutes later.

At 7:42, the taped interview made it onto the launch programme of *Daybreak*, along with a live interview with Hamish and his parents.

In the last eighteen hours, I had drunk about eleven cups of tea and three cans of Coke, eaten more than my fair share of cheese and onion crisps, service station sandwiches and an entire tin of biscuits, and raided the hospital vending machine for all its remaining snacks. I had met three new babies, seen an expectant father's tattooed chest and lain in a disused maternity wing, not sleeping a wink, but thankfully not meeting any maternity matron ghosts in the process.

I had done my job and produced a *Daybreak* baby. If I were giving an Oscar speech on this, I would like to say that all my past experiences had helped me to deliver this one-of- a-kind-production. Wrestling with junkies; solving police cases; dealing with amorous, sooty steamboat workers; covering terrorist attacks; fending off fake bishops and angry mobs waving sticks; wrangling with polite and not-so-polite popstars; negotiating with Namibian tribesmen; oh, and getting a unique view of Ben Shephard's bottom.

They had all been part of my amazing journey, but between you and me, my experience had nothing to do with it this time. No amount of planning or skill could produce a new baby. In this case, it was just down to luck and Mother Nature.

But as my Nanny Joan used to say, you make your own luck through hard work and kindness. I had been fortunate enough to work with and encounter hundreds, if not thousands of people who had helped me on my TV journey. From camera crew to presenters, nervous guests to deaf politicians, producers to production managers, and from railway station managers to singing Māori, all of them had helped me along the way, all had their own stories, and it was my job to tell them and produce them.

As far as I was concerned, I really was the luckiest Breakfast Telly Producer in the world.

Whether my new *Daybreak* bosses thought the same was another matter. They knew nothing about my wealth of experience. To them, I was just like any other producer paid to do my job. I soon realised I was going to have to prove myself all over again. I thought I had had some tough times in my career, but as I was to discover, things were about to get a whole lot tougher.

AFTERWORD

If you enjoyed this book please post a review, it means a lot!

You can sign up to my newsletter tellyontoast.com to hear more stories from behind the scenes working in Breakfast TV.

Also watch out for the next book which is coming soon.

Telly on Toast - Second Helpings will cover more adventures from my Daybreak and Good Morning Britain days working with all your breakfast TV favourites.

ACKNOWLEDGMENTS

I was lucky enough to work in a job which I loved. It was exciting, fun, interesting and really rewarding, but it also involved long hours, very early starts and some challenging situations involving guests, viewers and some very well-known faces.

This book is dedicated to all the people who work or have worked on Breakfast Television.

To all the presenters who got up early each morning to bring the news and a smile to millions of viewers around Britain. Also those who work behind the scenes at *GMTV*, *Daybreak* and *Good Morning Britain*, the producers, the researchers, the video editors, the directors, the studio crew, wardrobe and make up, the green room team, the camera and sound crews and all those who work on the outside broadcasts. Without them I would not have had such a fantastic journey.

I would also like to thank the people who helped me to get there.

To my parents Mike and Sandie who have always supported me and told me I can go anywhere and do anything.

To my lovely husband Ian who have always supported me and never stopped me when I did go everywhere and do everything.

To my sister Karen, who also experienced life working on Breakfast TV.

To all of my friends and family who have put up with me not turning up for events because of work and had to listen to my crazy stories.

To the people who inspired me to write this book, Omar and Rubina, who first told me I should write down my stories.

To Rosie Meleady, who inspired me to actually put pen to paper and helped me to produce it.

To Suzy Pope for her wise advice and editing.

To Gill Branca for fantastic memories from our days in TV and for her wise edits.

To Laurie Griffiths for being a great colleague and for your lovely cover design.

To Dave Barratt for the impressive website: www.tellyontoast. co.uk

And to you the readers and viewers of Breakfast Television who inspired us to make TV that is so fun to watch and work in.

ABOUT THE AUTHOR

Michelle Porter spent 22 years as a TV Producer on ITV Breakfast shows *GMTV*, *Daybreak* and *Good Morning Britain* working with TV household names like Dr Hilary Jones, Ben Shephard, Kate Garraway, Piers Morgan, Susanna Reid, Martin Lewis, Eamonn Holmes, Lorraine Kelly, John Stapleton, Richard Arnold, Andrew Castle, Andrea McLean and Clare Nasir.

This is her first book.